MANHATTAN
STREET NAMES
PAST AND PRESENT

A GUIDE TO THEIR ORIGINS

DON ROGERSON

Griffin Rose Press - 2013

ISBN-13: 978-0-9888137-2-4
ISBN: 0-9888137-2-6

Cover image: Viele, Egbert L. *Topographical map of the City of New York.* 1865. Digital image from the Library of Congress, Geography and Map Division.

CONTENTS

Acknowledgments   i

Introduction   iii

Using This Guide   vii

Alphabetical Guide to Street Names   1

Notes   117

Bibliography   147

ACKNOWLEDGEMENTS

The publication of this book was made possible by the support of the community at Kickstarter, the crowdfunding website. I want to thank all the backers who made contributions; it would not have happened without you. I would like to thank especially Michael Gornall, Gidget London, Tess Baldwin, Aneel, Ronald Cohen, W. Paul Morgan, Thomas Kula, Eric Hancock, Alex Kirkland, Charles Turner, Katrin Küchler and Kenneth Ouriel, MD, MBA for their particularly generous support.

INTRODUCTION

The researcher attempting to unravel the tangle of Manhattan's streets is soon bewildered. One looking for hard dates and data on the names of those streets may just as quickly become frustrated. Perseverance is rewarded, however, and a picture emerges of a city's fascinating history that is recorded in the names of the streets that define it.

From a modern standpoint, we might imagine the naming of streets as a simple administrative process; new streets are approved, surveyed, constructed, and suitable notable figures are chosen to be honored with a street name. Certainly this is how a few of Manhattan's streets were named, but only a few. In most cases the streets of Manhattan had names well before they were officially opened as public streets. These names were established through common usage or were proposed by property holders anticipating the development of their farmland as the city grew. Some of these names were officially adopted, some were not, and some were altered to avoid the confusion and duplication that followed naturally from such an unruly system.

Manhattan began as New Amsterdam, an outpost of the Amsterdam branch of the Dutch East India Company, situated among the sandy hills that once stood at the southern tip of the island. Official street names did not exist then in the same sense as today. Streets were usually indicated according to where they led, who lived on them, who laid them out, or some other characteristic. When circumstances changed, sometimes the street names changed as well. When residents of the Brewer's Street complained in 1655 that the wagons of the Company's brewery (located on the street) were creating excessive mud and dust, the Court of Burgomasters and Schepens ordered the street to be paved with stone. Shortly thereafter it became known as the Stone Street, the name it still carries, although a Dutch resident of the middle 17th Century would still have given you good directions had you asked for the *Straet van de Graft*, or "street to the canal" that ran through Broad Street.

The English took over the administration of the city in 1675, re-naming it after James Stuart, the Duke of York, and the old Dutch names were translated or transliterated. Thus the *Breedweg* became the Broadway and the *Tuyn Paat*, or "garden path," became Tin Pot Alley. The English continued the tradition of giving streets functional or descriptive names and added a tradition of their own: honoring the ruling monarchy of the colony's homeland. Crown Street, William, Nassau, King George Street, a couple of Queen Streets (Great and Little) and at least two Duke Streets were added to the growing city map. Many of these royal names were removed in 1794 by the council of the city that was now the largest in the new United States.

As the city grew northward, the landholders in its path saw the advantage of being prepared for its arrival. Families such as the Bayards, the Delanceys, the Stuyvesants and the Kips divided their farms into grids, often assigning the names of family members to the streets. While most of Nicholas Bayard's and James Delancey's streets still exist today, some with the same names they assigned them in the 18th Century, by the time the city reached the boweries of Peter Gerard Stuyvesant and the Kip family a great change had taken place.

In 1811 the Common Council put an end to the haphazard method of freelance street naming when it adopted a system of numbered streets and avenues oriented along the axis of the island. These streets would supersede any already laid out by private owners, and anonymous numbers would be used rather than the names of generals, statesmen or the members of propertied families.

Or so it first seemed. It was not long before developers and residents were before the council requesting special designations for the "places," "courts," and "terraces" that peppered the numbered grid as the city grew. As new avenues were deemed necessary they were inserted between the numbered thoroughfares and given names like Manhattan, Lexington and Madison. In the 1890s, Upper West Side property owners used their influence to rename the avenues near the newly-opened Central Park, hoping to attract a better class of resident with grand street names like Central Park West, Columbus and Amsterdam. Despite these occasional departures the number grid marched steadily northward, reaching its projected boundary at 155th Street by the turn of the 20th Century. Above this point many of the street names revert to an earlier tradition, taking the names of local landholders and nearby landmarks.

To trace the history of Manhattan's street names is to outline the growth of the city itself. A name like "Gramercy," for example, encapsulates several of the major changes in the city's history. A hook-shaped hill that once stood in the neighborhood reminded the Dutch settlers of a *krom-mesje*, a curved knife used to cut leather. To the English who followed, the word sounded like "Gramercy," and this name was given to the farm that included the hill. The numbered street grid of the aspirational yet practical Americans might have obliterated the name but for the efforts of a developer who sought to carve out an exclusive residential area in 1831, centered on a private garden he called Gramercy Park.

This book is intended to reconnect the street names of Manhattan's past and present and to serve as a starting point for further exploration of the city's fascinating history.

USING THIS GUIDE

Street names are listed alphabetically. Current street names are in regular bold type. Former street names and proposed names that were not adopted appear in bold italic type. In cases where a current street shares a name with a former or proposed street, or where part of a street has been renamed, separate entries have been made. Boldface names within entries indicate a separate entry for that street.

Although there was no formal method for distinguishing among streets, avenues, places, lanes, etc., the designations do follow some general patterns.

"Street" is the most common designation and indicates a residential, commercial or mixed street providing local access. Avenues are generally broader streets of greater length, often principally commercial. In the numbered grid plan, avenues were laid out along the north-south axis of the island and streets laid out perpendicularly east and west. Roads and lanes were usually routes between villages and farms that followed property lines and the topography of the land.

A "place" is usually a residential section of an existing street and often refers to a row of houses or related buildings given an official address different than the street on which it stands. Sometimes the name only applied to one side of the street, with the opposite side retaining the original street address, so that in practice two names were in use for the same stretch of street. Places were frequently named for the developer or property owner, or for well-known families or individuals. The designation of "place" was also commonly given to streets running in front of churches. "Rows" are similar to places and usually refer to one side of a street.

Alleys are normally narrow through passages between streets. Courts are similar to alleys but usually do not provide through access.

A "square" is an area around a wide intersection that is named independently of the streets that form it.

Along the waterfront, a "slip" referred originally to a squared-off inlet into which boats could be brought for loading and unloading. Keeping slips clear of mud was an ongoing problem in early Manhattan and they were all eventually filled in. Some have retained the designation and are now wide areas or parallel streets near the waterfront that indicate the location of the former slip. Wharves were generally mooring areas that ran parallel to the waterfront while docks and piers were structures built out perpendicular to the shore. Slips, wharves, docks and piers were usually called by their owners' names or by the names of nearby businesses. These names changed frequently and are not always attributable to a definite individual.

Some terms referring to the stages in a street's official existence will be useful to keep in mind. Dates given for when a street was laid out indicate the date it first appeared on a published map or in a description. It may only have existed on paper at this point and not yet surveyed and marked out on the ground. Opening a street was an official act that occurred sometimes after and sometimes in conjunction with surveying. This gave the street an officially-recognized path along which lots could be sold and buildings erected, although owners and builders did not always wait for official recognition before proceeding, and opening a new street usually involved moving or removing rogue structures. Regulating a street was the process of digging it out or filling it in as necessary to bring it to the level of intersecting streets while providing an appropriate slope for drainage. Regulation often meant cutting through the many hills of Manhattan, sometimes leaving buildings stranded on ledges several feet above the street surface.

Illustrations are drawn from contemporary maps and show historic streets and roads laid over the modern map to provide their relative locations. Because historic surveys do not usually match the modern maps exactly, these locations are sometimes approximate. Comparison of historic maps with modern tax maps will often reveal current property lines that still follow the boundaries of old streets and lanes, and this method has been used where possible in creating the illustrations.

A.

Avenue A. The first part of Avenue A opened in 1813 from North Street (now Houston) to the East River. The lettered avenues were proposed as part of the *Commissioners' Plan* of 1811, which laid out twelve avenues numbered from east to west and four avenues to the east of 1st Avenue lettered from west to east. Avenue A was laid out on the same line for the entire length of the island, although the contours of the East River interrupted its path in places, and by 1837 had been opened for most of its full length.

The section between East 57th and East 60th Streets was named **Sutton Place** in 1880, with South Sutton Place named shortly afterward. The portion between East 59th and 93rd Streets was renamed **York Avenue** in 1928. The section north of East 106th Street was first opened in 1837, with portions of it closed for construction of the **East River Drive** and Jefferson Park. The section between East 114th and 120th Streets was renamed **Pleasant Avenue** in 1879. In 1943, planning began for Stuyvesant Town and Peter Cooper Village, two private housing projects that closed part of Avenue A between East 14th and 23rd Streets. The small section cut off between East 23rd and 25th Streets was renamed **Asser Levy Place** in 1955.

A. Philip Randolph Square. A. Phillip Randolph (1889-1979) was a prominent civil rights leader and labor organizer. The name was changed from *Dewey Square* in 1964.

Abattoir Place. A name once used for the portion of West 39th Street between 11th and 12th Avenues. The H. C. Derby meatpacking operation occupied most of the street in the late 19th Century.

Abeel's Wharf. Garrit and John Abeel founded an iron foundry in 1765 at the corner of the *New Slip* and **Water Street**, about where Water Street turns to the north within the Alfred Smith Houses project.

Abingdon Place. Located on what is now West 12th Street between Greenwich Street and 8th Avenue. See *Troy Street*, **Abingdon Square**.

Abingdon Road. A now obsolete road that ran from 8th Avenue between 21st and 22nd Streets easterly to Broadway at 21st Street, then northeasterly to 23rd Street and 3rd Avenue. Also

1

mapped as *Rose Hill Lane* and *Love Lane*. See **Abingdon Square** and illustration on page 41.

Abingdon Square. Named for Willoughby Bertie, the 4th Earl of Abingdon, who married Charlotte Warren, daughter of Peter Warren, whose estate was at Greenwich. Abingdon received a portion of the Warren estate as dowry in 1768.

Abraham Kazan Street. Named after Abraham E. Kazan (1888-1971), a prominent advocate and organizer of cooperative housing. Formerly part of **Columbia Street**.

Academy Place. A former street that ran west of and parallel to the present Convent Avenue, between West 128th and West 130th Streets. Named after the Academy of the Sacred Heart, which was built nearby in 1847.

Academy Street. Named for the "Tubby Hook" school building that stood on the street at the corner of Broadway. The building was demolished in 1956 when the present Public School 52 was expanded. A portion of Academy Street between 10th Avenue and Nagle Avenue was closed in the 1940s for the Dyckman public housing project.

Achmuty Lane. Probably an alternate version of *Auchmuty Street*.

Achmuty Street. See *Auchmuty Street*.

Ackerly's Wharf. A former wharf along Water Street between Pike and Rutgers Streets. Named after the shipbuilder Samuel Ackerly (also Akerly) who operated at this location in the late 18th Century.

Ackerman Place. A name used for a portion of the obsolete *New Chambers Street* between Park Row and William Street, now part of the block where the New York City Police Headquarters is located. Of uncertain origin, however an attorney named P. C. Ackerman had set up offices in Ackerman Place in 1865.

Adam Clayton Powell, Jr. Boulevard. Named in 1974 for Reverend Adam Clayton Powell, Jr. (1908-1972), pastor and U.S. Representative for New York, 1945-1971. Formerly 7th Avenue.

Adams Place. Referred to a portion along the east side of **West Broadway** between Spring and Prince Streets. Of uncertain origin.

Adams Wharf. Formerly opposite 67 Washington Street, in the block now bounded by Washington, West, Rector and Joseph P. Ward Streets. The namesake is uncertain, but probably refers to a merchant or shipbuilder who operated there.

Agnew's Alley. A former alley that connected Front and Water Streets west of Roosevelt Street. William Agnew and Sons, a tobacco manufacturing firm, was located at 284 Front Street near Roosevelt Street.

Albany Avenue. See *West Road.*

Albany Basin. **Coenties Slip** was also called Albany Basin for a time, and the pier along its west side called Albany Pier. A "new" Albany Basin was located between Albany and Cedar Streets on the west side of Greenwich Street.

Albany Road. See *Eastern Post Road.*

Albany Street. An early pier serving Hudson River traffic between New York and Albany was located at the foot of Albany Street. The common use of the name Albany stems from the Duke of Albany, one of the titles held by James Stuart, Duke of York, after whom the city and state are named.

Albion Place. Referred to a section along the south side of East 4th Street between 2nd Avenue and The Bowery. Albion is a poetic reference to the island of Britain.

Allen Street. Named in 1817 for William Henry Allen (1784-1813) an officer in the U.S. Navy who died in the War of 1812. Previously called *Fourth Street.*

Allerton's Wharf. Also referred to as Allerton's Quay. An early wharf on the East River near the present Fulton Street. Isaac Allerton was a Mayflower pilgrim who lived in New York for a time. He operated a regular shipping trade with Virginia from this location.

Amersley Street. See *Hamersley Street.*

Amity Alley. An alley that formerly ran in the block between Wooster and Mercer Streets, now part of the New York University campus. The alley was a remnant of the closed *Amity Lane.*

Amity Lane. A country lane that originally ran from Broadway near Bleecker Street to West 3rd Street near Macdougal. The lane was first laid out in 1752 as an unnamed path to provide access to Elbert Herring's farm. The lower part of the lane was laid out by agreement between the heirs of the Herring and Bayard estates, and the name possibly refers to the spirit of cooperation in which it was designated. Ironically, the lane later became a matter of contention between the Herring family and the city over whether the land had been ceded for public use. The lane was closed in 1808 and at the same time the name was transferred to the newly-opened West 3rd Street, called *Amity Street.* See illustration on page 4.

Amity Place. Located along what is now La Guardia Place between Bleecker and West 3rd Streets. Named for its proximity to *Amity Street.*

Amity Street. A former name of West 3rd Street between Broadway and 6th Avenue. It takes its name from the former *Amity Lane,* which ended at the intersection of West 3rd and Macdougal Streets and ran diagonally to the intersection of Broadway and Bleecker Street. Opened in 1808 at the same time Amity Lane was ordered closed.

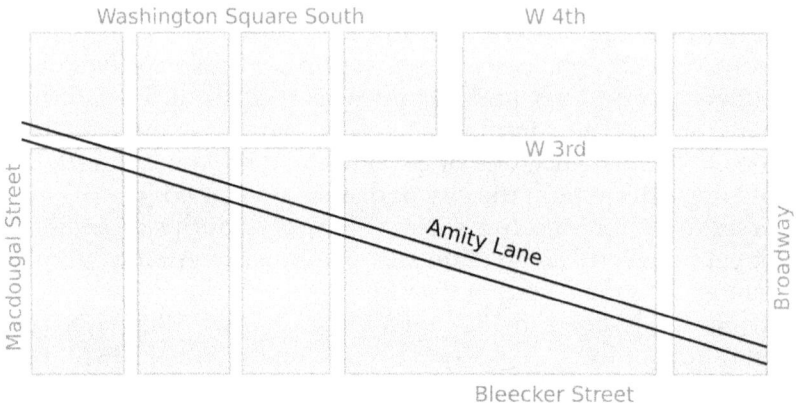

Amos Street. The former name of West 10th Street between 6th Avenue and West Street. The streets in this area were ceded to the city by Richard Amos in 1809. The name was changed to West 10th in 1857.

Amsterdam Avenue. 10th Avenue was laid out in the *Commissioners' Plan* and opened in 1816. In 1890, property owners and developers petitioned the Council to rename the upper portions of 8th, 9th and 10th Avenues to distance the area from the negative associations that had arisen with those street names. 10th Avenue between West 59th Street and Fort George Avenue was renamed Amsterdam in honor of the city's Dutch heritage and former name. 9th Avenue above 59th was renamed Columbus Avenue at the same time.

Amsterdam Street. A proposed east-west street in the *Mangin-Goerck Plan* that extended the *Stuyvesant Farm Grid* to the south.The plan included several streets named for European cities.

Ann Street, Anne Street. Several streets have held the name Ann or Anne. The portion of **Grand Street** between Broadway and the Bowery was mapped as Ann Street in 1799, possibly in reference to a member of the Bayard family, which owned the farm through which the street was laid. *Elm Street* between Reade and Franklin Streets was called Ann Street and Little Ann Street by 1797, also possibly in reference to a Bayard family member. By 1800, the street was mapped as Elm.

4

A portion of the present **William Street** was also sometimes called Ann or Anne Street in the mid 18th century, specifically the area at the intersection with present Ann Street.

Ann Street. The present Ann Street is most probably named for Ann Beekman, the wife of William Beekman. Another popular theory is that it was named after Ann White, the wife of Captain Thomas White, a merchant and land developer who owned lots along the street. White purchased the property in 1762, however, and the street is clearly called "Ann" on the Bradford Map of 1730. It was sometimes also referred to as *White Street* in deeds from the late 18th Century.

Anthony Street. A former name for **Worth Street** between Hudson and Baxter Streets. Named for Anthony Lispenard, the great-great-grandson of Anthony Lispenard the original landholder of what became the Lispenard estate. Laid out on the estate prior to 1799 between Hudson and Elm (now Elk) Streets. Extended to Orange Street (now Baxter) in 1817, at which time the name was also applied to *Little Water Street*, where Anthony terminated on its eastern end at the infamous *Five Points*. In 1855 the name was changed to remove its association with that notorious neighborhood.

Post indicates that **Duane Street** was formerly called Anthony Street, possibly for Anthony Rutgers, who had property in the area along Broadway.

Antwerp Street. A street laid out in the *Mangin-Goerck Plan* but never adopted. One of several east-west streets extending the *Stuyvesant Farm Grid* that were named for European cities.

Apthorp's Lane. A former lane that ran past the Apthorp Mansion which stood near present Columbus Avenue between 90th and 91st Streets. The lane ran from the Bloomingdale Road near the present intersection of Broadway and 93rd Street, southeasterly on a line between the present 93rd and 94th Streets to a point now within Central Park. Charles Ward Apthorp (1729-1797) was a loyalist merchant whose property was seized following the Revolution. Sometimes spelled Apthorpe. Also called *Turin Lane*.

Arch Place. Located on the south side of Canal Street between Church Street and West Broadway. Possibly named after a nearby bridge over the canal in Canal Street.

Arden Street. Named for Jacob Arden, a successful butcher who owned property in the area.

Arden Street. Former name of **Morton Street** between Bleecker and the bend in the street between Bedford and Hudson Streets. Also called Ardens Street. Jacob Arden, the same per-son after whom the present **Arden Street** is named, owned property nearby. The name was changed in 1829.

Arden's Wharf. A former wharf along present Washington Street between Battery Place and Morris Street. Named for the chandler James Arden, the brother of Jacob Arden. See also **Arden Street**.

Art Street. Former name of part of the *Sand Hill Road* between The Bowery and Waverly Place. The street extended from The Bowery at modern Astor Place to near the present intersection of 5th Avenue and Waverley Place where it turned to the north to meet 6th Avenue on the line of Greenwich Avenue. The section between Broadway and 6th Avenue was closed in 1825. The remaining section was renamed **Astor Place** in 1840. Named to honor one of the great human endeavors and Enlightenment ideals. *Science Street* was laid out nearby on the *Mangin-Goerck Plan.*

Arundel Street. A former name for **Clinton Street** between Division and Houston Streets. Originally part of the *Delancey Farm Grid* and possibly named after the London street of the same name. It is adjacent to several other streets in the Delancey plan that are named for English counties. Laid out prior to 1767 and opened in 1806. By 1831, the street had been joined with Clinton Street and was so called.

Ashland Place. Referred to **Perry Street** between Waverly Place and Greenwich Avenue.

Asser Levy Place. Asser (or Asher) Levy (d. 1680) was one of the first Jewish residents of New Amsterdam. A separated two-block section of **Avenue A** was named for him in 1955.

Astor Court. A former alley connecting West 33rd and 34th Streets west of 5th Avenue and along one side of the former Waldorf-Astoria Hotel. The Empire State Building now stands at the site.

Astor Place. Named in 1836 for John Jacob Astor (1763-1848), the prominent fur merchant. See also *Art Street.*

Asylum Street. A former name for West 4th Street between 6th Avenue and West 13th Street. Named for the New York Orphan Asylum, which built its first permanent building on four lots along the street in 1807. Prior to 1813 the street was called *William Street.* The name was changed to 4th Street in 1833.

Attorney Street. Possibly named for the presence of attorneys' offices on the street. The street was at one time a private street on property owned by Maturin Livingston, a prominent attorney, suggesting another possible origin.

Auchmuty Street. A former name for the present **Rector Street**. Named after the Reverend Samuel Auchmuty (1725-1777), the third rector of Trinity Church, from 1764 to 1777. Originally laid out as *Robinson Street*.

Audubon Avenue. Named for the famed naturalist John James Audubon (1785-1851), who established an estate in Washington Heights in 1841

Audubon Place. The former name of **Edward M. Morgan Place**. Named for nearby Audubon Park, which was part of the estate of John James Audubon. Name changed in 1926.

Augusta Street. A misspelling of *Augustus Street*.

Augustus Street. A former street that ran just north of **Cardinal Hayes Place** between Centre and Pearl Streets. Laid out prior to 1767, but not named. Known as Augustus Street by 1786, when it was regulated. The name was changed to *City Hall Place* in 1834. Of uncertain origin, but possibly in reference to Augustus Van Cortlandt.

Avenue of the Americas. The official, if rarely used, name of 6th Avenue. The name was changed in 1945 as a symbolic effort to promote trade, with the nations of the Western Hemisphere represented by signs along the street.

Avenue of the Finest. Named for "New York's Finest," the New York City Police Department, whose headquarters are located here.

B.

Avenue B. Laid out as part of the *Commissioners' Plan* as one of the lettered avenues running to the east of the numbered avenues. The northern portion of Avenue B was originally laid out as a waterfront street between 73rd and 89th Streets. This section was renamed **East End Avenue** in 1890.

Bache Street. Original spelling of the present **Beach Street**. Named for Paul Bache, who married Helena Lispenard, daughter of Anthony Lispenard.

Bailey Street. A former street that ran from the Bloomingdale Road near 26th Street to near what is now 26th Street and Madison Avenue. Named after Theodore Bailey, whose property along the Bloomingdale Road was crossed by the street.

Bancker Street. A former name for **Madison Street**. Originally part of the Rutgers estate and named by Hendrick Rutgers after

William Bancker, husband of his daughter, Anna. Sometimes spelled Bankers Street.

Bancker Street is also given as a former name of **Duane Street**, probably referring to *Colden Street*, which met Bancker obliquely at its western end and later became part of Duane.

Bancker's Wharf. A former wharf located on the East River between Clinton Street and Montgomery Street. Operated by Evert Bancker, Jr. See also *Bancker Street*.

Bank Street. In the early 19th Century, the Bank of New York and a branch of the Bank of the United States relocated from lower Manhattan to the village of Greenwich to escape being quarantined during an outbreak of yellow fever. Bank Street is named for the new location of these banks. Ironically, in another outbreak in 1822, several cases of the disease were noted among residents of the street.

Bank Street. An obsolete street that ran parallel to the Bowery in the area of what is now Union Square in the early 19th Century. Named for the Bank of Manhattan which stood on the east side of Broadway between 17th and 18th Streets. The bank had established the location around 1805 to escape an outbreak of yellow fever in lower Manhattan. See illustration on page 107.

Barclay Street. Named for Reverend Henry Barclay (1746-1764), the Rector of Trinity Church from 1711-1764. Sometimes spelled Barkly, Bartley or Bartly's Street. The street was first called *Mortkile Street*. See also *Barley Street*.

Barley Street. A former name for the portion of **Duane Street** west of Broadway. Possibly named in association with the Rutgers family, a brewing family with property nearby. Sometimes misspelled as Barclay Street. The street was combined with Duane and *Colden Street* in 1809 and the resulting street named Duane.

Barrack Street. A former street located in what is now City Hall Park. Named for the British barracks that stood nearby until the late 18th Century. See also *Tryon Row*.

Barrick Street. A short version of *Flatten Barrack Street*.

Barrow Street. Named in 1807 for Thomas Barrow, vestryman of Trinity Church from 1790-1820. Barrow Street was originally laid out between West and Hudson Streets, extending east of Hudson to the point where it now bends northward. In 1828, *Reason Street* was extended from Bedford Street to meet with Barrow and form a through street. Around the same time the name Barrow was extended to the whole street. See also *Gilbert Street*.

Barrow Street. A former name of **West Washington Place**. See **Barrow Street**.

Baruch Drive. A drive within the Baruch Houses project named for the financier and political advisor Bernard Baruch (1870-1965).

Baruch Place. Two short segments of street share the official name Baruch Place, one connecting the north and south lanes of Delancey Street beneath the Williamsburg Bridge and another forming one leg of a U drive in the Baruch Houses development. Both segments are generally along the line of the former *Goerck Street.* See **Baruch Drive**.

Batavia Lane and *Batavia Street.* A one-block street that connected Roosevelt and James Streets between Oak and Cherry Streets. Named for the Batavia region of the Netherlands. Laid out prior to 1767 as Batavia Lane, the name was changed to Batavia Street in 1817. Closed for construction of the Alfred E. Smith Houses, which were completed in 1953. See illustration on page 78.

Battery Place. Opened in 1857 and named for the defensive fort that once stood on the lower tip of Manhattan. See also **Marketfield Street**.

Battoe Street. A name sometimes used for **Dey Street**. An anglicized version of *batteau*, a French style of boat. Also some-times spelled Bateau and Batteaux. Perhaps so called in reference to a boatyard on the street.

Baxter Street. Named in 1854 for Lt. Col. Charles Baxter, an officer killed in the Mexican War. Formerly called *Orange Street* and *Mary Street*.

Bayard Place. A section of **Greenwich Street** between Jane and Horatio Streets. Named for the prominent Bayard family.

Bayard Street. Named probably for Nicholas Bayard II, descendent of the former mayor of New York of the same name, who laid out the streets on the Bayard Farm some time prior to 1754. *Fisher Street* was incorporated into Bayard Street in 1809, extending it east of Bowery to Division Street. This portion was closed in the 1960s.

Bayard's Lane. A former lane on the Bayard Estate that ran near the present **Broome Street**.

Beach Street. Formed from the original name, *Bache Street*. Laid out prior to 1799 between West and Hudson Streets, the street was ceded by Trinity Church to the City in 1802. In 1808 it was extended from Hudson to Chapel Street (now West Broadway.) The street appears as Beach Street on the 1799 Mangin-Goerck plan, but is referred to as Bache Street in the records of 1802 when the land was ceded. In 1808, when the street was extended, it was referred to as Beach.

Beach's Wharf. Also Bache's Wharf. A wharf operated by Theophylact Bache east of the present Old Slip.

Beak Street. Of uncertain origin.

Beaver Lane. A former name of **Morris Street**. The lane met Broadway opposite and north of Beaver Street. Laid out prior to 1730, the name was changed in 1829 after a petition of residents of the street, who requested the name Morris. See also *Goelets Street.*

Beaver Street. The English version of Bever Straat, the Dutch name for the street. The street was initially laid out partly along a branch of the Heere Graft in present day Broad Street. Also called Beaver Ditch, Bever Graft, Bever Straat, Beaver Path, Bever's Paatje. and Beaver Graft. Named for the animal that was the primary economic resource of the early colony.

Bedford Street. Of uncertain origin, but possibly after the London street of the same name.

Bedlow Alley. An alley that once connected Madison and Monroe Streets between Catherine and Market Streets. Named for its connection to the former *Bedlow Street.*

Bedlow Street. A former name of a portion of **Madison Street**. Named for William and Catherine Bedlow. Catherine Bedlow had inherited a portion of the Rutgers estate from her father, Henry Rutgers. Previously called *William Street* and changed to Bedlow in 1792 to avoid confusion with the present William Street.

Beekman Place. Named for its location on the former Beekman farm. Opened prior to 1869.

Beekman Street. Opened some time before 1730 and ordered to be laid out in 1750 as Beekmans Street. The street passed through what was known as Beekman's Pasture, an area bounded roughly by Gold, Fulton, Pearl and Ferry (now closed). Named for Willem Beekman or Beeckman, an early commissioner of New Amsterdam who owned the pasture as well as Beekman's Swamp to the north of it and a house to the west. The street was originally laid out to the waterfront at Pearl Street, extended to Water Street in 1803, to Front Street 1816 and to South Street in 1818. The portion between Gold and Pearl Streets was closed in 1971 for the construction of housing projects. Sometimes called *Chapel Street*. See also *George Street.*

Belvidere Place, also *Belvedere Place.* Located on West 30th Street between 9th and 10th Avenues. Of uncertain origin, but a common Irish and English place name.

Bennett Avenue. Named for James Bennett (1795-1872), founder of the New York Herald, who had an estate in the area.

Benson Place. Named for Egbert Benson, a former Attorney General for New York. Also called Benson Street. See *Benson's Lane.*

Benson's Lane. Given as a former name for *Elm Street*, now **Elk Street** and **Lafayette Street**. In 1791, the City negotiated with Egbert Benson, a representative of the Rutgers estate, to purchase land that stood under and around the western part of the Collect Pond. The former Elm Street ran directly through this land, and it is likely the name is a reference to Benson's part in obtaining the land. The present **Benson Place** is located at what was then the very western edge of the pond. It is possible, perhaps likely, that this a remnant of Benson's Lane, as the name Elm was already in use by the time Benson Place was first mapped in 1827.

Bethune Street. Named for Johanna Graham Bethune, a philanthropist and one of the founders of the New York Orphan Asylum. Bethune ceded her property for the street in 1827, when it was opened.

Beurs Straat. Literally "Purse Street" in Dutch, or Exchange Street. A former name of **Whitehall Street**, where one of the first markets was established. See also **Marketfield Street**.

Bialystoker Place. Named for the Bialystoker Synagogue situated in the street. Located in **Willett Street**.

Billings Row. West 50th Street between 8th and 9th Avenues. Possibly named for Henry M. Billings, president of a manufacturing company, who lived on West 50th near 6th Avenue.

Birmingham Street. A short street that connected Henry and Madison Streets in the block between Market and Pike Streets. Sometimes called Birmingham Alley. Renamed *Livingston Place* in 1954 when the original Livingston Place on Stuyvesant Square was renamed for Nathan D. Perlman. Closed in 1962.

Bishop's Lane. A former lane that connected Chambers Street and Warren Street west of Greenwich Street. Of uncertain origin, however probably named for a nearby property holder.

Bleecker Street. Named for Anthony Bleecker (1770-1827), who ceded the land for the street where it was originally laid out between the Bowery and Broadway in 1805. The street was later connected to *David Street* which ran between Broadway and Hancock Street (now at 6th Avenue) and to *Herring Street* beyond Hancock Street, and the name was extended to the entire street.

Bloomfield Street. Opened in 1873 and named for General Joseph Bloomfield, a veteran of the Revolutionary War and the War of 1812.

Bloomingdale Road. An early road serving the west side of the island, much of which now corresponds with modern **Broadway** above Union Square. The road ran from a point now within Union Square at about 16th Street northward to the Kings Bridge Road at about modern 147th Street and 9th Avenue. The name is an anglicization of *Bloemendaal,* which the Dutch used to refer to the collection of small villages along the western side of the island, including the village of Bloomingdale located around 110th Street. *Bloemendaal* is a city in the Netherlands. See illustration on page 13.

Bogardus Place. Probably refers to the Robert Bogardus family, who owned a farm near present day West 183rd Street east of Broadway.

Bogart Street. An obsolete street that once connected West Street and West 13th Street north of Gansevoort. Opened and named in 1873 for Lt. Colonel Joseph Bogart, a commander in the War of 1812.

Bolton Road. A former road that led to the Reginald Bolton estate in what is now Inwood Hill Park. Much of the road is now a pedestrian walkway within the park.

Bond Street. Of uncertain origin, but possibly named after the London street of the same name. The street had been so designated when it was ceded to the city by Samuel Jones in 1806. It was probably Jones who had given the street its name.

Bonsall's Wharf, also *Bonsall's Basin, Bonsall's Dock.* Located on the Hudson River between Dey Street and Cortlandt Street. Named for John Bonsall, a lumber dealer who operated there. Bonsall's Dock extended into the river at the south side of Dey Street.

Boorman Place. A former name for part of West 33rd Street, between 8th and 9th Avenues. James Boorman was a successful New York merchant and philanthropist, and the founder of the Hudson River Railroad. The name is possibly in reference to him.

Boorman Terrace. West 32nd Street between 8th and 9th Avenues. See *Boorman Place.*

Boston Road. See *Eastern Post Road.*

Bott Street. Given as a former name for *Elm Street.* Origin uncertain.

Boulevard Place. Referred to West 130th Street between Lenox Avenue and 6th Avenue.

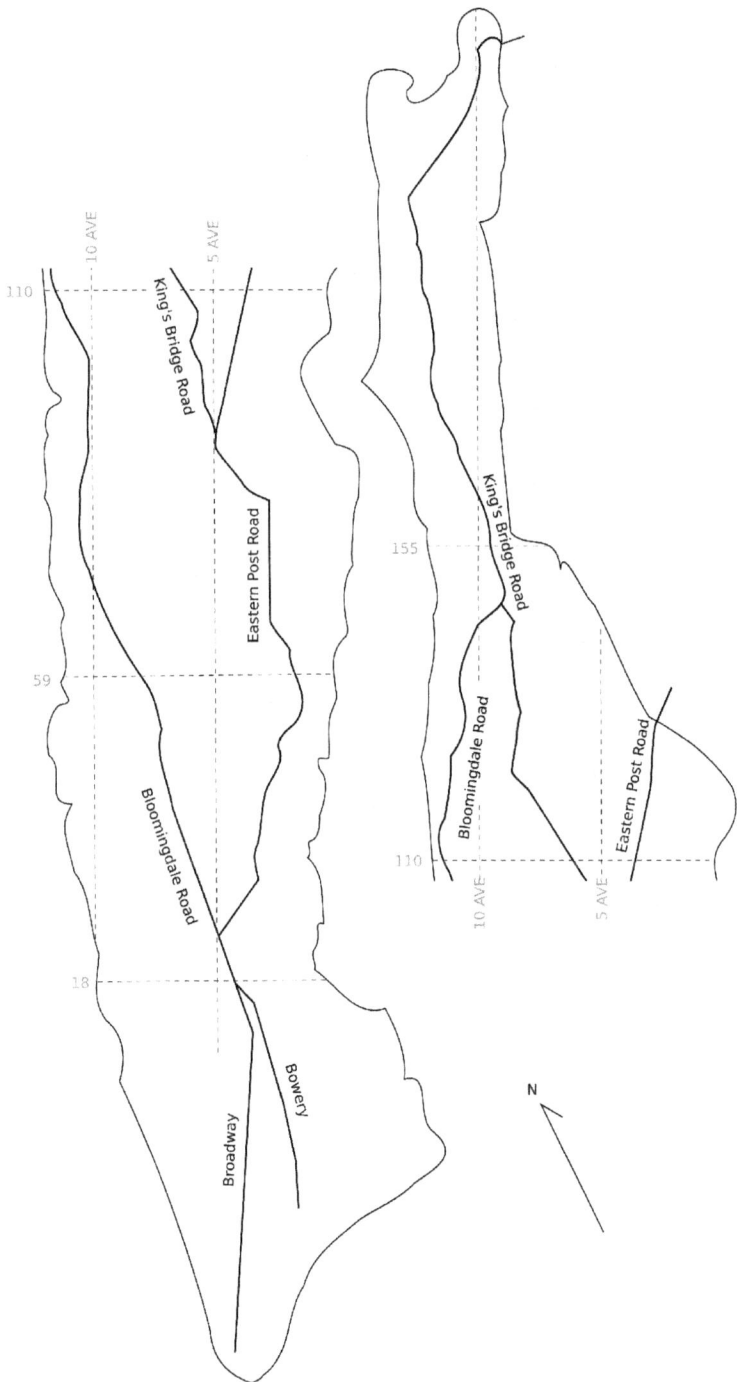

10 AVE

5 AVE

110

King's Bridge Road

Eastern Post Road

155

King's Bridge Road

59

Bloomingdale Road

Bloomingdale Road

110

Eastern Post Road

10 AVE

5 AVE

18

Bowery

N

Broadway

North-South Roads of Manhattan c.1807

The Boulevard. Beginning in 1867, parts of the *Bloomingdale Road* and West 11th Avenue between West 59th and 155th Streets were widened and improved along the path of modern **Broadway**. The Bloomingdale name was dropped and the street was referred to simply as the "Road or Public Drive." This new drive came to be called "The Boulevard," or sometimes "Broadway Boulevard" for its connection with Broadway at 59th Street. In 1873 the road was extended from 155th Street to the Kings Bridge Road (now St. Nicholas Avenue). Officially named part of Broadway in 1899. See also the illustration on page 13.

Prior to 1893 a branch of the Boulevard was laid out beginning just above West 155th Street and winding along the riverside to meet the Broadway line at Dyckman Street. This portion was named *Lafayette Boulevard* in 1894, and in 1905 became part of **Riverside Drive**.

The Bowery. "Bouwerij" is the Dutch word for "farm," and the road once served a collection of farms established by the Dutch East India Company, particularly that of Peter Stuyvesant. Often called the Bowery Lane and the Bowery Road, the street ran from modern Park Row to about East 23rd Street and included what is now 4th Avenue and part of **Broadway** between Union Square and East 23rd Street. The name The Bowery was officially assigned in 1813.

Bowling Green. The nearby park has been a public space since the earliest days of the city, having first served as a square and public market. It was formally designated in 1732 when it was leased to three citizens at the sum of one peppercorn per year in return for improving the field for public use as a bowling green. The adjacent street was formally laid out and named for the park in 1817.

Bowne's Wharf. A former wharf on the East River between John and Fulton Streets. Named after the nearby shop of stationer and printer Robert Bowne, who started operations in 1775. Sometimes spelled Bown, Baume, Bowen and Browne.

Bradhurst Avenue. Dr. Samuel Bradhurst was a physician, pharmacist and merchant who had large estate north of 145th Street in the area of present Bradhurst Avenue. Named in 1889. See also *Coogan Avenue*.

Brannon Street. A former name for **Spring Street** west of modern 6th Avenue. Named for Charles John Brannon, an innkeeper and loyalist whose property was seized following the Revolution. Also sometimes spelled Bannon Street. The name was changed in 1807 when Brannon Street was renamed as an extension of Spring Street.

Breedweg and *Breedwegh.* Literally, "broad way." A Dutch name for what is now lower **Broadway**.

Breevoort Place. The former name of West 10th Street between Broadway and University Place. The Brevoort family owned property in this area from New York's Dutch settlement days. The land on which Grace Church currently stands at 10th and Broadway was purchased from Henry Brevoort, Jr.

Brewer Street. Also sometimes Brouwer Straat or other variants, and so called by 1653. A former name for **Stone Street** west of Broad Street, where the Dutch East india Company's brewery was established prior to 1646. The street was paved with cobblestone in 1655, the first such paved street in the city. The name Brewer Street continued to be used for some years after it was paved. Also called the *Straet van de Graft.*

Brewers Hill. An alternate name for *Rutger's Hill,* now part of **Gold Street** between Maiden Lane and John Street. Anthony Rutgers established a brewery on this hill in the late 18th Century.

Bride Street. A former name of **Minetta Street** between Bleecker Street and the bend in the street. Of uncertain origin, possibly named after the London street of the same name.

Bridge Street. Named for the bridge that crossed the *Heere Graft* canal in the center of Broad Street. Sometimes called Brugh Street or Brugh Straet, using the original Dutch. The name remained in use after the canal was filled in 1767 and the bridge became part of **Broad Street**. Also known as *High Street.* See also *Hull Street.*

Broad Street. In the days of Dutch settlement a canal, the *Heere Graft,* ran in the center what is now Broad Street from the waterfront about to present day Exchange Place. The canal was filled by the English in 1676, creating an extra wide street that became known as the "broad street." The section above Beaver Street was formerly called *Princes Graft.*

Broadway. The present Broadway was officially created from several main streets in 1899, although the street had come to be commonly called Broadway before that. The name given to the street is taken from its oldest portion, one of the first streets established in New Amsterdam. On the northern side of the first Dutch fort was a large open area that formed the foot of "De Breede Wegh," literally, "The Broad Way." This open area corresponds to modern Bowling Green Park. The street extended to the city wall at Wall Street, where one of the two wall gates was located. The early street was referred to by various names in public documents, including The Public Wagon Road, The Great Highway, De Heere Wegh (The Gentlemen's Way), De Heere Straet (The Gentlemen's Street), The Common Highway, and The Great Public Road. Above Ann Street it was called *Great George Street* until 1794.

From its intersection with the Bowery to West 59th Street, Broadway follows the path of the former *Bloomingdale Road*. Between West 59th and 155th Streets, it follows the path of the *Boulevard*, laid out in 1867, which also largely followed the Bloomingdale Road, as well as the line of 11th Avenue. In 1873 the Boulevard was extended to the *Kings Bridge Road*, the path of which Broadway follows above 169th Street. See also the illustration on page 13.

Broadway Alley. Presumably named after Broadway, but located several blocks from the street.

Broadway Terrace. Named for **Broadway**, which it abuts.

Brook Street. A former name for **Hancock Street**, which later became the portion of 6th Avenue that extends south of Bleecker Street. A reference to the Minetta Brook that ran nearby. Also called *Cottage Place*. See illustration on page 73.

Brooks Street. A private street located on the property of a man named Brooks that was ceded in 1808 and made part of *Collect Street*, now **Centre Street**.

Broome Street. Named after John Broome (1738-1810), a successful New York merchant and Lt. Governor of the state. Formerly *Bullock Street*. The section between the Bowery and Sullivan Streets was also called *William Street*.

Browne's Wharf. See *Bowne's Wharf*.

Bruce's Wharf. Located at the foot of Pine Street. Robert Bruce and his family were successful merchants of early British New York. Bruce's Wharf was infamous for its unhealthy conditions and was the center of the regular outbreaks of yellow fever that plagued the city in the late 18th and early 19th Centuries.

Brugh Steegh. "Bridge Lane." A short lane between Stone and Bridge Streets that ran along the eastern side of the Company's Brewery on Stone Street. See illustration on page 115.

Brugh Straat. See **Bridge Street**.

Budd Street. A former name for **Vandam Street**. Possibly named for Nathaniel Budd, a ferryman who was active at the time on the Hudson River. Laid out prior to 1799, the name was changed from Budd to Vandam in 1807, but was referred to by both names in official records for some time afterward.

Bullock Street. A former name for the eastern part of **Broome Street**. Of uncertain origin, but probably simply a reference to the rural nature of the area when the street was laid out some time prior to 1767. Name changed in 1806.

Burgher's Path. Once ran at what is now William Street and Old Slip between Wall Street and Hanover Square. Also called Burger Jousens Path, Boyer Jori's Path, Boyer Jorisen's Path, and other variants. Named for the early settler and smith Burger Jorissen, who built one of the first houses in New Amsterdam.

Burling Lane. Also called Burlings Lane. An obsolete lane that ran approximately from present day Broadway and East 16th Street to near the present intersection of West 15th Street and 6th Avenue. It served the property of Thomas and Samuel Burling.

Burling Slip. A slip located at the foot of John Street. James Burling had a storehouse near the slip prior to 1754, and other members of the Burling family owned property along the waterfront nearby.

Burnet Street, also *Burnett Street.* A former waterfront street between Maiden Lane and Wall Street that is now part of **Water Street**. Laid out in 1722 and so called in 1730. See *Burnet's Key*.

Burnet's Key. A wharf that was established in 1722 on the East River between Maiden Lane and Wall Street. Now part of **Water Street**. Also sometimes called Burnet or Burnett Street. Probably named after William Burnet (1688-1729), governor of New York at the time the street was opened.

Burr Street. A name sometimes used for **Charlton Street**. Named for Aaron Burr, who owned the Richmond Hill mansion that stood near the present intersection of Charlton and Varick Streets. See *Hetty Street*.

Burr's Corners. The former intersection of the *Middle Road* and the *Cross Road*, corresponding nearly exactly with the present intersection of 5th Avenue and 42nd Street. Named for the family of Isaac Burr, who purchased part of the adjacent property in the early 19th Century.

Burrows Street. A former name for **Grove Street**. Originally called *Columbia Street* and named Burrows Street in 1813 after Lieutenant William Burrows (1785-1813), a naval officer in the War of 1812. Changed to Grove Street in 1829.

Burton Street. A former name for the portion of **Leroy Street** between Bleecker Street and the bend in the street near 7th Avenue. Extended to meet Leroy in 1845 and renamed as part of Leroy Street around 1848. Of uncertain origin.

Bushwick Street. A name sometimes used for *Tompkins Street*, which ran between Grand and Rivington Streets along the East

River. Now part of **East River Drive**. Possibly related to the former Bushwick Street in Brooklyn (now North 2nd Street), which was connected with Tompkins Street by William Woodhull's ferry that landed at the foot of Grand Street.

Bussing's Wharf. A former wharf at the foot of Cortlandt Street. Abraham Bussing was a dry goods merchant who operated the wharf around 1800.

Byvanck Street. An obsolete street that once connected Grand Street and the East River and which ran between and parallel to the present Gouverneur and Jackson Streets. The street was laid out near the water lot of Peter Byvanck. Also known as *Fir Street*.

C.

Cabrini Boulevard. Named in 1938 for Saint Frances Xavier Cabrini (1850-1917), the first American canonized by the Catholic Church. Previously called *Northern Avenue*.

Camden Place. A former name for part of East 11th Street between Avenue B and Avenue C. A popular place name, possibly referring to the borough in London.

Canal Street. Named for the canal that once ran through the center of the street between the old Collect Pond and the Hudson River. The canal was first proposed in 1796 and ordered to be surveyed in 1803. In 1805 a plan was finalized to run an open canal through a street of 100 feet in width between the Collect Pond and the Hudson River and for the next several years the city was involved in the legal processes of obtaining the necessary land from affected property holders. The Collect Pond was filled in 1810 and by 1820 the open canal had been converted into an enclosed sewer.

Canal Street. The *Straet van de Graft*, presently **Stone Street** between Whitehall and Broad Streets, is sometimes translated from Dutch records as Canal Street. The name refers to the canal formerly located in Broad Street. Also called *Brewer Street*.

Cannon Street. Named for John Cannon, a ship captain and merchant who had a store and dock nearby at the foot of Broome Street. Originally laid out from Grand Street to North Street (now Houston,) an extension of Cannon Street north of Houston was proposed on the Stuyvesant property but never adopted.

Cannon's Dock. The dock at the foot of Broome Street where John Cannon operated a ferry to Long Island. See **Cannon Street**.

Cannon's Wharf. A wharf along several lots owned by John Cannon located north of Water Street east of present day Fulton Street.

Cardinal Hayes Place. Named in 1941 for Patrick Joseph Hayes (1867-1938) a former Archbishop of New York.

Carlisle Street. Carlisle Pollock, a member of a successful New York merchant family, owned waterfront property along Greenwich Street near Carlisle Street in 1797. In 1816 his widow was living at 54 Greenwich Street, near the present intersection of Carlisle and Greenwich Streets.

Carlisle Street Wharf. A wharf at the foot of Carlisle Street at about present day West Street. See **Carlisle Street**.

Carman Street. Part of **Beaver Street** east of Broad Street was called Carman or Carman's Street in the late 17th Century. Of uncertain origin, but the family of Jan Carman were early settlers of New Amsterdam.

Carmine Street. Possibly from an alternate spelling of Carman, the name is of uncertain origin. Sometimes spelled "Germain." Laid out on the Herring farm prior to 1799.

Caroline Street. A former street that connected Duane and Jay Streets between West and Washington Streets. Of uncertain origin.

Carroll Place. Formerly located in Bleecker Street between Thompson Street and La Guardia Place. Named after Charles Carroll (1787-1832), the last surviving signer of the Declaration of Independence.

Cart and Horse Street. See *Horse and Cart Lane*.

Cathedral Parkway. Named after the Cathedral of St. John the Divine. West 110th Street was ordered by the state legislature to be widened in 1891 to create the parkway, at which time the name was also designated.

Catherine Lane. Laid out prior to 1797 north of *Catherine Street* (now Worth) between Broadway and the Collect Pond. Later connected to Elm Street (now Lafayette) after the Collect Pond was filled. Sometimes mapped as Catherine Place and Catherine Alley.

Catherine Market. Located at the foot of **Catherine Street**.

Catherine Slip. Named for its location at the foot of **Catherine Street**.

Catherine Street, also **Catharine Street.** The present Catherine Street and Catherine Slip are named for Catherine Desbrosses, a member of a prominent family whose distillery was located at the foot of James, Oliver and Catherine Streets. James and Oliver were brothers of Catherine.

Catherine Street. The name Catherine or Catharine has been used for several streets, including **Worth Street**, and **Waverly Place**. These are of uncertain origin, but are probably in reference to the wives or daughters of nearby property owners.

    Mulberry Street was first laid out as Catherine Street on the Bayard Farm. Nicholas Bayard II 's mother was named Catherine, as was his daughter-in-law.

Cato's Lane. A section of the *Eastern Post Road* between about East 43rd and 63rd Streets. Named after Cato's Tavern, a popular inn that stood near modern 54th Street between 1st and 2nd Avenues. This fashionable roadhouse was owned and operated by Cato Alexander, a former South Carolina slave whose remarkable talents as a chef were said to have allowed him to purchase his freedom.

Cedar Street. Formerly called *Little Queen Street.* The street was renamed in 1794 when several streets that referred to the city's former colonial status were removed.

Center Drive. A drive through the lower part of Central Park, named for its location between West Drive and East Drive.

Central Park West. Forms the western border of Central Park. Opened in 1816 as 8th Avenue, the portion above 59th Street was renamed Central Park West in 1890, after property owners and developers petitioned the Council. See also **Amsterdam Avenue**.

Centre Market Place. The Centre Market was located along this street and Centre Street between Grand and Broome Streets. Named in 1839.

Centre Street. Named for the Centre Market, which stood on the east side of the street between Grand and Broome Streets, and for its central location between Broadway and the Bowery. Formerly called *Collect Street* between Pearl and Hester Streets, where it had been built over the filled-in Collect Pond. Collect Street was joined with *Rynders Street* in 1823, extending it to Broome Street, at the same time the full street was renamed Centre.

Chambers Street. Named for John Chambers, a lawyer and officer of Trinity Church. Ceded to the city by the Church in 1761, the street was originally laid out between the Hudson River and William Street. It was extended to Chatham Street (now Park Row) in 1811. In 1855 it was further extended under the name *New Chambers Street.*

Chapel Street. A former name for part of **West Broadway** south of Canal Street, named for St. John's Chapel. A portion of the street was later named *College Place.*

Chapel Street was also once used as the name of **Beekman Street** in reference to St. George's Chapel. Sometimes spelled Chappell. Sometimes called *Little Chapel* to distinguish it from the other Chapel Street.

Charles Lane. Named for its proximity to **Charles Street**. Also called Charles Alley.

Charles Street. Named for Charles Christopher Amos. See **Amos Street**.

Charlotte Slip. A former name of **Pike Slip**. See *Charlotte Street.*

Charlotte Street. A former name of **Pike Street**. Situated near the former George Street and George Slip (now Market), and named after the bride of King George III. Laid out before 1797, the name was changed in 1813 at the same time George Street was changed to Market.

Charlton Street. Named in 1807 for Dr. John Charlton, (c.1731-1806), a former president of the Medical Society of the State of New York and a warden of Trinity Church from 1794-1806. Ceded to the city by Trinity Church in 1808. Originally laid out prior to 1799 as *Hetty Street.*

Chatham Row. A former name of **Park Row** between Broadway and Murray Street (now at the intersection of Park Row and Centre Street). See *Chatham Street.*

Chatham Square. Surveyed as part of *Chatham Street* in 1790 and fenced in as a public park in 1812, Chatham Square was opened and paved in 1816. Sometimes called Chatham Park or The Park in Chatham Street.

Chatham Street. Former name of **Park Row**. Named in 1774 after William Pitt, Earl of Chatham (1708-1778), Prime Minister of England. Prior to 1797 the portion fronting the Common between Broadway and Murray Street was referred to as *Chatham Row*, and called Park Row by 1829. In 1886 the name Park Row was extended to the whole street.

Cheapside Street. Former name of *Hamilton Street*, an obsolete street that connected Catherine and Market Streets south of Monroe. Possibly named for the street in London. Cheapside was also a common English name for market streets. See illustration on page 22.

Cheeseman Street. A former street located west of the present intersection of West 41st Street and Broadway. The name is of uncertain origin, but possibly associated with Forman Cheeseman, a prominent and successful shipbuilder.

Chelsea Lots. A series of lots along West 24th Street between 9th and 10th Avenues. The Chelsea district was so named by Captain Thomas Moore, who established a country estate in the area in 1750, naming it after the neighborhood in London from which he came. Moore's grandson, Clement C. Moore, developed the property after inheriting it in 1813.

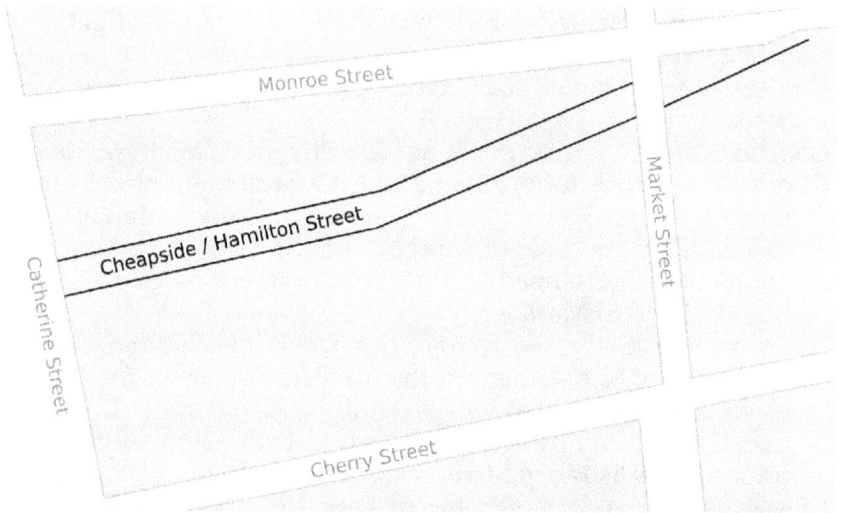

Cherokee Place. Named for the Cherokee Club, a meeting house that was built at this location in the early 20th Century. The Cherokee Club was a Democratic association affiliated with Boss Tweed's Tammany organization. The street once ran through from East 76th to 78th Street. The portion between East 76th and East 77th Streets was closed in the 1940s.

Cherry Street. Named for Richard Sackett's grove of cherry trees, through which the street was first laid out. The grove stood on Sackett's property at the west end of the street, which at the time was at Pearl Street near Dover Street.

Chester Street. A former name for what is now West 4th Street between Christopher and Bank Streets. Of uncertain origin. See also *William Street* and *Asylum Street*.

Chestnut Street. Formerly connected Madison and Oak Streets between Pearl and Roosevelt Streets through what is now James Madison Plaza. See illustration on page 78.

Christopher Street. Named for Charles Christopher Amos. See also *Skinner Road*, **Charles Street** and **Amos Street**.

Chrystie Street. Named in 1817 for Lt. Colonel John Chrystie, an officer in the War of 1812. Previously called *First Street*.

Church Street. Named for St. Paul's Chapel, which stands at what was once the foot of Church Street at present Fulton Street. Originally laid out prior to 1767 between Fulton and Duane Streets. Extended in 1869 to meet **Trinity Place** at Liberty Street and extended south to the Battery. Formerly called *Lumber Street* and *Lombard Street* below Liberty Street.

City Hall Lane. Another name for *Coenties Lane.* The first public building in Dutch Manhattan was the Stadt Huys, or City Hall, built in 1642 near what is now the corner of Pearl Street and Coenties Slip. Coenties Slip was also sometimes known as City Hall Slip.

City Hall Place. Augustus Street was renamed City Hall Place in 1834 in reference to the nearby city building and park.

Claremont Avenue. Refers to the Claremont Mansion of Michael Hogan, a navigator and successful merchant. The house stood in what is now Riverside Park. Hogan was from County Clare, Ireland, suggesting a possible origin. Another possibility is that Hogan named the mansion after the county seat of his friend and fellow sailor, Prince William, Duke of Clarence, who became King William IV. The name was given to the newly-opened avenue in 1880.

Clark Street. The spur of 6th Avenue that forms a triangular island between Broome and Spring Streets was originally called Clark Street. The street was laid out and named by Trinity Church, which ceded the street to the city in 1809. The origin of the name is uncertain, but possibly named after Thomas Clark, a vestryman and warden of the church.

Clarkson Street. General Matthew Clarkson was a vestryman of Trinity Church from 1788-1792. The street was named by Trinity Church in 1807 and ceded to the City the following year. Formerly called *Morton Street.*

Clendening's Lane. A former lane that twisted from about modern West104th Street and Amsterdam Avenue to about West 105th Street and Columbus Avenue. The mansion of the John Clendenning family once stood at what is now the southwest corner of Columbus and West 104th Street, and the surrounding region was known as Clendening Valley. Sometimes spelled Clendenning or Clenderring.

Clermont Street. The name Clermont was used for several streets in Manhattan including the present **Hester Street**, **Howard Street** and **Mercer Street**. Possibly named for the Hudson River estate established by Robert Livingston in 1728 for his son, who was called Robert of Clermont, and whose son and grandson, also both named Robert, were a prominent judge and state chancellor, respectively. Robert Fulton's steam ship, the *Clermont*, was also named for the Livingston estate.

Cleveland Place. Named in 1908 in memory of former New York Governor and U.S. President Grover Cleveland (1837-1908). Previously *Marion Street*.

Cliff Street. Named for Dirck Van der Clyff, who laid out the street on his own land some time prior to 1686. The street formerly extended past present Fulton Street to the former Ferry Street, with a section extending to the former Vandewater Street, now obscured by the Brooklyn Bridge ramps. A small portion of *Skinner's Street* east of Frankfort Street was renamed part of Cliff Street in 1827. Sometimes appears spelled as Clift Street. Also called *Elbow Street*.

Clinton Alley. A former alley connecting Clinton and Suffolk Streets between Rivington and Delancey Streets. Named for its connection to **Clinton Street**.

Clinton Market. The Clinton Market was established in 1829 along Washington Street between Spring and Canal Streets.

Clinton Place. A former name of 8th Street between 6th Avenue and Broadway. Probably named in reference to George Clinton. Clinton Court was located at 120 Clinton Place. See **Clinton Street**.

Clinton Street. Named for George Clinton, the first governor of New York. The portion south of East Broadway was originally called *Warren Street* and was renamed Clinton in 1792 to avoid confusion with the Warren Street in Greenwich Village. The section between East Broadway and Houston Street was called *Arundel Street* until the 1830s.

Coenties Lane. A short alley that ran between Pearl and Stone Streets, just west of where the present Stone Street meets Pearl. The large house of Coenraet Ten Eyck stood on the east side of this lane. See **Coenties Slip**, *City Hall Lane*.

Coenties Slip. The name is a contraction of Coenraet and Antje, sometimes spelled Coentjes or referred to as "Coen and Anty's Slip." Named for Coenraet and Antje Ten Eyck. Ten Eyck was a prosperous tanner whose house stood near the intersection of Coenties Slip and Pearl Street. The slip after which the street takes its name originally extended inland to Water Street. See also *Ten Eyck's Wharf*.

Coffee House Slip. A slip at the foot of Wall Street that extended to the present Front Street. The name was used for the portion of **Wall Street** below Pearl Street even after the slip had been filled in. The coffee house referred to is the Merchants Coffee House, which opened on the southeast corner of the present

Wall and Water Streets some time in the 1740s. The Tontine Coffee House was built on the opposite corner in 1792.

Colden Street. A former name of the part of **Duane Street** east of Broadway. Probably refers to Cadwallader Colden (1688-1776), Lt. Governor governor of colonial New York. Renamed in 1809.

Collays Place. A former place located in East 3rd Street between Avenues B and C. Of uncertain origin.

Collect Street. A former name of **Centre Street**, which was laid out through the center of the site of the Collect Pond. One popular theory of the origin of the name holds that the pond took its name from the Dutch *Kalck Hoek,* or "chalk hook," supposedly a reference to the piles of oyster shells left there by the Native Americans in the region. A more probable and simpler explanation is suggested by the Old Dutch word *kolch* (*kolk* in Modern Dutch), which means a pond or small lake. Opened from Pearl to Worth Streets in 1808.

College Place. A former name of **West Broadway** between Barclay and Canal Streets. Columbia College was originally located in the block bounded by the present Barclay, Church and Murray Streets and West Broadway. Previously *Chapel Street,* this portion was changed to College Place in 1831. Changed to West Broadway in 1866.

Collister Street. Thomas Collister was a sexton of Trinity Church. Regulated in 1818.

Colonnade Row. See *La Grange Terrace.*

Columbia Lane. See *Columbian Alley.*

Columbia Street. The name is a popular poetic reference to the New World. Laid out on the Delancey farm prior to 1767, a portion of Columbia Street between Grand and Broome Streets was renamed **Abraham Kazan Street** in 1969.

Columbia Street. Former name of **Grove Street** between Bedford and Bleecker Streets. Laid out prior to 1799 and extended in 1811 westward to Hudson Street and joined with *Cozine Street* to extend eastward to Christopher Street. Renamed *Burrows Street* in 1813, which is the present **Grove Street**.

Columbian Alley. A former name for **Jersey Street**. Of uncertain origin, but possibly after the Columbian Order, a common name for the Tammany Society. The street was also sometimes called Columbia Lane.

Columbus Avenue. 9th Avenue north of 59th Street was named Columbus Avenue in 1890 after the well-known explorer.

Columbus Circle. Named for Christopher Columbus. The statue of Columbus that is central to the circle was dedicated as part of the commemoration of the 400th anniversary of Columbus' voyage in 1892. The circle was laid out as a turnaround for carriages in 1869 as part of the Central Park Plan.

Commerce Street. Reportedly named for the commercial district that sprung up along the street when businesses relocated during an outbreak of yellow fever in 1798. First mapped in 1799 from Bleecker to the edge of the Herring Farm just west of Bedford Street. The street was connected to Barrow at the same time Reason Street was extended to meet Barrow in 1827.

Commissioners' Plan. In 1807 the Common Council of New York appointed three commissioners to oversee the creation of a comprehensive plan for the city's streets. In 1811 the commission presented a plan surveyed by John Randel Jr. that proposed a rectilinear grid of streets and avenues aligned with the axis of the island. Rather than names, the plan simply assigned numbers and sometimes single letters to the orderly grid. The plan was adopted and has shaped the growth of the city for over two centuries.

Common Ditch. See *Heere Graft.*

Commons Street. According to Post, a name once used for **Park Row**. City Hall Park, which the street borders, was once called the Commons.

Concord Street. Another name for *Laurens Street,* now **La Guardia Place** and **West Broadway** between Canal Street and West 4th Street. Of uncertain origin, but possibly, like Lexington Avenue, a reference to the famed Revolutionary War battle.

Congress Place. A former alley that adjoined *Congress Street.* Also called *Smith Place.*

Congress Street. A former street that ran just west of 6th Avenue between King and Houston Streets. The street was incorporated into 6th Avenue when the avenue was extended south in the 1920s and survives today as a turn lane. Named for the American legislative assembly. Labeled as *Smith Street* on maps into the mid-19th Century but is listed concurrently as Congress in city directories.

Convent Avenue. Named for the Convent of the Sacred Heart convent that stood along the street between 125th and 136th Streets.

Coogan Avenue. An unofficial former name of **Bradhurst Avenue**. Although the street was marked with signs reading Coogan, in 1889 it was discovered that the street had never been so named officially. James J. Coogan, a failed mayoral candidate in 1888, had real estate holdings in the area.

Cooper Square. Named for Peter Cooper (1791-1883), builder of the first steam locomotive and founder of Cooper Union. The park around which Cooper Square runs was originally laid out in 1828 and by 1850 was called Stuyvesant Square. It was later called 4th Avenue Park in the 1870s before being named Cooper Park in 1883. The streets now called Cooper Square were originally parts of the **Bowery** and 3rd and 4th Avenues.

Cooper Street. Named for the American author James Fenimore Cooper. Two nearby streets, *Hawthorne Street* and *Emerson Street* were also named for prominent American authors. Cooper Street is the only one of the three that retains its original name. The streets were laid out prior to 1889 and were regulated and opened in 1896.

Cooper Street. A name used for the lower part of present **Fletcher Street**. Of uncertain origin but probably referred to a local merchant or craftsman. The name Fletcher was extended to the entire street in 1794.

Copsey Street. Also sometimes *Copsie* or *Cropsie Street.* A former name of **State Street**. The name is given as a corruption of the native word for the rocks that stood at the southern point of the island, above which a battery was constructed. In 1793, the street was filled in with earth from the wall of the "old fort" and renamed State Street.

Corlears Street. A former street that ran from Grand Street to South Street, east of the present Jackson Street, partially through what is now Corlears Hook Park. Corlears Hook was a point of land extending into the East River that has since been obscured by landfill. The hook and the street were named for the early Dutch schoolmaster Jacobus von Corlaer, whose plantation was at this point. The British called this hook Crown Point. Sometimes called *Crown Point Street.*

Cornelia Street. The present Cornelia Street is named for Cornelia Herring, wife of Samuel Jones and one of the heirs of the Herring Farm property. The street formed the boundary between lots on the property.

Cornelia Street. A name used for what is now West 12th Street between Greenwich Street and Hudson Street. The street coexisted with the present Cornelia Street for a time in the early 18th Century. Of uncertain origin.

Cornelia Street was also a proposed street in the *Stuyvesant Farm Grid* that was never officially adopted. Named for Cornelia Stuyvesant, daughter of Petrus Stuyvesant (1727-1805) and wife of Dirck Ten Broeck after whom the proposed *Ten Broeck Street* was named. See illustration on page 103.

Cornelius Street. A former street laid out in the *Kip's Bay Farm* around 1805. Named for Cornelius Kip, son of Samuel

Kip. See illustration on page 60.

Cornelius Street was also the name of a proposed street in the *Mangin-Goerck Plan* that was never adopted. Its proposed path corresponds roughly with modern East 18th Street between Broadway and 5th Avenue.

Cortlandt Alley. See **Cortlandt Street.**

Cortlandt Street. Named after the Van Cortlandt family, early Dutch settlers descended from Oloff Stevenson van Cortlandt, (d. 1684). Originally laid out and named between Broadway and the Hudson River in 1733 by Phillip and Frederick Van Cortlandt. A three-block portion of Cortlandt Street between West and Church Streets was closed for the construction of the original World Trade Center in 1965. The portion between Church Street and a reopened section of Greenwich Street is planned to be reopened as Cortlandt Way in 2015. Formerly *Leary Street* and *Windmill Lane*.

Cottage Place. Located in *Hancock Street,* now part of 6th Avenue between about Bleecker and Houston Street. See also *Brook Street.*

Cottage Place was also used to refer to part of East 3rd Street between Avenues B and C.

Countess' Slip. A former slip at the foot of Maiden Lane named in honor of the Countess of Bellomont, wife of Governor Richard Coote, First Earl of Bellomont (1636-1700). Later called the *Fly Market Slip*.

Cozine Street. A former name for part of **Grove Street** east of Bleecker Street. In 1808 William W. Gilbert and his wife, the former Catherine Cozine (called Betsy), ceded the land for Gilbert and Cozine Streets. See also *Gilbert Street, Burrows Street, Columbia Street.*

Crabapple Street. A former name for **Pike Street**.

The Crane Wharf, also *Crane Wharf.* A former wharf at the foot of present day Beekman Street. Established by 1767 and so called by 1797, the name is a reference to the presence of a crane used for loading and unloading vessels.

Crosby Street. Sometimes said to be named for William Bedlow Crosby (1786-1865), a philanthropist and heir to the Henry Rutgers estate. The name appears in a deed dated 1794, however, when the street was first laid out between Hester Street and Prince Street on Nicholas Bayard's East Farm. Crosby was but 8 years old at the time. Opened to Bleecker Street in 1808.

Cross Road. The same as *Low's Lane* and *Steuben Street.* So called because it crossed the city-owned Common Lands between the Eastern Post Road and the Bloomingdale Road.

Cross Street. A former street that ran from the present location of Reade Street at Centre Street easterly to Mott Street at Mosco Street. **Mosco Street** is a surviving remnant of the street. So named because it crossed the large tract of land developed by John Kingston, who laid it out in lots in 1771. Cross Street intersected Anthony Street (now Worth) at Orange Street (now Baxter), forming the *Five Points*. The name was changed to *Park Street* in 1854.

Croton Street. Former name of the westbound portion of West 165th Street between Amsterdam and Audubon Avenues. The Croton Aquaduct crossed the Harlem River about ten blocks to the north and passed about one block east of Croton Street.

Crown Point Road. Also called The Road to Crown Point. A former name for **Grand Street** east of the Bowery. Crown Point was the British name for Corlaer's Hook, the point that jutted into the East River near the east end of the street. See also *Corlears Street.*

Crown Point Street. A name used for **Water Street** east of Montgomery Street. Refers to the point of land at the eastern end of the street. See also *Corlears Street.*

Crown Street. Named in reference to the British monarchy, Crown Street was renamed **Liberty Street** in 1794 to remove reference to America's former colonial status.

Cruger Street. A street in the *Mangin-Goerck Plan* that was never officially adopted. It was laid out as an east-west street in an extension of the *Stuyvesant Farm Grid* and ran parallel to White Street one block to the north. Several members of the Cruger family owned property in the area through which the street was proposed.

Cruger's Wharf. A wharf operated by brothers Henry and John Cruger, located along the western side of Old Slip.

Cumming Street. Of uncertain origin, but probably named for a local property owner.

Custom House Street. A name used for part of **Pearl Street** between Whitehall Street and Hanover Square. The old custom house once stood at the present intersection of Pearl and Moore Streets. This section was also called *Dock Street.*

Cuyler's Alley. A former alley that connected Water Street and South Street between Coenties Slip and Old Slip. Named for Henry Cuyler, who owned the surrounding property in the late 18th Century. Also called *Messier's Alley.* Peter Messier purchased the adjacent lot from the estate of Henry Cuyler in the 1770s.

D.

Daniels Street. Originally called D Street, the name was changed to Daniels in 1921 to honor a local World War I veteran who had died in action. The name was suggested by the Inwood Post of the American Legion and the first name of the veteran is not known. The Henry Hudson Parkway now runs over the path of the former street.

David Street. A former name of **Bleecker Street** between Broadway and Hancock Street, which appears in records from 1818 as "Samuel David's Street." Samuel David was presumably a property holder in the area and may have been associated with the David family of Montreal, who were prosperous fur merchants. Appears in records from 1819 as St. David Street.

David Street is also given as a former name of **Clarkson Street** between Varick Street and Hudson Street.

Davies Place. Listed in 1877 as part of West 36th Street between Broadway and 6th Avenue. Hopkin B. Davies, a successful coal merchant, was in operation at 125 West 36th Street at this time.

Decatur Place. A former name for the section of East 7th Street between 1st Avenue and Avenue A. Named for Stephen Decatur (1779-1820), a naval commander in the War of 1812. In 1837, a petition to change the name of East 7th Street between 3rd Avenue and Avenue A to Decatur Place was flatly denied by the Board of Aldermen. Nevertheless, the name appears in city directories from the same year, suggesting it was widely recognized unofficially.

Delafield's Wharf. A former wharf located at the foot of Broad Street at South Street, operated by John Delafield.

Delameter Square. A former designation of the area between Little West 12th Street and West 14th Street, and between 10th and 11th Avenues. Named for the former location of the Delameter Iron Works operated by Cornelius Delameter, co-builder of the warship *Monitor* with John Ericsson. The square was named at the same time a section of Beach Street was renamed for Ericsson. See also **Ericsson Place**.

Delancey Farm Grid. The Delancey family property was bounded by modern Division Street, The Bowery, Houston Street and the East River. Prior to the 1767, the family had laid out and named a grid of streets on the property, centered around a grand square. James Delancey, a loyalist, left the city for England during the Revolution and the property was seized and sold in the 1780s. The street grid was retained, along with most of the original names.

Delancey Street. James DeLancey (1703-1760) was a chief justice and colonial governor of the Province of New York. His son, also named James, established a large estate on the family's property on the lower east side of Manhattan. The younger James abruptly left New York on the eve of the Revolution and his property was confiscated by the state. Delancey Street runs through this property. Laid out and named prior to 1788.

Depau Place and *Depau Row.* De Pau Place was an alley that connected to the south side of Bleecker Street west of Thompson Street. It served a line of houses on Bleecker known as Depau Row. Named for the builder of the houses, Francis Depau, a shipper, who also resided there.

Depew Place. Named for Chauncy Depew (1834-1928), president of the New York Central Railroad and U.S. Senator for New York. It was officially closed as a city street in 1905 when construction on the present structure was begun and used as an access street by the New York Central Railroad Company. The path was re-opened in the 1920s when the Park Avenue Viaduct was extended around the east side of the terminal in an effort to reduce traffic congestion.

Depeyster Street. An obsolete street that connected Water and South Streets between Pine Street and Maiden Lane. In 1784 the City granted a water lot at this location to Pierre Van Cortlandt and Cornelia Depeyster.

Depeyster's Lane. An obsolete road near what is now Columbia University. The road ran from about present day Riverside Drive and West 111th Street due east to West 113th Street where it followed roughly the path of present day 113th Street about to the midpoint between Amsterdam Avenue and Morningside Drive. The lane ran along the southern border of the farms of Nicholas, James and Gerard Depeyster, providing access to the Bloomingdale Road. See illustration on page 32

Desbrosses Street. Elias Desbrosses was a vestryman and warden of Trinity Church. Laid out on the *Commissioners' Plan* to extend from the river at West Street to intersect with Canal Street just east of Hudson Street, the portion between Hudson and Varick Streets was never completed. The short section of **Grand Street** between Varick and Sullivan Streets was originally named as part of Desbrosses Street. It was changed to Grand in 1823 on petition of the inhabitants of the street.

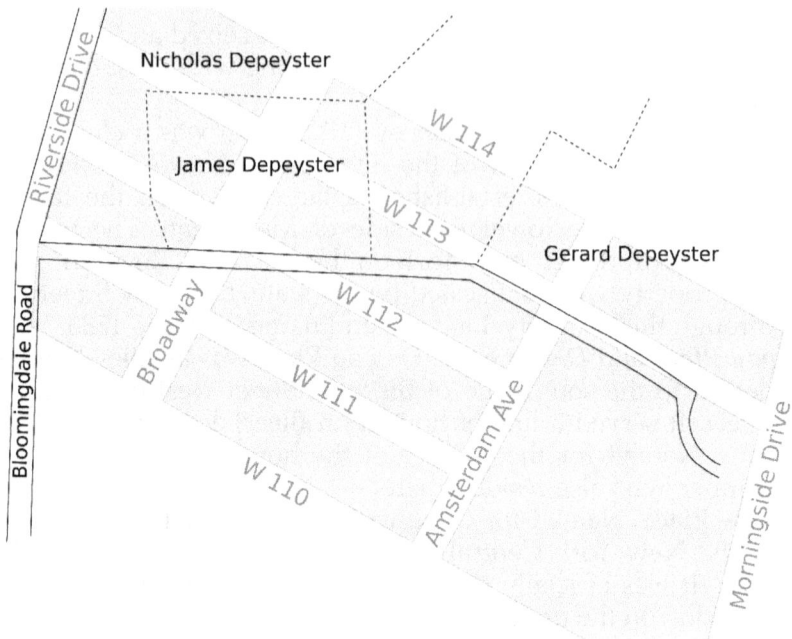

Depeyster's Lane c.1820

Dewey Square. Former name of **A. Philip Randolph Square**. Named for Admiral George Dewey (1837-1917).

Dey Street. Laid out prior to 1767 and named for Dirck Dey, who owned a tract of property along Dey Street between Broadway and the Hudson River. Sometimes spelled Dye, Dyes, Dies and Dyers. Also known as *Battoe Street*. A portion of the street west of Church Street was closed for construction of the original World Trade Center. A reopened section between Church Street and the reopened extension of Greenwich Street is proposed as part of the new World Trade Center development.

Dirty Lane and *Ditch Street.* Former names for **South William Street**. Dirty Lane is the English version of the Dutch name *Slyck Steege*.

The Ditch. See **Broad Street**.

Division Street. Used as a name for the present **Fulton Street** west of Broadway. The street marks the southern border of the original Company Farm, later the Trinity Church Farm. Also called *Partition Street*.

Division Street. The present Division Street marks the division between the original Delancey and Rutgers farms. Division Street originally extended between Bowery and Grand Streets. The portion between Canal and Grand was closed for the creation of a park in 1897 (now Seward Park) and cooperative housing projects in the 1950s.

Dixon's Row. Located in West 110th Street (**Cathedral Parkway**) from Broadway to Columbus Avenue. Of uncertain origin.

Dock Street. A former name for **Pearl Street** between Whitehall Street and Hanover Square. Named for the "Great Dock" that once stood near Whitehall. The street was also called Great Dock. Named part of Pearl Street in 1794.

Dock Street was also used as the name of **Water Street** between Fulton Street and Coenties Slip.

Dominic Street. Given as a former name of **Downing Street**. Of uncertain origin.

Dominick Street. Ceded by Trinity Church in 1813 and named for George Dominick, a vestryman of the church.

Dongan Place. Named for Colonel Thomas Dongan (1634-1715), governor of New York and the 2nd Earl of Limerick.

Donovan's Lane. An alley located off Pearl Street near Park Row. Of uncertain origin.

Dove Street. A street in the *Mangin-Goerck Plan* that was never officially adopted. It was laid out as an east-west street in an extension of the *Stuyvesant Farm Grid* and ran parallel to Livingston Street one block to the north. Of uncertain origin.

Dover Street. Named for the English port. Originally laid out between Pearl and Water Streets some time prior to 1766, Dover was extended to the East River in 1818.

Dow Street. A street in the *Mangin-Goerck Plan* that was never officially adopted. It was laid out as an east-west street in an extension of the *Stuyvesant Farm Grid* and ran parallel to Ten Broeck Street one block to the north. Of uncertain origin.

Downing Street. Laid out prior to 1799. Of uncertain origin, possibly named for the street in London.

Doyers Street. Sometimes also Doyer Street. Probably named for Henry Doyer, a merchant who owned property at 3 Doyer near the Bowery in 1808. Sometimes called *Shinbone Alley*.

Dry Dock Street. Former name of **Szold Place**. Opened in 1847 on the property of the Dry Dock Company.

Duane Street. Named for James Duane, the first mayor of New York after the evacuation of the British. Referred to as "the street ... by the windmill" in 1740, in 1767 Duane Street ran for three blocks between the waterfront and Hudson Street, where it formed a three-way intersection with Hudson and Barley Streets. In 1809 *Barley Street* and *Colden Street* were combined with the original Duane Street, and the entire street was designated Duane Street.

Duffy Square. Named in 1939 for Father Francis Duffy (1871-1932), a decorated military chaplain and former pastor of the nearby Holy Cross Church.

Duggan Street. A former name of **Canal Street** between Center and West Streets. Named for Thomas Duggan, whose property the street crossed.

Duke Ellington Circle. Named for Edward "Duke" Ellington (1899-1974), noted musician, composer and band leader whose memorial statue stands at the circle. Previously called **Frawley Circle**, both names still appear on maps.

Duke Street. A former name for **Stone Street** between Broad and William Streets, a section that is now partially closed. Named prior to 1730 for James Stuart, Duke of York, after whom the city and state are named, and who became King James II. The name was changed from Duke to Stone in 1794, when most street names referring to the city's former colonial status were removed. Some sources appear to confuse the former Duke Street with *Mill Street* (now **South William Street**), which is one street to the north.

Duke Street is also a former name of *Vandewater Street*, which ran between Frankfort and Pearl Streets one block south of the present Rose Street.

Duncomb Place. Refers to East 128th Street between 2nd and 3rd Avenues. Of uncertain origin.

Dunham Place. A former alley that connected to the south side of West 33rd Street between 6th and 7th Avenues. Of uncertain origin.

Dustan's Wharf. A former wharf near Coenties Slip. Early records show a Peter Dustan who lived nearby at 104 Pearl Street, suggesting a possible source for the name.

Dutch Street. The specific origin is uncertain, but certainly a reference to the original European settlers. Possibly named by John Harpendingh, after whom John Street is named. Harpendingh was a benefactor of the Dutch Church and one of the owners of the surrounding property.

Dwars Street. A former name for a portion of **Exchange Place** between Broadway and Broad Streets. "Dwars" is a Dutch word that means "cross" or "transverse." A cross street between the Broadway and the Princes Graft, now Broad Street.

Dyckman Street. The Dyckman family were early settlers on the island and owned a farm in the region of Dyckman Street. The farmhouse of William Dyckman, the oldest on the island, still stands nearby on the corner of Broadway and West 204th St.

The street was originally called *Inwood Street* and was changed to Dyckman in 1888.

Dyer Avenue. George Rathbone Dyer (1869-1934), the son of a governor of Rhode Island, chaired the Port of New York and the State Bridge and Tunnel Commission. Dyer Avenue, an approach to the Lincoln Tunnel, was named for him.

E.

Eagle Street. Former name of **Hester Street** between Bowery and Division Street. Named for the bird, however the use of the name precedes its adoption as the Federal symbol.

East Bank Street. An obsolete street that ran perpendicularly from the present Greenwich Avenue at about the intersection with 7th Avenue northeast to about the location of the present 14th Street. Named in reference to **Bank Street**.

East Broadway. *Harman Street* was renamed East Broadway in 1831 after a petition by some of the residents and property owners on the street. Named in reference to Broadway.

East Clinton Place. Formerly located behind 50 **Clinton Street**, between Stanton and Rivington Streets. Named for its connection to Clinton Street.

East Drive. A drive on the eastern side of Central Park.

East End Avenue. So named for its location at the east end of several east-side streets. Laid out as **Avenue B** on the *Commissioners' Plan*. The name was changed in 1890.

East George Street. A former name for **Market Street**. See also *George Street*.

East Place. A name for part of East 3rd Street between Avenues B and C. Also called *Cottage Place*. Named for its eastern location.

East River Drive. Officially renamed **Franklin D. Roosevelt Drive** in 1945, the name still appears on many modern maps. Named for its location along the East River.

East Rutgers Street. Referred to the present **Rutgers Street**. It was so called to distinguish it from the older *Rutgers Street* that existed for part of the same time.

East Street. An obsolete waterfront street that once ran from the eastern end of Water Street northerly to a point near modern East Houston Street and Baruch Drive. Named for its former location on the eastern waterfront. Also given as a former name of *Mangin Street*, possibly out of confusion.

35

East Tompkins Place. A name once used for part of East 11th Street between Avenues A and B. Probably a reference to Daniel Tompkins (1774-1825), Former Governor of New York and U.S. Vice President under James Monroe. Tompkins, after whom the nearby Tompkins Square Park is named, owned property in this area.

Eastern Post Road. A major early road up the east side of Manhattan forming the western border of many of the farms located along the East River. The road connected to the Bloomingdale Road near the present intersection of 23rd Street and 5th Avenue and ran to the village of Harlem. This lower section was usually referred to as the Eastern Post Road. Also referred to as the Boston Road, the Boston Post Road, and the Road to Albany and Boston. See illustration on page 13.

Eden Street. Given as a former name of **Morton Street**. Probably a misspelling of *Arden Street*.

Eden's Alley. Named in reference to Medcef Eden, who acquired the property north of the alley and east of Gold Street in his marriage to Martha Pelletreau in 1775. This short leg off **Ryder's Alley** that connects to Gold Street is often mapped as part of Ryder's Alley through the 20th Century, although references through the 19th Century usually distinguish between the two. A historic street sign restoring the distinction was placed in the early 21st Century. The alley does not appear on the 1730 Bradford map, but is shown (although not named) on the Duyckinck Plan in 1754.

Edgar Street. The street is first mentioned by name in public records in 1795, when it was regulated. It was laid out in March, 1795 when *Lumber Street* was extended southward to the edge of a lot owned by William Edgar, and the short street was created along the edge of the lot to connect with Greenwich Street. William Edgar was a successful merchant who lived nearby at *Edgar's Alley*.

Edgar Street. Given as a former name of **Morris Street**, but this may be a mistake given the proximity of the two streets.

Edgar's Alley. A name for **Exchange Alley**. William Edgar, a successful merchant, lived at 39 Broadway in 1808, where Exchange Alley meets Broadway. See also *Edgar Street*.

Edgar's Wharf, and *Edgar's Basin.* Formerly located along the Hudson River between Morris and Rector Streets and Washington and West Streets. William Edgar, a prominent merchant in the late 18th Century, owned lots in this area near Morris Street. See **Edgar Street.**

Edgecombe Avenue. Originally Edgecombe Road. Named for its location along the crest of high land in upper Manhattan. The name was in use prior to 1884. Opened from West 155th Street to Amsterdam in 1898 and not officially named Edgecombe Avenue until after that. Often spelled Edgecomb.

Edward M. Morgan Place. Named in 1926 for the former Postmaster of New York City, Edward M. Morgan (1855-1925). Formerly *Audubon Place*.

Elbert Street. A street that was laid out on the *Kip's Bay Farm* but never adopted officially. Named for Elbert S. Kip (1769-1827), son of Samuel Kip. See illustration on page 60.

Elbow Street. A name sometimes used for **Cliff Street**. The street originally extended past Beekman Street where it took a turn to the east, forming an elbow.

Eldridge Street. Named for Lt. Joseph Eldridge who was killed in Canada in the War of 1812.

Elephant Wharf. A former wharf east of Dover Street constructed in 1823. Of uncertain origin.

Eliza Street. A street named for Elizabeth Kip, daughter of Samuel Kip, was laid out on the *Kip's Bay Farm* about 1805 but never officially adopted. See illustration on page 60.

Eliza Street was also a proposed street in the *Stuyvesant Farm Grid* but never officially adopted. Named for Elizabeth Stuyvesant, daughter of Petrus Stuyvesant (1727-1805).

Eliza Street is also a former name for part of **Waverly Place** between Christopher Street and Broadway, possibly named for Elizabeth Herring, wife of Elbert Herring. The street ran through the northern part of the Herring farm.

Elizabeth Street. Laid out between Bayard and Prince Streets prior to 1754 on Nicholas Bayard's farm and named for Elizabeth Bayard, his first wife. Extended north to Bleecker Street in 1816.

Elk Street. Named in 1939 for the Order of Elks, a fraternal organization that had its first lodge on the street. In 1968 a section between Duane and Worth Streets was closed. Formerly *Elm Street*.

Ellet's or Elliotts Alley. A former name for **Mill Lane**, referring to Richard Elliott, a cooper who owned the surrounding property in the late 17th Century.

Ellwood Street. Of uncertain origin. Frequently spelled Elwood Street.

Elm Street. Former name of **Elk Street**. The street began as *Ann Street* or Little Ann Street between Reade and Worth Streets and was mapped as Elm Street by 1800. In 1806 it was joined with *Pitt Street* to extend it to Spring Street, apparently with a gap between Canal and Hester Streets (the site of the old Collect Pond) which was connected in 1811. In 1905, the portion north of Worth Street was renamed **Lafayette Street**. Elm Street was extended a block south to Chambers Street in 1923, and the street was renamed **Elk Street** in 1939.

Emerson Street. A former name of West 207th Street. Emerson Street originally extended into what is now Inwood Hill Park under the name Emerson Place, curving northeasterly and forming a U shape. Like the neighboring *Hawthorne Street* and **Cooper Street**, the street was named for a prominent American author, in this case Ralph Waldo Emerson. Laid out prior to 1889 and opened and regulated in 1896.

Ericsson Place. Named for John Ericsson (1803-1889), the designer of the ironclad ship *Monitor*. Ericsson lived on the street until his death in 1889. Formerly part of **Beach Street**. See also *Delameter Square*.

Erie Place. Former name for the section of **West Street** between Duane and Reade Streets. Named for the New York and Erie Railroad, which had its offices here.

Essex Market Place. An alley that ran along the north side of the *Essex Market* in Grand Street between Essex and Ludlow Streets.

Essex Market. Located on Grand Street between Essex and Ludlow Streets.

Essex Street. Named for the English county of Essex. Laid out on the Delancey Farm prior to 1767, Essex Street is one of several in the area named for English places, such as Norfolk and Suffolk Streets and possibly Arundel Street.

Everett Row. Former name for part of West 34th Street near 6th Avenue. Of uncertain origin.

Exchange Alley. An extension of **Exchange Place**.

Exchange Place. Named for the Merchants Exchange building constructed in 1827 at the corner of William and Wall Streets. Formerly *Tuyn Street* then *Garden Street*. Also once called *Flatten Barrack* between Broadway and Broad.

Exchange Street. A name for *Slote Lane*. Renamed *Merchant Street* in 1835. One part of this L-shaped street is now incorporated into **Beaver Street** between William and Hanover Streets and the other section is incorporated into **Hanover Street** between Beaver and Pearl Streets. The Merchants Exchange building at William and Wall Streets was completed in 1827, when the street was given the name Exchange. In 1835, the exchange building burned down and the name was changed.

Exterior Street. A frontage street laid out along the Harlem River in 1858 from 89th Street to the Hudson River. Now part of **FDR Drive** and **Harlem River Drive.**

Extra Place. After Philip Minthorne divided his estate into nine equal plots to be left to his nine children, a small triangular plot was left over as "extra," giving this short lane its name.

F.

Factory Street. A former name for the present part of **Waverly Place** between Bank Street and the east-west section of that street. Changed from *Catherine Street* in 1813. Presumedly named for a manufacturer located on or near the street.

Fair Street. Former name of **Fulton Street** east of Broadway. One of the oldest streets in Manhattan, it was laid out prior to 1696 between Broadway and Cliff Street. It was extended to the river in 1814. Of uncertain origin, but a common street name of the time. The name was changed to Fulton in 1816.

Father Demo Square. Named in 1941 for Father Antonio Demo (1870-1936), pastor of Our Lady of Pompei Church.

Fayette Street. Former name of **Oliver Street** between Park Row and Madison Street. The street was laid out prior to 1792 and is possibly named for the Marquis de La Fayette who had visited the city in 1784.

Feitner's Lane. Former name of *Verdant Lane.* Catherine Feitner, the wife of Francis Feitner, was given property along the lane by her father, Charles Kelly, in the late 18th Century. Also called *Leggett's Lane.*

Ferry Place. Former name of **Jackson Street** between Water and South Streets. Named for the ferry landing at the foot of *Ferry Street.*

Ferry Street. Former name of **Jackson Street**. Named for the ferry landing at its foot. See also *Walnut Street.*

Ferry Street was also the name of a former street that ran along the line of the present **Peck Slip** northerly to Gold Street. So named in 1749, the lower part of this street was called Peck Slip, and Ferry Street between Gold and Pearl Streets. Closed between Gold and Pearl in the 1960s.

Scammel Street was also sometimes referred to as Ferry Street.

Field Street, Fieldmarket Street. Alternate names for **Marketfield Street.**

Finn Square. Named in 1919 for Philip S. Finn, who died the preceding year in World War I as a member of New York's 69th Regiment, the "Fighting Irish." Finn was the son of Tammany politician Daniel Finn.

Fir Street. Never officially adopted as a public street, Fir Street was mapped between Grand Street and the East River, beginning at a point at about the present intersection of East Broadway and Grand and running parallel to Jackson Street. Also referred to as *Byvanck Street.*

First Street. A former name for **Chrystie Street**. The six blocks east of the Bowery were laid out some time prior to 1767 and given numbered names. After the Commissioner's Plan of 1811 was adopted, creating the now familiar grid of numbered streets and avenues, it was realized that confusion would ensue from duplicate numbers. In 1818 the Common Council resolved to rename the old numbered streets (with the exception of Fifth Street, which had already been named **Orchard Street**). They chose the names of officers killed in the recent War of 1812.

Fisher Street. Former name for a portion of **Bayard Street** that once extended east of Bowery to Division Street. Made part of Bayard Street in 1809 and closed in the 1960s. Probably named for George Fisher, who was one of the purchasers of the Delancey Farm, where the street was located.

Fitzroy Road. A former road that ran north from about West 14th Street between 7th and 8th Avenues to West 42nd Street, roughly along the line of present 8th Avenue. The name is also used on some maps for the upper part of *Greenwich Lane*, now **Gansevoort Street**. Named for Charles Fitzroy, Baron Southampton, son-in-law of Sir Peter Warren, who had an estate at Greenwich Village. The road was closed beginning in 1830 in preference to 8th Avenue, which was laid out in the *Commissioners' Plan*. See also *Southampton Road* and illustration on page 41.

Five Points. A broad square formed by the former intersection of *Orange, Anthony* and *Cross Streets* that stood at the modern intersection of Baxter and Worth Streets. Formed over land reclaimed from the Collect Pond, the area became notorious for poverty and crime. In an effort to clean up the neighborhood and improve its image, the city closed some of the surrounding streets and renamed others.

Flatten Barrack Street, also *Flatten Barrack Hill.* A former name for **Exchange Place** between Broadway and Broad Street. The name is an English approximation of the Dutch "Verlettenberg," meaning "Verlett's Hill." See *Verlettenberg*.

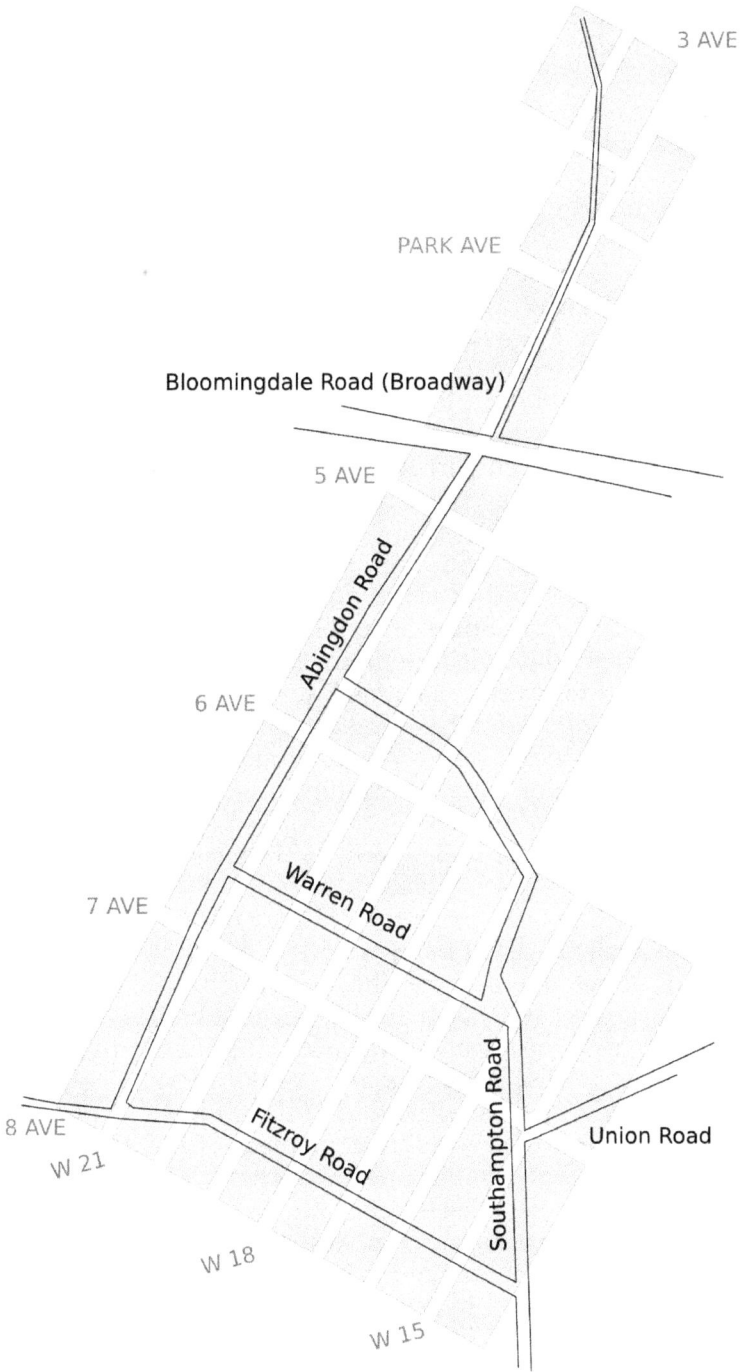

Former Roads on the Warren Estate

Fletcher Street. Probably a reference to Benjamin Fletcher (1640-1703), colonial governor of New York from 1692 to 1697. Laid out between Pearl and Water Streets prior to 1730 and mentioned by name in records of 1736.

Fly Market Street, Fly Market Slip. Formerly located along the present Maiden Lane between Pearl and South Streets. The marshy meadow that was originally located here was called *Smiths Vly*, a "vly" being a valley or meadow. The name was anglicized to "Smith's Fly" and the meat and seafood market located here was called, perhaps aptly, the Fly Market. The name **Maiden Lane** was extended to include Fly Market Street in 1824.

Foley Square. Named in 1926 for Thomas F. Foley (1852-1925), a Tammany district leader.

Forsyth Street. Named for Lt. Col. Benjamin Forsyth, who was killed in 1814 in the War of 1812. Called *Second Street* prior to 1817.

Fort George Avenue and **Fort George Hill.** Named for Fort George, which stood near the present intersection of Audubon Avenue and 192nd Street. The fort was built by the British in 1776 and named for George III, the King of England.

Fort Washington Avenue. Named for the American fort built nearby during the Revolutionary War. The fort itself was named for General George Washington. First referred to as Fort Washington Ridge Road or simply Ridge Road, the name was changed officially in 1888.

Fort Washington Place. Between 1921 and 1923 the name of **Magaw Place**.

Fourth Street. Laid out prior to 1767 and until 1817 the name of **Allen Street**. See also *First Street*.

Frankfort Street. Named for the German birthplace of former New York governor Jacob Leisler. Leisler obtained the adjacent property from the family of his wife, Elsie Lockerman, in 1682. Sometimes spelled Frankford and Frankfurd.

Franklin Alley. Alternate name for **Franklin Place**.

Franklin Delano Roosevelt Drive. Named for the 32nd President of the United States and former Governor of New York.

Franklin Market. Established in 1821 at the Old Slip between Front and Water Streets. Originally called Old Slip Market, the name was officially changed to Franklin Market in 1822.

Franklin Place. Named in association with **Franklin Street**. Also called Franklin Alley. Formerly *Scotts Alley*.

Franklin Square. Named in 1817 for Benjamin Franklin, the square was formed by the intersection of Pearl, Cherry and Dover Streets. Formerly *St. George's Square*.

Franklin Street. Named for the founding father Benjamin Franklin (1706-1790). Formerly *Sugar Loaf Street* between Centre Street and West Broadway and *Provost Street* between West Broadway and West Street. Sugar Loaf Street was changed to Franklin Street in 1816. The former Provost Street was renamed as part of Franklin Street in 1833.

Franklin Terrace. Formerly located behind 364 West 26th Street.

Frawley Circle. Named in 1926 for James J. Frawley, a former Tammany leader and state senator. The name is shared with **Duke Ellington Circle**.

Frederick Douglass Boulevard. Frederick Douglass (1818-1895) was a runaway slave who became a distinguished author and social reformer. 8th Avenue north of Central Park is officially named in his honor.

Frederick Douglass Circle. Dedicated in 1950 in honor of the abolitionist, author and statesman Frederick Douglass.

Freedom Place. Named in 1967 to honor three civil rights activists, Andrew Goodman, Michael Schwerner and James Chaney, who were murdered in Mississippi in 1964. Goodman and Schwerner were from New York.

Freeman Alley. Of uncertain origin. Mapped without a name as early as 1859, the alley is first referred to in documents as Freeman's Alley in the 1890s. It is likely the name comes from one of the tenants or owners of the buildings that had access to the alley.

French Church Street. A former name used for **Pine Street** between Broadway and William Street. *La Temple du Saint-Esprit* was built at the corner of the present Pine and Nassau Streets in 1704 when the church founded by French Huguenots outgrew its first building on Petticoat Lane (now part of Battery Place). The street was laid out as *King Street* in 1685, which was its official name until it was changed to Pine Street in 1794.

Front Street. Named for its waterfront location along the lower eastern edge of the island. Front Street was first regulated in 1787 between the Old Slip and the Fly Market (at Maiden Lane) and by 1805 had been extended to Roosevelt Street, near the present location of the Brooklyn Bridge. From this point, Front Street was laid out on the *Commissioners' Plan* to run in a straight line parallel to the waterfront eastward to East Street at Corlear's Hook. At that time, the city anticipated the waterfront would eventually extend another block south of Front Street, and laid out South Street as the waterfront street between Roosevelt Street and East Street. In the end, the waterfront did not extend past Front Street for much of this section except for a portion at Corlear's Hook between Montgomery Street and Corlears Street (now Jackson). By 1865, the name of South Street had been extended to the stretch of Front Street between Roosevelt and Montgomery Streets, where the street resumed the name Front and where South Street jogged one block to the south where the waterfront was built out.

Fulton Market. Established in 1816, the Fulton Market was opened in 1822 in the block bounced by South, Front, Fulton and Beekman Streets. Closed in 1914. The Fulton Fish Market was established on South Street opposite the Fulton Market in 1835.

Fulton Street. Named for Robert Fulton (1765-1815), builder of the first commercial steam ship. In 1816, shortly after his death, *Fair Street* was renamed Fulton Street in his honor.

G.

Gansevoort Street. Named in 1837 for Fort Gansevoort, a fort constructed near the intersection of Washington and Little West 12th Streets. The fort was named for Peter Gansevoort (1749-1812), a Revolutionary War officer. Formerly part of *Greenwich Lane*. Also formerly called *Great Kill Road*.

Garden Row. A former name for 140 to 158 West 11th Street between 6th and 7th Avenues.

Garden Street Alley. Former name of **Exchange Alley**. Also known as *Tin Pot Alley*, an English interpretation of the Dutch "Tuyn Paat," or "Garden Path." See *Garden Street*.

Garden Street. Former name for **Exchange Place**. "Garden" is the English translation of the original Dutch name for the street, *Tuyn Street*. A formal garden was established by the early Dutch settlers along the west side of Broadway opposite and just north of the present intersection with Exchange Alley (formerly *Garden Street Alley*).

Garden Street is also the former name of **Cherry Street** between Jackson Street and the East River (now the bend where Cherry becomes FDR Drive).

Gardiner Street. Former name of *Tompkins Street*. Of uncertain origin.

Gates Street. A street in the *Mangin-Goerck Plan* that was never officially adopted. It was laid out as an east-west street in an extension of the *Stuyvesant Farm Grid* and ran parallel to Cruger Street one block to the north. Perhaps named in honor of General Horatio Gates.

Gay Street. Of uncertain origin. A deputy surveyor named Calvin Gay was active in the 1820s and '30s, when Gay Street was named. One common claim is that the street was named for abolitionist and newspaper editor Sydney Howard Gay. Gay was born in 1814, however, and was only 14 years old when the street is first mentioned in public records in 1828.

General Green Street. Given as a former name of **Gouverneur Street**. Probably a reference to Revolutionary War General Nathanael Greene.

George Slip. A former slip at the foot of *George Street*, renamed **Market Slip** in 1813.

George Street. Several streets in Manhattan have borne the name George Street, after the British monarch. Following the Revolution and the War of 1812, most references to the monarchy were removed from New York place names.

    Spruce Street was called George Street until 1817, and sometimes referred to as *Little George Street*.

    Market Street between Division and Cherry Streets was called George Street until 1813.

    The portion of *Herring Street* (now **Bleecker Street**) above Christopher Street was called George Street until 1813. George Street is also reported to be a former name for **Hudson Street, Rose Street** and **Beekman Street**.

Gerard Street. A proposed street in the *Stuyvesant Farm Grid* that was never officially adopted. Gerard was a common name among the Stuyvesant family. Probably named in reference to Peter Gerard Stuyvesant (1778-1847), the son of Petrus Stuyvesant (1727-1805). It was Petrus who laid out the proposed streets about 1788. See illustration on page 103.

Germain Street. Probably an alternate spelling of **Carmine Street**. Sometimes spelled Germaine.

Gibbs' Alley. An alley that formerly ran northwesterly from Madison Street between Oliver and James Streets to a point at about the center of the block. Possibly named for Isaac Gibbs, a grocer who lived at the corner of Madison and James Streets in 1798.

Gilbert Street. Original name of **Barrow Street** between Bleecker and West 4th St. Named for William W. Gilbert, who ceded the land for the street in 1808. Joined with *Reason Street* and extended to meet Barrow in 1827, at which time the whole street was given the name Barrow.

Gilford Place. Former name for part of East 45th Street between 3rd and Lexington Avenues. Named in 1899 in reference to the Gilford family estate, which was located in the area.

Glass House Farm. A small development of lots on the Hudson River dating from the early 19th Century. The original farm stretched from the Fitzroy Road (near present day 8th Avenue) westward to the Hudson River, roughly between the lines of modern West 32nd and 34th Streets. A glass works had been established on the farm at least as early as 1732 and perhaps much longer before that, giving the farm its name. See illustration below.

Glass Makers Street. See *Glaziers Street.*

Glaziers Street. A former name for part of *South William Street.* Evert Duyckinck was an early Dutch glass maker who received a grant of land along the north side of **Slyck Steege** in 1643 and set up operations there. Also called *Dirty Lane, Mill Street,* and *Jews Alley.*

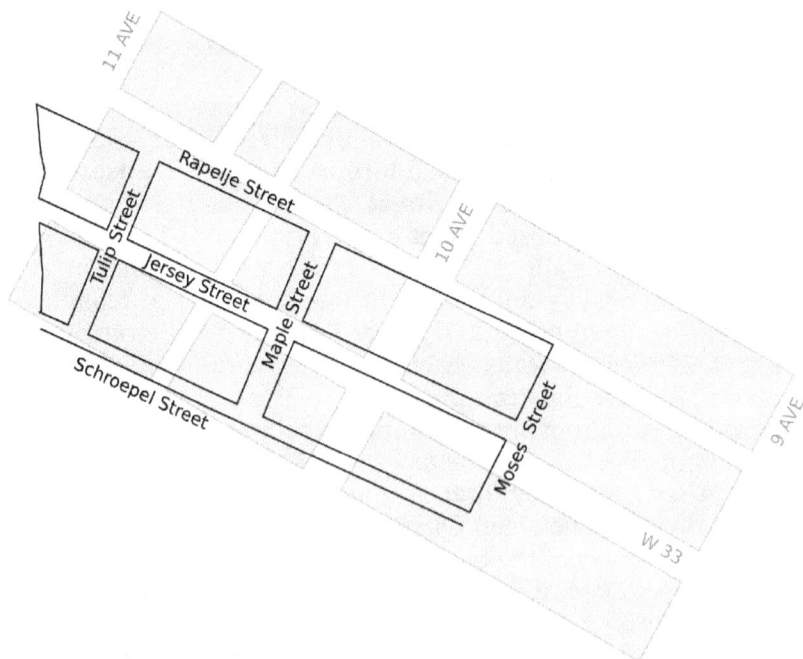

Glass House Farm

46

Glover Place. Former name for part of **Thompson Street** between Spring and Prince Streets. Possibly in reference to Thomas Glover, Jr., a butcher whose business was located on the east side of present Thompson Street just north of Spring Street in 1848.

Goelets Street. Former name of **Morris Street**. Laid out prior to 1729 and probably named for Francis or Jacobus Goelet. Jacobus Goelet was adopted by Frederick Philipse after his father, Francis, died at sea. The Philipse family owned the property through which Goelets Street was first laid out. By 1797 the street was known as *Beaver Lane*, and in 1829 was changed to **Morris Street**.

Goerck Street. A former street that originally ran one block east of and parallel to present-day Lewis Street. Goerck Street was laid out from Grand Street north to the waterfront at a point about halfway between Rivington and Stanton Streets. Named for Casimir Goerck, an 18th-century surveyor and partner of Joseph Mangin. See also *Mangin Street*.

Gold Street. Appears mapped in 1730 as Gold Street between Ann Street and the Beekman Swamp, between present Spruce and Frankfort Streets. Named in reference to *Golden Hill*. Called *Vandercliffes Street* between modern Fulton Street and John Street and *Rutgers Hill* between John Street and Maiden Lane.

Golden Hill Street. Former name for the part of **John Street** east of William Street. See *Golden Hill*.

Golden Hill. A hilled pasture in the vicinity of present day Gold Street and in 1770 the site of an early skirmish between the Sons of Liberty and English troops. Both *Golden Hill Street* and **Gold Street** were named after this area, which was originally named "Gouwenberg" (literally "Golden Hill") around 1644 by Cornelius van Tienhoven, who built a residence there. The most common account of the name claims it refers to yellow wildflowers that grew on the hillside. Anthony Rutgers later established a brewery on the hill, providing alternate names of *Rutgers Hill* and *Brewers Hill*.

Gouverneur Alley. Former name of **Gouverneur Lane**.

Gouverneur Lane. Once served the house of Isaac Gouverneur, located on Pearl Street, near Hanover Street. Gouverneur's counting house and storehouses were located near the foot of the lane, near Gouverneur's Wharf.

Gouverneur Slip. Named for its location at the foot of **Gouverneur Street**.

Gouverneur Street. Named for Nicholas Gouverneur, who owned part of the land ceded to the city for the street in 1798. See also *General Green Street.*

Gouwenberg. See *Golden Hill.*

Governor Street. A proposed street in the *Stuyvesant Farm Grid* that was laid out in 1788 but never officially adopted. Named in honor of Governor Petrus (or Peter) Stuyvesant (c.1612-1672), the last Director General of New Netherland under the Dutch and the original owner of the farms which formed the Stuyvesant estate. See illustration on page 103.

Gracie Square and **Gracie Terrace.** Named for Archibald Gracie (1755-1829) a successful New York businessman whose estate stood along the East River and whose former mansion now serves as the official residence of the Mayor of New York.

Gramercy Park. The streets surrounding Gramercy Park are named for the park itself. "Gramercy" is an English approximation of the Dutch *krom-mesje*, literally "curved blade." It is a reference to the hook-shaped hill that stood in the area where Gramercy Park is now situated. A portion of Gramercy Park South has also been referred to as Gramercy Place.

Grand Army Plaza. Designed as an entrance to Central Park, the plaza was named in 1923 for the Grand Army of the Potomac, i.e. the Union Army of the Civil War.

Grand Street. Originally laid out as a road to Crown Point and called the *Crown Point Road*, by 1767 the street was referred to as Grand in reference to its breadth and central position in James Delancey's proposed street grid. First laid out between Mulberry Street and the East River, Grand was extended in 1818 to Broadway and in 1819 to Sullivan Street, where it intersected opposite *Desbrosses Street*. In 1823, the short section of Desbrosses Street west of Sullivan was added to Grand Street.

Great Dock Street. See *Dock Street.*

Great George Street. Former name of **Broadway** between Ann Street and Astor Place. Renamed as part of Broadway in 1794. Called Great George Street to distinguish it from the existing *King George Street.*

Great Graft. See *Heere Graft.*

Great Jones Alley. Named for its connection to **Great Jones Street** at its northern end.

Great Jones Street. Named for Samuel Jones, who ceded the land for the street in 1806. The street was called "Great Jones" to distinguish it from **Jones Street**.

Great Kill Road. Former name of **Gansevoort Street** until it was changed in 1837. The Great Kill was a stream that flowed into the Hudson River near present-day 42nd Street. Gansevoort formerly extended to the *Fitzroy Road,* which led to the stream. Sometimes called Great Kiln Road and Old Kiln Road, but this is most probably a variant and not a reference to the presence of a kiln, as some sources speculate.

Great Queen Street. Former name for **Pearl Street** between Hanover Square and Park Row. Named for the British monarch and referred to as "Great" to distinguish it from "Little" Queen Street, now Cedar Street. Renamed as part of Pearl Street in 1794.

Greeley Square. Named in 1894 for Horace Greeley (1811-1872), influential editor of the New York Tribune.

Green Lane. An early alternate name of **Maiden Lane** that never gained common usage and was later used for the short lane between Maiden Lane and Crown Street west of Nassau Street, the present **Liberty Place**.

Greene Street. Named some time between 1797 and 1799, probably for Revolutionary War figure Nathanael Greene (1742-1786). Sometimes Green Street. Formerly *Union Street.*

Greenwich Avenue. Named after the village of Greenwich, to which the road led. Formerly called Greenwich Lane, Greenwich Road or the Road to Greenwich, the road was laid out in 1707 and ran along the line of the present Gansevoort Street to its present course as far as Astor Place. The portion between Broadway and 6th Avenue was closed in 1825, and the portion between 13th Street and 8th Avenue the following year. The name was changed to Greenwich Avenue in 1843. See *Sand Hill Road.*

Greenwich Lane, Greenwich Road. Former names for **Greenwich Avenue**. See also *Sand Hill Road.*

Greenwich Street. First laid out along the high water mark of the Hudson River in 1739, Greenwich Street was once the main waterfront thoroughfare between Manhattan and Greenwich Village. The street underwent several extensions after the Revolution, reaching its present length about 1810. In 1973, a portion of the street between Liberty and Vesey Streets was closed when the World Trade Center was erected. Plans for the newly constructed World Trade Center will reconnect the north and south sections of the street by 2016.

Grove Court. This small, unmarked L-shaped court at the bend in Grove Street near Hudson serves the houses in the back of the block.

Grove Street. Named for the rows of poplar trees that once lined the street on the Timothy Whittemore estate, the name being suggested by one of his daughters. Originally called *Columbia Street* between Bedford and Bleecker Streets, the street was then renamed *Burrows Street* in 1813. Confusion with Barrow Street occasioned the renaming to Grove Street in 1829.

H.

Hague Street. Sometimes *Hage Street.* A former street that ran between Skinner (later Cliff) Street and Pearl Street, intersecting with Pearl just north of the Brooklyn Bridge. Probably named for the Dutch city. Laid out prior to 1755. Closed for the construction of the Murray Bergtraum High School in 1973.

Hall Street. Originally *Hall Place.* Former name of **Taras Shevchenko Place**. Named for Charles Henry Hall, who ceded the street to the city in 1828 as part of the sale of several nearby lots for the establishment of the Tompkins Market.

Hamersley Place. A section of the former *Hamersley Street* (now **Houston Street**) near its intersection with Bedford Street.

Hamersley Street. Former name of **Houston Street** between 6th Avenue and West Street. Named in 1807 for Andrew Hamersley, who served as a vestryman of Trinity Church from 1787 to 1807. Trinity Church ceded the street to the city in 1808. The name also appears as Hammersely and sometimes Amersley. Renamed Houston in 1858. Originally *Village Street.*

Hamill Place. The diagonal pedestrian walkway between Centre and Worth Streets along the northwestern edge of the State Supreme Court Building was once a street by this name. Named for the Tammany leader Peter J. Hamill. Closed in the late 1990s.

Hamilton Place. Named for Alexander Hamilton, whose country home The Grange was located near the northern end of the street. The house was moved from its location on Convent Avenue to St. Nicholas Park in 2008.

Hamilton Street. An obsolete street that once ran between the present Catherine and Market Streets just south of and roughly parallel to Monroe Street. Closed in 1933 for the construction of Knickerbocker Village. Named in 1827 after Alexander Hamilton, a founding father and the first U.S. Secretary of the Treasury. Originally called *Cheapside Street.* See illustration on page 22.

Hamilton Terrace. Named for Alexander Hamilton. See **Hamilton Place.**

Hammond Street. Former name of West 11th Street between Greenwich Avenue and West Street. Named for Abijah Hammond, who laid out the street on his farm around 1796. Changed to West 11th Street in 1865. Sometimes appears as Hammonds Street.

Hancock Place. Named for General Winfield Scott Hancock in 1886. Originally part of *Manhattan Street.*

Hancock Street. A former street that is now part of 6th Avenue between Bedford and Bleecker Streets. Also called *Brook Street* and *Cottage Place.* Laid out prior to 1811. Of uncertain origin, but possibly named in reference to John Hancock, President of the Second Continental Congress. The street paralleled Macdougal Street, which, like the other parallel streets between Hancock and Broadway, was originally named for a Revolutionary War figure. See illustration on page 73.

Hanover Square. Named for the house of Hanover, which assumed the British throne in 1714 with King George I. So called by 1730, the name originally applied to the large area created by the intersections of the former *Dock Street, Duke Street,* and *Queen Street.* In 1794, when most references to the British monarchy were eliminated from New York place names, the square was renamed as part of **Pearl Street.** Although it was officially removed, the name continued to be used, particularly for the short street south of Pearl leading to the Old Slip. The name Hanover resurfaced in 1830 when the present **Hanover Street** was opened and named.

Hanover Street. Opened and named in 1830 for its connection to **Hanover Square.** The lower part of Hanover Street was originally part of *Slote Lane.*

Hariot Street. A street in the *Mangin-Goerck Plan* that was never officially adopted. It was laid out as a north-south street in an extension of the *Stuyvesant Farm Grid* and ran along the waterfront of the East River. Also called Harriott. Of uncertain origin.

Harlem Bridge Road. A former road that connected the Eastern Post Road with the village of Harlem, crossing the Harlem Creek. The road intersected with the Post Road near where modern 5th Avenue meets 91st Street. It ran in a nearly straight line northeasterly to the center of Harlem, at present Sylvan Place, crossing the creek near present-day Park Avenue at East 106th Street.

Harlem Lane. A former lane that followed the path of present day **St. Nicholas Avenue** between 8th Avenue and a point now within the Harlem Meer in Central Park about on a line with West 108th Street. Named for the nearby village of Harlem.

Harlem River Drive. The road runs along the western edge of the Harlem River.

Harlem Road. A former road that ran from the center of the village of Harlem (or Haerlem) to the north and northwest. From west to east, the road began at present St. Nicholas Avenue about two blocks south of West 133rd Street and ran southeast to a point in West 127th Street just east of 7th Avenue. It followed West 127th for about half a block, then turned southeast again to West 124th Street at the northwest corner of Mt. Morris Park. The road followed 124th Street east to what is now the intersection with Lexington, then turned southeast again, ending at Harlem, near the present intersection of East 120th and Sylvan Place.

Harman Street. The name of **East Broadway** until 1831. Named for Harman (or Harmanus) Rutgers, patriarch of the Rutgers family.

Harrison Street. Named for George Harrison, a successful brewer whose operation was located near the present intersection of Greenwich and Jay Streets, which was at the water's edge in the 1770s when the brewery was active. Laid out and named prior to 1797.

Harry Howard Square. The area around the intersection of Canal and Walker Streets between Baxter and Mulberry. Named for Harry Howard (1822-1896), former Chief of the Volunteer Fire Department of the city.

Harsen's Road. A former road that followed the path of present 71st Street from near present Amsterdam Avenue and extending on the same line through what is now Central Park to 5th Avenue at East 71st St. The road ran through the center of Jacob Harsen's property. His house stood near the western end of the road, in the block now bordered by East 70th and 71st Streets and Amsterdam and West End Avenues.

Harwood Place. Referred to East 78th Street between 3rd and Park Avenues. A family named Harwood lived at 1365 3rd Avenue in the 1870s, at the corner with East 78th.

Haven Avenue. Named for John Haven, who owned property in the area of what is now Fort Washington Park. In 1897 some of Haven's property was made part of the park including his house. He continued to live in the house, paying rent to the Park Board.

Hawthorne Street. Former name of West 204th Street. Named for the American author Nathaniel Hawthorne. See also *Emerson*

Street and **Cooper Street**. Laid out prior to 1889 and opened and regulated in 1896. Renamed 204th Street by 1916.

Hazard Street. Former name of the present **King Street**. Laid out prior to 1799, renamed in 1807 and ceded to the City by Trinity Church in 1808. Of uncertain origin, but possibly named for Ebenezer Hazard, Postmaster of New York and later Postmaster of the United States.

Heere Graft, Heeren Gracht. Dutch for the "gentlemen's canal" that ran inland from the harbor in early New Amsterdam. The canal was filled in 1676 and became what is now **Broad Street**. See also *Princes Graft*.

Hell Gate Road. A former road that led from the Eastern Post Road to the Hell Gate Ferry near what was the foot of East 86th St, now within Carl Schurz Park. Also called the Hell Gate Ferry Road. The source of the name Hell Gate is obscure, but is an anglicization of the original Dutch Hellgat or possibly Hellegat, referring to the entry to the Harlem River, which has been translated as "open passage" and "bright passage" as well as "gate to hell." The ferry is called the Holle Gat on the 1811 *Commissioners' Plan*, which could translate as "hollow passage." Other versions of the origin are based on variations in spelling and translation, but the English name Hell Gate was in common use by the early 19th Century, although more polite society sometimes referred to the location as "Hurlgate."

Henderson Place. Named for John C. Henderson, a fur importer who purchased the surrounding property in the 1850s and began developing it in the 1880s. The brick buildings along the east side of Henderson Place were built by Henderson. The street gives its name to the historic district that includes the street and parts of East End Avenue and East 86th and 87th Streets.

Henry Hudson Parkway. Named for the English explorer who navigated the Hudson River on behalf of the Dutch East India Company.

Henry Street. Former name of **Perry Street**. The origin of the name of this Henry Street is uncertain. The area was originally part of the Peter Warren estate, which bordered on that of Elias and Henry Brevoort, suggesting a possible connection. One also notes that there was formerly a Warren Street laid out on the Henry Rutgers estate. Mapped as *Ogden Street* in 1799. Named Perry Street in 1813.

Henry Street. Laid out prior to 1797 and named for Henry Rutgers, whose land the street passed through.

Henshaw Street. In 1921, the Inwood Post of the American Legion proposed names for three short streets to honor local World War I veterans who had died in action. Henshaw Street, originally called B Street, was one of the names suggested, however the first name of the veteran is not known. See also **Staff Street** and *Daniels Street.*

Herald Square. Named for the New York Herald, whose offices were in the Herald Building at Broadway and 34th Street.

Herman Place. A former place behind 220 East 4th Street. Of uncertain origin.

Herring Street. Former name of **Bleecker Street** west of 6th Avenue. The street passed through the farm of Elbert Herring. Also spelled Herrings, Haring and Harinck. Originally laid out from the western end of *David Street* to Christopher Street, in 1813 the name was extended north of Christopher when *George Street* was renamed.

Hester Street. Named for Hester Bayard, daughter of Nicholas Bayard II. Laid out on the Bayard farm prior to 1754 between Mulberry Street and the Bowery, the street originally included what is now **Howard Street**. See also *Clermont Street.*

Hetty Street. The name of **Charlton Street** prior to 1808. Of uncertain origin. The name "Hetty" is usually short for Harriet or Henrietta. See also *Burr Street.*

Hevins Street. Also *St. Hevins Street.* A former name of **Broome Street** between Broadway and Hudson. Originally laid out between the Bowery and about Mulberry Street prior to 1754. Of uncertain origin.

High Street. Former name of part of *Madison Street* between Montgomery and Grand Streets. Also a name formerly used for **Bridge Street** and **Stone Street** between Broad Street and Hanover Square. The designation of "high street" was commonly used for streets that were near but not directly on the waterfront, i.e. on "high" ground. Before most of lower Manhattan was surrounded by infill, Bridge Street and the eastern part of Stone Street were one block inland from the waterfront, which was at modern Pearl Street. Present day Madison Street began as a short "high street" near the waterside at Corlear's Hook.

Hillside Avenue. Named for its location running along Fort George Hill.

Hoboken Street. The eastbound section of **Canal Street** between West and Washington Streets was formerly called Hoboken Street. John Stevens was granted the use of the street in 1823 to operate a ferry to Hoboken, from which the street takes its name.

54

Hoffman Street. A former street that once ran between 3rd and 4th Avenues about on the line of East 69th Street. Named for Martin Hoffman, whose farm was bordered on the south by the street.

Hogan Place. The section of **Leonard Street** between Baxter and Centre Streets was designated Hogan Place in 1980 after Manhattan District Attorney Frank S. Hogan.

Hopper's Lane. A former road that ran from near what is now 6th Avenue and West 50th Street, where the house of Andrew Hopper stood, westerly to a point on the river now within Dewitt Clinton Park about on a line with West 53rd Street. Another Hopper household stood at the west end of the lane.

Horatio Street. Named for General Horatio Gates (1727-1806), a Revolutionary War commander. Originally laid out between Greenwich Street and Greenwich Lane (now Avenue) prior to 1811, it was extended to the Hudson River in 1834.

Horse and Cart Lane also *Horse and Cart Street, Cart and Horse Street*. Former name of part of **William Street**. A reference to the Cart and Horse, a popular tavern on the corner of William and Ann Streets in the mid 18th Century.

Houston Street. Named for William Houstoun (1755-1813), a delegate to the Constitutional Convention from Georgia and the son-in-law of Nicholas Bayard. Houston Street was originally laid out between present day 6th Avenue and Broadway. In 1823 it was extended eastward to meet with *North Street*, which was extended westward from the Bowery at the same time. North Street was renamed Houston in 1833. The portion of Houston west of 6th Avenue was called *Hamersley Street* until 1858, when it was renamed as part of Houston.

Howard Street. Of uncertain origin. Originally named as part of **Hester Street**, the name was changed to Howard in 1820 after a petition by residents of the street. Some sources claim the street is named for Harry Howard, the former Fire Chief of New York City after whom Harry Howard Square is named. Harry Howard was born in 1822, however, after the present Howard Street was named.

Hubert Street. Named for Hubert Van Wagenen, a vestryman of Trinity Church. The street originally included what is now **York Street**.

Hudson Place. Referred to West 34th Street between 9th and 10th Avenues.

Hudson Street. A main north-south thoroughfare that parallels the Hudson River. Laid out prior to 1797 between Barley (now Duane) and North Moore Streets, and between Vestry (now

Hubert) and Desbrosses Streets. By 1817, the street had been opened as far as 9th Avenue.

Hull Street. The Miller Plan of 1695 shows Hull Street for what is now **Bridge Street** between Whitehall and Broad Streets. A proclamation in 1693 that calls for the paving of common streets refers both to "the street commonly called the bridge street," as well as "the street that Hull lives in."

Hunter's Key. A former wharf along what is now **Water Street** between Old Slip and Wall Street. Possibly named for Robert Hunter, governor of New York in the early 18th Century when the key was established. Also called *Rotten Row.*

Hurlgate Road. See *Hell Gate Road.*

I.

India Wharf. A former wharf near Dover Street where Thomas H. Smith operated his trade in tea with the East.

Indian Road. Named for the nearby presence of Native American archaeological findings. The street was laid out in the early 20th Century and followed along an inlet of the Harlem River in what is now part of Inwood Hill Park.

Inwood Street. Former name of **Dyckman Street**. Of uncertain origin, but this area has been called Inwood for some time, probably in reference to its wooded and hilly terrain.

Irving Place. Laid out in 1832 and named in 1833 after the American author Washington Irving.

Isham Street. Named for the William B. Isham family, whose estate stood at what is now Isham Park. The street once curved and extended through the park, partly following the path of the present **Indian Road**.

J.

Jackson Avenue. From about 1833 to 1836 the name of **University Place**. Named for Andrew Jackson, who was serving as President at the time. Previously part of **Wooster Street**.

Jackson Place. A former place behind behind 16 Downing Street. Of uncertain origin, but possibly named for Andrew Jackson.

Jackson Street. Named around 1850 after Andrew Jackson (1767-1845), 17th President of the United States. Originally laid out as *Ferry Street*, the street was mapped as *Walnut Street* by 1799.

Jacob Street. A former street that connected Frankfort and Ferry Streets between Gold and Cliff Streets. Probably named for Jacob Lorillard, who owned property nearby, lived on Ferry Street and operated a tanning operation on Jacob Street. The area was for many years the center of the tanning industry in the city and the street was previously known as *Leather Street*. Laid out but not named prior to 1776, it appears as Jacob Street on a map of 1798. Closed in the 1960s.

James Slip. A former slip named for its location at the foot of **James Street**. Also called St. James Slip. Closed for the construction of the Alfred E. Smith Houses.

James Street. Commonly thought to have been named for James Desbrosses, who had a distillery on the river at the foot of James, Oliver and Catherine Streets. The street was called *St. James Street* in official documents and maps prior to 1755, however adding and dropping the "saint" for streets with Christian names was common. The portion between Madison Street and the East River was closed for construction of the Alfred E. Smith Houses which were completed in 1951.

Jane Street. Probably named for a nearby landowner, but of uncertain origin. Laid out and named prior to 1811, and opened in 1827.

Jauncey Court. A former court including 37, 39, 41 and 43 **Wall Street**. Named for William Jauncey, a wealthy English merchant who owned the property.

Jauncey Lane. A former lane near Apthorp Lane named for William Jauncey, who purchased the nearby property from Charles Apthorp in 1799. See also *Jauncey Court, Apthorp's Lane.*

Jay Street. Named for John Jay, Governor of New York and first Chief Justice of the U.S. Supreme Court. It was probably Jay's service as a Warden of Trinity Church that occasioned the naming of the street in the 1790s, when it was laid out on church property.

Jefferson Market. A former market located at the intersection of 6th Ave and Greenwich Avenue. Established in 1833.

Jefferson Street. Named for Thomas Jefferson, founding father and third President of the United States. Formerly called *Washington Street.*

Jersey Street. A proposed street on the *Glass House Farm* that was never officially adopted. See illustration on page 46.

Jersey Street. Of uncertain origin, but named for the neighboring state or the English island. Changed from *Columbian Alley* to Jersey Street in 1829.

Jew Street. One of several former designations of the present **South William Street**. The first synagogue in the city was constructed on this street prior to 1730.

Jews Alley. A former alley that ran northwesterly from near the present intersection of Madison and Oliver Streets about to the center of the block. This was the location of an early Jewish cemetery. Also called *Gibb's Alley.*

Joe DiMaggio Highway. Ceremonial name of the West Side Highway. Named in 1999 for the baseball legend Joe DiMaggio (1914-1999) who played thirteen years for the New York Yankees.

John Street. Named for John Harpendingh, one of five shoemakers who purchased the surrounding property and developed it into lots in about 1696. Harpendingh built a house at the corner of Maiden Lane and Broadway. The name originally applied to the portion of the street west of William Street, with the part east of William Street called *Golden Hill Street.* The two names were used interchangeably for the eastern portion of the street into the early 19th Century, when it became known as John Street for the full length.

Jones Alley. The current Jones Alley is part of a very old alley that zig-zagged from Bleecker Street northerly, then westerly, crossing Lafayette Street, then northerly again crossing Bond Street and ending at Great Jones Street. The section connecting Lafayette and Bond Streets is designated *Shinbone Alley* on current official city maps. The section connecting Bond and Great Jones Streets is called **Great Jones Alley**, which provides Jones Alley with its current name.

Jones Lane. A former street that ran from Front Street to the East River at South Street between Gouverneur Lane and Wall Street. The lane was located where Jones' Wharf once stood.

Jones Street. Named for Dr. Gardiner Jones, who ceded the property for the street. When Samuel Jones ceded land for a street in 1806, the Common Council resolved that Jones Street would keep its name and the new street be called Great Jones.

Judith Street. Former name of **Grand Street** between Bowery and Centre Streets. Named for Judith Bayard, daughter of Nicholas Bayard II.

Judith Street was also the name of a proposed street in the *Stuyvesant Farm Grid* that was never officially adopted. Named for Judith Stuyvesant, daughter of Petrus Stuyvesant (1727-1805). See illustration on page 103.

Jumel Terrace and **Jumel Place.** Named for Stephen Jumel, who purchased the mansion and property along Jumel Terrace in 1810.

K.

Kenmare Street. Named for the Irish village where the mother of Tim Sullivan, a Tammany leader, was born. The street was cut through four blocks between Lafayette Street and the Bowery beginning in 1905 to extend access to the Williamsburg Bridge.

King George Street. Laid out prior to 1730, King George Street ran between Frankfort and Pearl Streets. William Street once extended north along its present line to Frankfort Street at the point where King George Street also met Frankfort. From this point it ran northeast to Pearl Street to a point just south of the present intersection with Park Row. The street was merged with **William Street** in 1794, and this portion has since been closed. Sometimes shortened to *King Street.*

King Street. A former name for **Pine Street**. King Street was also used as a short version of *King George Street.* In both cases, the name is a reference to the monarch of England.

King Street. Named in 1807 for Rufus King (1755-1827), one-time U.S. Senator for New York and presidential candidate, and warden of Trinity Church at the time the street was ceded by the church to the city in 1808. Formerly *Hazard Street.*

Kings Bridge Road. A former road that followed part of the present path of **St. Nicholas Avenue** and **Broadway**. The Kings Bridge was located at the northern tip of Manhattan near what is now the southern end of Kingsbridge Avenue in Marble Hill. The road to the bridge branched from the Eastern Post Road at about present-day 110th Street and followed the route of St. Nicholas Avenue to 170th Street, where it followed the path of modern Broadway to the southern end of current Kingsbridge Avenue. Sometimes also spelled Kingsbridge. See illustration on page 13.

Kings Road. A name used for what is now **Pearl Street** between Franklin Square and Park Row. A reference to the English monarch.

Kip Street. A former name for **Nassau Street** between Maiden Lane and Spruce Street. Named for Jacob Kip. The name is applied to the whole of Nassau Street on the Miller Plan in 1695.

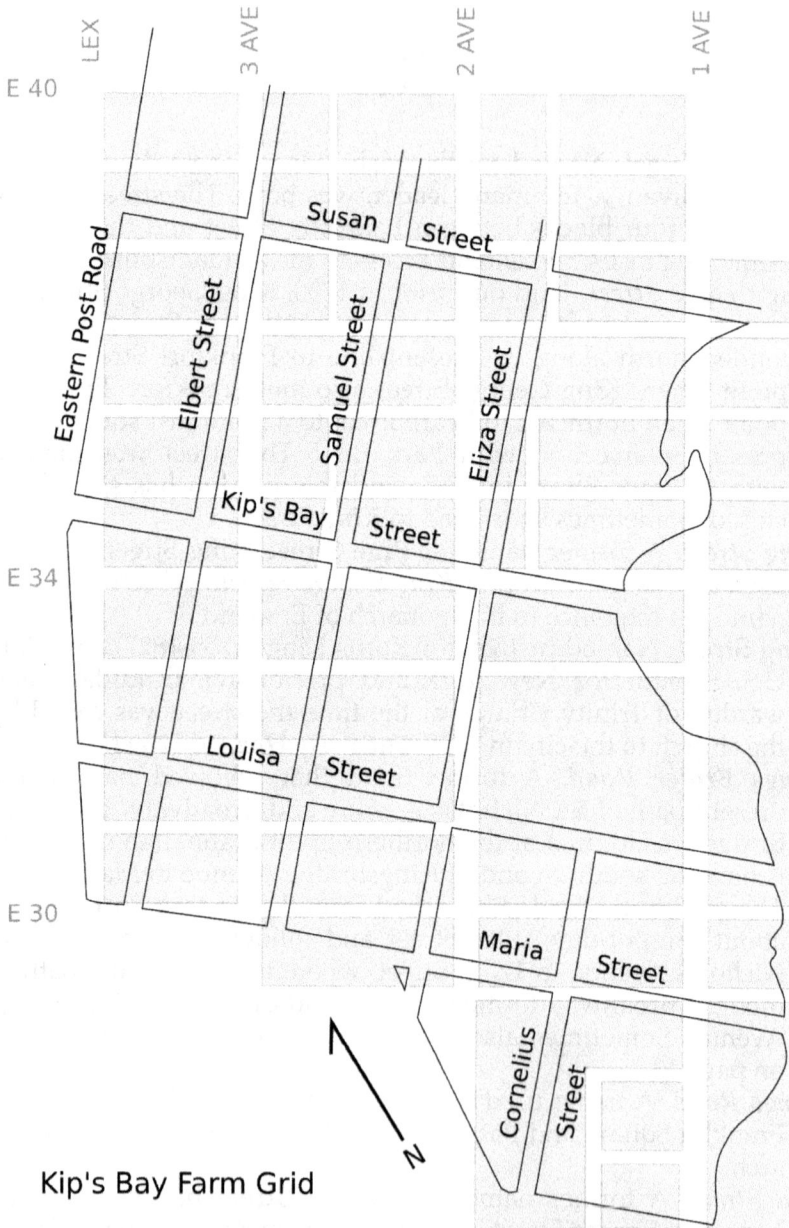

Kip's Bay Farm Grid

E 40

LEX

3 AVE

2 AVE

1 AVE

Eastern Post Road

Susan Street

Elbert Street

Samuel Street

Eliza Street

Kip's Bay Street

E 34

Louisa Street

E 30

Maria Street

Cornelius Street

N

Kip's Bay Farm Grid. Around 1805 the Kip family began selling lots on their farm along streets named for the children and in-laws of Samuel Kip. Laid out between what is now East 26th and 39th Streets, the grid was oriented parallel to the Eastern Post Road (about where Lexington Avenue now stands) and ran to the East River at Kip's Bay, which at that time reached inland west of 1st Avenue. See illustration opposite.

Kip's Bay Street. The central street of the *Kip's Bay Farm Grid* laid out about 1805 but never officially adopted.

Kirkpatrick Place. Part of East 74th Street between 5th and Madison Avenues. Of uncertain origin.

Knapp's Place. Former place behind 422 East 10th Street. Of uncertain origin.

L.

La Guardia Place. Named in 1967 for Fiorello LaGuardia (1882-1947), Mayor of New York from 1934 to 1945, who was born in Greenwich Village. Previously *West Broadway*. Originally *Laurens Street* and *South Fifth Avenue*.

La Grange Terrace. A row of colonnaded houses built on *Lafayette Place* in 1827 and named for the Marquis de Lafayette's French estate. The buildings became known later as *Colonnade Row*. A portion of the row still stands on the west side of **Lafayette Street** between East 4th Street and Astor Place.

Lasalle Street. Named in 1921 for Jean-Baptiste de la Salle (1651-1719), French priest and founder of the Lasallian Brothers, the order that established Manhattan College. The college moved to this Manhattanville location in 1853 from a school on Canal Street. It was located here until 1922 when it moved to its present location in The Bronx. Formerly part of 125th Street.

Lafayette Boulevard. Former name of part of the **Henry Hudson Parkway** and **Riverside Drive** north of West 155th Street. Lafayette Boulevard was originally laid out around 1893 as a branch of the *Boulevard*, which later became part of Broadway. It branched westward from Broadway just above West 155th Street and ran along the riverside to meet Broadway again at Dyckman Street. It was renamed Lafayette Boulevard in 1894 in honor of the Marquis de Lafayette. In the early 20th Century, Riverside Drive was extended to meet Lafayette Boulevard near West 161st Street and the name of Riverside was extended to the whole street.

Lafayette Place. Former name of **Lafayette Street** between Great Jones and East 8th Streets. Named for the Marquis de Lafayette, who served as a general in the Revolutionary War and who had visited the city in 1824 and 1825, shortly before the street was opened in 1826.

Lafayette Street. *Lafayette Place* was extended and connected to *Elm Street* and renamed Lafayette Street in 1905.

Laight Street. Named in 1794 by Trinity Church for William Laight, a successful merchant and vestryman of the church.

Lamartine Place. Former name of West 29th Street between 8th and 9th Avenues, now a historic district. Named in honor of Alphonse de Lamartine (1790-1869), the French poet and statesman.

Lambert Street. Probably a misspelling of *Lombard Street*.

Laurens Street. Former name of **West Broadway** north of Canal Street. Laid out prior to 1797 and called Laurens Street by 1800. In 1870 the name was changed to *South Fifth Avenue*, and it was incorporated into West Broadway in 1896. Named for former President of the Continental Congress, Henry Laurens (1724-1792).

Leanderts Place. Referred to part of East 7th Street between Avenues A and B. Named for the Leandert Farm, which stood in this area.

Leary Slip. A slip on the Hudson River that stood at the foot of *Leary Street*.

Leary Street. Also *Leary's Street.* Alternate name of **Cortlandt Street**. Referred to John Leary, who owned a livery stable on the street beginning in the mid 1700s. Although first designated as Cortlandt, the two names appear to have been used concurrently for many years. See also *Windmill Lane*.

Leather Street. A former narrow street that was laid out connecting Ferry and Frankfort Streets between Gold and Cliff Streets. Named for the presence of tanning pits and leather-related industry centered around the Street. Later called *Jacob Street*.

Legget's Lane. A former name for *Verdant Lane*. Barbara Leggett was given property along the lane by her father, Charles Kelly, in 1798. Also called *Feitner's Lane*.

Lennox Place. Formerly West 22nd Street between 8th and 9th Avenues. Sometimes spelled Lenox. Of uncertain origin.

Lenox Avenue. Named in 1887 in reference to the family of Robert Lenox (1759-1839), who first purchased property in the area. James Lenox, Robert's son, divided the property into lots and sold them in the 1860s and 70s. Formerly 6th Avenue.

Leonard Street. Named for Leonard Lispenard, great-great-grandson of Anthony Lispenard, the patriarch of the Lispenard family in New York City. Laid out between Hudson Street and Broadway before 1797, and extended to Orange Street (now Baxter) in 1813.

Leroy Place. Stood on the south side of **Bleecker Street** between Mercer and Greene Streets. Named for Jacob LeRoy, a city alderman.

Leroy Street. Named in 1807 for Jacob LeRoy, a city alderman and vestryman of Trinity Church from 1795-1815. Extended in 1845 to meet *Burton Street,* the entire street was called Leroy shortly afterward.

Lewis Street. Named possibly for Morgan Lewis, who served as Chief Justice of the Supreme Court of New York at the time the street was laid out some time between 1797 and 1799. Regulated in 1807, the street originally ran through from Grand Street to what is now Houston Street and was later extended to East 8th Street. Most of it was closed for the construction of housing projects.

Lexington Avenue. Named in July 1836 to commemorate the Battle of Lexington. The avenue was laid out as a "new street" in 1832 between East 21st and 30th Streets, then extended to 42nd Street in 1833, to 66th Street in 1838, and to the Harlem River in 1870. Labeled on one 1836 map as an extension of **Irving Place**.

Liberty Court. Referred to Numbers 4 and 6, Liberty Place.

Liberty Place. Named for its location connecting Liberty Street and Maiden Lane. See **Liberty Street**.

Liberty Street. *Crown Street* was renamed Liberty Street in 1794 in reference to America's independence from the crown of England.

Lillian Wald Drive. Named for Lillian D. Wald (1867-1940), founder of the Henry Street Nurses Settlement. This short drive serves the Lillian Wald Houses housing projects that were completed in 1949. The street runs about on the line of **Lewis Street**, which was partly closed for construction of the project.

Lispenard Street. The street runs through what was once a swampy lowland called Lispenard's Meadow, named after Anthony Lispenard, its owner. Originally laid out between what is now West Broadway and Mercer Street, which ex-tended south of Canal to end at an intersection with Lispenard. In 1809, Lispenard Street was extended to meet Broadway.

Little Ann Street. See Ann Street, Anne Street.

Little Chapel Street. A name sometimes used formerly for **Beek-man Street**. See *Chapel Street.*

Little Division Street. Former name of **Montgomery Street**. Laid out prior to 1767 and surveyed in 1790, the street marked the eastern border of the Herman Rutgers farm. It was called "Little" to distinguish it from the existing Division Street. By 1792 it was referred to as Montgomery Street.

Little Dock Street. Former name of **Water Street** between Broad Street and Old Slip. So named to distinguish it from *Great Dock Street,* part of the present Pearl Street.

Little George Street. A name used for **Spruce Street**. By 1813, Manhattan had at least three streets bearing the name George. The term "little" was sometimes added to distinguish this street from the others. The street was renamed Spruce in 1813. See *George Street.*

Little Green Street. Former name of **Liberty Place**. Named in reference to *Green Lane,* an alternate name for the present Maiden Lane.

Little Queen Street. Former name of **Cedar Street**. Called "Little Queen" to distinguish it from *Queen Street.* Laid out prior to 1695 and regulated in 1755. Name changed to Cedar Street in 1794. Also sometimes called *French Church Street.*

Little Stone Street. Former name of **Thames Street**. Sometimes mapped as *Stone Street.* Laid out prior to 1730 and mapped as Little Stone Street in 1767. The term "little" was added to distinguish it from the existing **Stone Street**.

Little Water Street. A former street that made up the western part of the *Five Points.* The water referred to was the Collect Pond which stood nearby, with "Little" added to distinguish it from the Water Street along the lower East River. It was officially named part of *Anthony Street* in 1809, but continued to be known by its original name. After 1850 it was also called *Mission Place.*

Little West 12th Street. This short street lies on the same line as the middle section of West 12th Street but does not connect through. "Little" is added to distinguish it from West 12th.

Little West Street. Named in reference to West Street, which it parallels.

Livingston Place. Former name of **Nathan D. Perlman Place**. Named for the Livingston family descended from Robert Livingston (1654-1728), which had a long association with the Stuyvesant family. Margaret Livingston was the wife of Peter Stuyvesant (1727-1805). The land for Stuyvesant Square Park was donated to the city by the Stuyvesant family in 1836. The street forms the eastern border of the park. See also **Rutherford Place**.

At the same time the original Livingston Place was renamed in 1953, the City Council gave the name to *Birmingham Street*.

Livingston Street. A street in the *Mangin-Goerck Plan* that was never officially adopted. It was laid out as an east-west street in an extension of the *Stuyvesant Farm Grid* and ran parallel to Gates Street one block to the north. The Livingston family were an old New York family closely associated with the Stuyvesant family.

Locust Street. Original name of **Sullivan Street**. First laid out on the Bayard West Farm, the name probably referred to the presence of locust trees, which grew native on the island. Mapped as Sullivan Street by 1799.

Lombard Street. Former name of **Monroe Street**. Of uncertain origin, but possibly in reference to the storage of goods near the waterfront. Because of confusion with *Lumber Street*, the name was changed to *Lombardy Street* in 1809.

Lombardy Street. Former name of **Monroe Street**. Originally *Lombard Street*, the name was changed in 1809 to avoid confusion with *Lumber Street*.

London Terrace. A row of 36 houses along the north side of West 23rd Street between 9th and 10th Avenues. Named for the English city. The original London Terrace was developed by Clement C. Moore and completed in 1845. In 1928, demolition of the houses began and the present London Terrace Towers were completed on the site in 1935.

Long Acre Square. A former name of **Times Square**. The area was once home to several carriage makers and stables and was named after the similar district of London, called Long Acre. Officially changed to Times Square in 1904.

Lord's Court. Formerly located in the rear of 51 Beaver Street. Of uncertain origin.

Lorillard Place. Formerly located on **Washington Street** between Charles and Perry Streets. The name referred to a row of houses set back from the street behind iron fences. Some of the houses of Lorillard Place are still present on the Street. Established in 1834, the development was named for the Lorillard family, prominent tobacco merchants.

Louisa Street. A former street in the Kips Bay Farm grid laid out about 1805. Probably named for Ann Louisa Kip, grand-daughter of Samuel Kip. See illustration on page 60.

Love Lane. A former street that followed closely the line of present 21st Street between 8th Avenue and Park Avenue, then curved northerly to end at 23rd Street and 3rd Avenue. Closed in 1826 when 21st Street was opened. Also mapped as *Abingdon Road*. The two names appear to have been used concurrently. *Love Lane* was also the name of a former lane on the Rutgers Farm corresponding about to the line of the present **Henry Street**. In both cases, the roads were shady country lanes that were popular paths for strolling couples.

Low's Lane. Also called the *Cross Road* and *Steuben Street*. A former street that ran between Broadway and the East Post Road. The road was closed in the 1830s and the roadbed granted to adjacent property owners in 1848. Named for a Mr. Low, who owned a tract south of the road, along the *Middle Road*, near what is now East 42nd Street and Madison Avenue.

Lower Robinson Street. Former name of part of **Park Place** between Greenwich Street and West Broadway. The street was in line with the former *Robinson Street*, separated by the one-block campus of Columbia College. In 1813, when Robinson Street was changed to Park Place, Lower Robinson was at the same time renamed Robinson. When Park Place was extended through the former college campus and joined with Robinson, the entire street was named Park Place.

Ludlow Place. Part of **Houston Street** between Sullivan and Mac-Dougal Streets. Of uncertain origin, but probably named after the property owner or developer.

Ludlow Street. Named after Lt. Augustus C. Ludlow (1792-1813) who was mortally wounded in the capture of the *Chesapeake* in the War of 1812. Previously called *Sixth Street*. Name changed in 1817.

Lumber Street. Former name of **Trinity Place** between Edgar and Liberty Streets. The name of the street was the source of some confusion among New Yorkers, who used the name Lumber and Lombard interchangeably for the street. In 1792, the Common Council ordered that the street officially be called Lumber. The name was changed to Trinity Place in 1843. Of uncertain origin, but its location near the old waterfront may have made the area convenient for the piling of items being loaded or unloaded from boats. See also *Lombard Street.*

M.

Maagde Paatje. See **Maiden Lane**.

Macdougal Alley. Named for its connection to **Macdougal Street**. Laid out prior to 1850.

Macdougal Street. Named for Revolutionary War General Alexander McDougal (1731-1786), a leader of the Sons of Liberty. Laid out prior to 1799, the street was regulated between Spring and Houston Streets in 1813. In 1828 it was extended to Clinton Place, now West 8th Street. In 1858 the portion along Washington Square Park was renamed **Washington Square West**. The portion below Prince Street was closed in the 1920s for the extension of 6th Avenue.

Macomb's Lane. Former name of **Macombs Place**.

Macombs Place. Named for Robert Macomb, who built a dam on the Harlem River in 1813 to power his grist mill. Macomb built a toll bridge over the dam in 1816. Originally called Macomb's Lane, the road led to the bridge on the Manhattan side.

Madison Avenue. Named for James Madison (1751-1836), fourth President of the United States. The avenue was established between East 23rd and 42nd Streets in 1833 by act of the state legislature. It was extended to 86th Street in 1860, to 120th in 1867, and to the Harlem River in 1869.

Madison Court. A short street north of Madison Street between Jefferson and Clinton Streets. Named in association with **Madison Street**.

Madison Square North. The portion of East 26th Street that borders Madison Square Park on the north is named after the park. Madison Square Park is a remnant of the large parade ground laid out in the *Commissioners' Plan* that extended from 23rd to 34th streets and between 3rd and 7th Avenues. The parade ground was named for James Madison in 1814.

Madison Street. Named for James Madison (1751-1836), fourth President of the United States. Formerly called *Bancker Street*, *Bedlow Street*, and *William Street*. The name was changed from Bancker in 1826 after the street fell into disrepute.

Magaw Place. Named for Colonel Robert Magaw (1738-1790), who surrendered Fort Washington in 1776 and was made prisoner of war by the British. Called *Fort Washington Place* between 1921 and 1923.

Magazine Street. A former street, part of which is now part of **Pearl Street**. The street was originally laid out before 1797 between Broadway and Chatham Street (now Park Row) and passed by the British powder magazine on the south shore of the Collect Pond. It was renamed as part of Pearl Street in 1811. The portion between Broadway and Lafayette Street was closed when the Federal Plaza was built in 1968.

Maiden Lane. The English translation of *Maagde Paatje*, "Maiden's Path," the Dutch name for the lane that ran along a stream leading to the East River. The stream was used for washing clothes, a task usually performed by young women. Also called *Green Lane*, Maidens Valley, and Maids Path.

Maiden Slip, also **Maiden Lane Slip.** An alternate name for the *Fly Market Slip.*

Mail Street. A former street that ran across what is now the southern tip of City Hall Park, east of the triangular City Hall Post Office building. Opened after the completion of the building in 1880. The post office was demolished in 1939 and the street was closed when the park was extended to include the former site.

Mangin-Goerck Plan In 1797 city surveyors Joseph Mangin and Casimir Goerck were charged by the City with producing a map and plan of the city streets. The plan was completed, printed and presented to the Common Council in 1803. Mangin, who had completed the work following the death of his partner, overstepped his authority, however, and projected several city streets that had not been officially approved. Concerned that property holders might begin selling lots based on the unofficial plan, the Council ordered the plans be recalled and a disclaimer pasted on them disavowing any official endorsement of the projected streets. Just a few years later the Council would adopt the numbered grid plan that shaped the future growth of the city.

In general, the Mangin-Goerck plan preserved the private street grids of the Delancey and Stuyvesant farms, extending them to meet at a point about where East 4th now intersects with the Bowery. Broadway was extended in a straight line past its junction with the Bowery at Union Square and a grid of parallel streets were laid out west of it. The plan retained the proposed street names of the *Stuyvesant Farm Grid* and the *Delancey Farm Grid* and assigned additional names to the streets that extended them.

Mangin Street. Named for Joseph Francis Mangin, a surveyor and partner of Casimir Goerck. Mangin Street originally ran through from Grand Street north to Houston Street. Portions of it were closed for the Baruch Houses. See also *Goerck Street.*

Manhattan Alley. A later name for the former *Republican Alley.* Same as *Manhattan Place.*

Manhattan Avenue. A name used for the *Middle Road.*

Manhattan Avenue. First proposed by the Commissioners of Central Park in 1868, Manhattan Avenue was laid out in 1871 and originally referred to as *New Avenue.* In 1890, the West Side Association proposed the name be changed to Manhattan Avenue in reference to its intersection with Manhattan Street (now West 124th Street) in the north. See also *Manhattan Street*.

Manhattan Lane. A former lane that led southwest out of the village of Haarlem and met with the *Manhattan Road*.

Manhattan Place. A later name for the former *Republican Alley*. Usage of the two names appears to have overlapped.

Manhattan Road. A former road that ran from the village of Haarlem at about East 121st Street and Lexington Avenue, easterly to the village of Manhattanville. The eastern portion was also called Manhattan Lane.

Manhattan Street. Former name of West 125th Street, **Hancock Place** and West 124th Street between Hancock Place and St. Nicholas Avenue. Laid out prior to 1806 as the main street through the settlement of Manhattanville, most of the street was incorporated into 125th Street in 1920.

Manhattan Street was also the name of a former alley that connected East Houston Street and East 3rd Street, running about one half block east of Columbia Street. An access street west of the public school building on Houston corresponds to the location of the former street, the northern part of which has been closed.

Mansfield Place. Located in West 51st Street between 8th and 9th Avenues.

Maple Street. A proposed street on the *Glass House Farm* that was never adopted. See illustration on page 46.

Marckvelt Steegie. See **Marketfield Street**.

Marckvelt. Former name of **Whitehall Street**. See also **Marketfield Street**.

Margaret Corbin Drive and **Margaret Corbin Circle.** Named in 1977 for Margaret Corbin (1751-1800), who fought the British at Fort Washington in 1776, stepping into the fray to take over for her fallen husband.

Margaret Street. Former name of **Willett Street**. Probably named for Margaret Bancker, the wife of Colonel Marinus Willett (1740-1830). Willett purchased several lots in the area along Grand Street in 1785. Margaret and Marinus Willett also had a daughter named Margaret.

Margaret Street was also the name of a proposed street in the *Stuyvesant Farm Grid* that was never officially adopted. Named for Margaret Stuyvesant, daughter of Petrus Stuyvesant (1727-1805). See illustration on page 103.

Maria Street A street in the *Kip's Bay Farm Grid* laid out about 1805 but not officially adopted. Named for Mary Kip, daughter of Samuel Kip. See illustration on page 60.

Marie Curie Avenue. In 1935, the former *Exterior Street* was re-named for the Polish scientist Marie Curie (1867-1934). The street was later incorporated into the *East River Drive.*

Marion Street. Former name of **Cleveland Place** and **Lafayette Street** between Spring Street and about Jersey Street. Originally laid as part of *Mary Street,* later *Orange Street,* the name of which was changed to Marion north of Broome Street in 1839. Named in honor of General Francis Marion (1732-1795), a Revolutionary War figure.

Market Slip. Named for its location at the foot of **Market Street.** Previously *George Slip.*

Market Street. Named in 1813 in reference to the *Catherine Market,* which stood along the waterfront between Catherine and Market Streets. Previously called *George Street.*

Marketfield Street. A *marckvelt,* or "market field" stood outside the original Dutch fort on the southern end of the island, near the present Bowling Green. The street originally ran from the waterfront at present day West Street, along the south side of Bowling Green and on to Broad Street. The portion west of Broadway is now occupied by **Battery Place.** A segment of the street between Broadway and Broad was closed in 1880 and the street was extended north to Beaver Street to provide through access. Also called Marketfield Lane, Marketfield Path, and Marckvelt Steegie or Steegh. The name Marckvelt was also used for Whitehall Street, which led to the market field, but which also had a market of its own near Pearl Street.

Maretta Street. A street laid out on the *Mangin-Goerck Plan* that was not adopted. It was laid out as a north-south street running from about the modern intersection of Thompson Street and Washington Square South. The name is of uncertain origin, but is a woman's given name.

Martha Street. A street in the *Mangin-Goerck Plan* that was never officially adopted. It was laid out as a north-south street in an extension of the *Stuyvesant Farm Grid* and ran parallel to Cornelia Street one block to the east. Of uncertain origin.

Martin Terrace. Referred to East 30th Street between 2nd and 3rd Avenues. Of uncertain origin.

Mary Street. Former name of **Baxter Street** and **Centre Market Place** between Bayard and Broome Streets, and a portion of *Lafayette Street* north of Prince Street. Originally laid out on the Nicholas Bayard farm prior to 1794, Mary Street extended along the line of modern Baxter Street from Bayard to just north of Prince Street where it dead-ended just south of present-day Jersey Street. South of Bayard the street was called

Orange Street and by 1803 the name Orange had been extended to include Mary Street on many maps, although official records continued to refer to Mary Street for several years afterward. In 1839 the section north of Broome Street was renamed *Marion Street,* and in 1854 the section of Orange south of Broome was renamed Baxter. Marion Street was then absorbed into *Elm Street* when it was extended and later renamed part of **Lafayette Street**.

McCreas Dock. Formerly located along Water Street between Clinton and Montgomery Streets.

McKees Dock. Formerly located at the foot of North Moore Street.

Meadow Street. A name used for the present **Grand Street** between Broadway and West Broadway. Laid out prior to 1797, but by 1799 not used. The street ran along the northern edge of Lispenard's Meadow.

Mechanics Alley. Laid out prior to 1836 connecting Monroe and Cherry Streets west of Pike Street, the original Mechanics Alley was closed around 1905 when the Manhattan Bridge was built. It appears at that time the name was applied to a new alley formed by the supports of the bridge in the blocks to the north, between Henry and Monroe Streets. It is this section that is now mapped as Mechanics Alley Named for the skilled manual workers who commonly lived and worked near the waterfront. See also *Mechanics Place.*

Mechanics Place. Two short alleys have borne the name Mechanics Place. One was located at 28 Avenue A between East 2nd and 3rd Streets. Another was south of Rivington Street between Lewis and Goerck Streets (now within the Baruch Houses development). "Mechanic" was once a more general term for anyone who performed manual manufacturing work, such as shipbuilders. See also **Mechanics Alley.**

Meeks Court. Formerly located behind 58 Broad Street. A Robert F. Meeks is listed as living nearby on Broad Street in 1877.

Mercer Street. Mapped as "First or *Clermont Street*" in 1797 and as Mercer Street in 1799. Named in honor of General Hugh Mercer (1726-1777), a figure in the Revolutionary War who died from wounds incurred in the Battle of Princeton.

Merchant Street. When the Merchant's Exchange building burned down in 1835, the name of the street was changed from Exchange to Merchant. See *Exchange Street.*

Merchant's Court. Formerly located behind 48 1/2 **Exchange Place**. Probably in reference to the Merchant's Exchange that stood nearby.

Merchant's Place. Formerly located behind 28 Avenue A.

71

Messier's Alley A former alley that connected Water Street and South Street between Coenties Slip and Old Slip. Named for Peter Messier, who purchased the adjacent lot from the estate of Henry Cuyler in the 1770s. Also called *Cuyler's Alley*.

The Mews. Former name of **Theatre Alley**. Mews were rows of stables and carriage houses, often with living quarters above them. The street became known as Theatre Street, now Theatre Alley, after the construction of the Park Theater which opened on Park Row near Ann Street in 1798.

Middle Road. A former road that ran from the Eastern Post Road at about the present Park Avenue and East 29th Street northerly to the Cross Road at about the present 5th Avenue and 42nd Street. So called because of its location between two major north-south roads, the Eastern Post Road and the Bloomingdale Road. The road also passed through the center of the lower part of the Common Lands, a large tract of land once owned by the City of New York. Also called *Manhattan Avenue*.

Middle Street. Former name of **Monroe Street** between Montgomery and Grand Streets. The street ran through the middle of a small grid of streets laid out prior to 1797 at Crown Point. Middle Street was between *High Street* and *Garden Street*.

Mill Lane. Laid out prior to 1657, this short lane connected *Mill Street* (now **South William Street**) to Stone Street. Also called Mill Street Lane.

Mill Street. One of many former names of **South William Street** west of Mill Lane. A horse-powered bark mill was established at this location around 1626. Bark was used in the process of tanning leather, a significant early industry on the island.

Miller Place. Formerly located behind 4 **Macdougal Street**. Of uncertain origin. Sometimes also Miller's Place.

Milligan Lane. Referred to West 10th Street between Greenwich Avenue and 6th Avenue. See **Milligan Place**.

Milligan Place. This short alley off 6th Avenue between West 10th and 11th Streets was named for Samuel Milligan, who owned the surrounding land. Milligan's house is labeled on the Commissioners' Plan and is shown standing near what is now the end of **Patchin Place**.

Millward Place. Formerly located in West 31st Street between 8th and 9th Avenues. Of uncertain origin.

Minetta Lane. Named for the Minetta Brook, which it crossed. Laid out prior to 1836. See also **Minetta Street**.

Minetta Place. Formerly located behind 2 Minetta Street and named for its connection to that street.

Minetta Street. The name is believed to be an English approximation of the Dutch word *mintje,* meaning "small." The Mintje Kill,
or "small stream" ran through this part of Manhattan and
Minetta Street follows part of the path of this old waterway.
Sometimes called *Bride Street.*

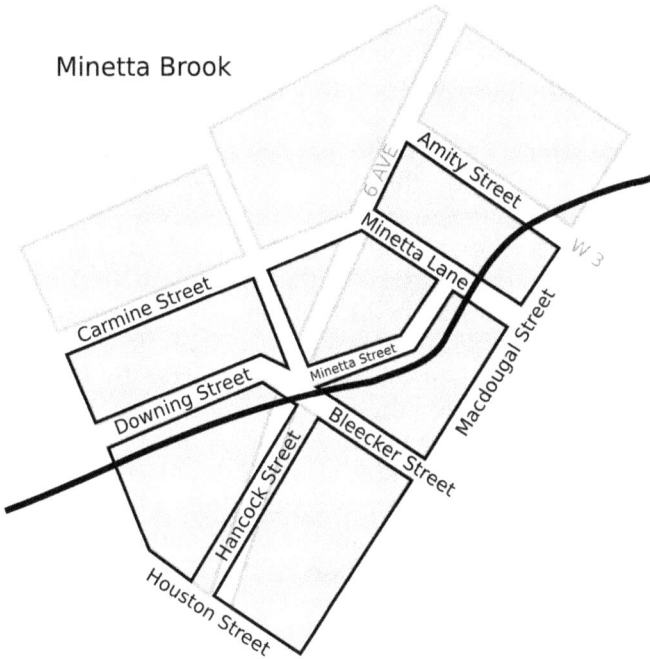

Minetta Brook

Minthorne Street. A proposed street in the *Mangin-Goerck Plan*
that ran parallel to East Houston Street from the East River to
the Bowery just opposite Great Jones Street. The street was laid
out through what was the Philip Minthorne farm.
Mission Place. A former street that was closed for the construction
of the New York Supreme Court building. The street met Worth
Street about halfway between Center and Baxter Streets and
ran south, parallel to Baxter, to Park Street (also now closed).
Named for the Five Points Mission, established in 1850 on Park
Street opposite the southern end of Mission Place. Also called
Little Water Street.
Mitchell and Agnew's Basin. Formerly located on the East River
between Roosevelt and Dover Streets. An alley by the same
name served the basin, according to Post.
Mitchell Place. Of uncertain origin. The designation appears first
to have been applied to East 49th Street between 1st Avenue

73

and Avenue A (now Beekman Place). It was officially opened as an adjacent but separate street in 1899.

Moll Street. Most likely a misreading of **Mott Street**.

Monroe Place. Referred to part of **Monroe Street** between Gouverneur and Scammel Streets. Now closed.

Monroe Street. Named in 1831 for President James Monroe. Previously *Lombardy Street*.

Montgomery Street. Probably named for Brigadier General Richard Montgomery (1738-1775) who died in Quebec during the Revolutionary War. Laid out prior to 1767 and called *Little Division Street*, by 1792 the street was known as Montgomery, possibly so called by the heirs of the Rutgers estate where it was located. Often also spelled Montgomerie.

Monument Lane. A former lane that followed what is now **Greenwich Avenue**, extending on the same line past 8th Avenue about to the north side of 14th Street. At this spot was located a monument to General James Wolfe, British hero of the Battle of Quebec in 1759. The monument was erected by Oliver de Lancey in 1761. Also called the *Obelisk Road*.

Moore Street Moore Street once extended from Pearl Street to the waterfront and was the site of the first wharf in the city. Some sources speculate the name is a variation of "moor" in reference to the moorage of ships at the location, but it is most certainly named for Colonel John Moore (1686-1749), a successful merchant who owned the surrounding property including the house known as Whitehall that stood near the wharf, and "Moore's Wharf" at the foot of Moore Street. The street originally extended through to South Street. Formerly *Weigh House Street*.

Moore's Row. An alternate name for *Torbert Street*. Of uncertain origin.

Moore's Wharf. The wharf of Colonel John Moore located at the foot of **Moore Street**.

Morningside Avenue and **Morningside Drive.** Named for Morningside Park, which is bracketed by the two streets. The name Morningside refers to the eastern exposure of the ledge of schist upon which the park is built.

Morris Place. Formerly located in West 42nd Street between 10th and 11th Avenues. Of uncertain origin, but possibly in reference to Gouverneur Morris.

Morris Street. Possibly named for Gouverneur Morris, one of the Commissioners appointed in 1807 to lay out a street plan for Manhattan. Previously called *Beaver Lane*, the name was changed in 1829 after residents of the street petitioned the City Council to call it Morris.

Mortkile Street. Former name of **Barclay Street**. Of uncertain origin, but possibly formed from a Dutch name for the Street. A "moord-kuil" in old Dutch is a smugglers' or robbers' cave. The word "kill" refers to a stream or brook, many of which crossed the island.

Morton Street. Former name of **Clarkson Street**. Laid out on Trinity Church land, the street was renamed Clarkson in 1807 and ceded by the church to the City in 1808. At that time, the name was transferred to the present **Morton Street** which had been laid out as an extension of *Arden Street*. Both the original and later Morton Streets were named for General Jacob Morton (1762-1837).

Morton Street. Named for General Jacob Morton (1762-1837). Morton Street had been the name of the present Clarkson Street prior to 1807, when the church proposed transferring the name to the present Street. The street was extended to meet *Arden Street* around 1813 and in 1829 the entire street was called Morton.

Mosco Street. Named in 1982 for Frank Mosco, a community activist. Previously *Park Street*, Mosco is the last remnant of the original *Cross Street*, which was one of the streets that formed the *Five Points*.

Moses Street A proposed street on the *Glass House Farm* that was never officially adopted. Named for Isaac Moses, who owned adjoining property to the east of the farm. See illustration on page 46.

Mott Street. Commonly said to be named for Joseph Mott, a New York butcher and innkeeper, but the name is of uncertain origin. The street was first laid out between present day Worth Street and the bend at Pell Street around 1751 when property owner John Kingston laid the parcel out in lots. One source indicates that one of these lots was sold to Jacob Mott, after whom the adjoining street was named. The streets of the Kingston property were ceded to the city in 1763. What is now Mott Street between Bayard and Broome Streets was laid out before 1754 as *Winne Street*. Some time before 1805 the entire street became known as Mott. Extended to Bleecker Street in 1809.

Mott's Lane. A short lane at the eastern end of *Hopper's Lane* that ran from what is now 11th Avenue between West 52nd and 53rd Streets northwesterly to point near the present northwest corner of Dewitt Clinton Park. The lane led to the riverside country house of the Mott Family at Mott's Point.

Mount Carmel Place. Named for the Mt. Carmel Church that stood on East 28th Street.

Mount Morris Park West. Named for Mount Morris Park, the former name of Marcus Garvey Park. The name of the park was changed in 1973.

Mount Morris Place. Referred to West 124th Street between 5th Avenue and Lenox Avenue/Malcolm X Boulevard. Named for its proximity to Mount Morris Park (now Marcus Garvey Park), itself named for the family of Gouverneur Morris.

Moylan Place. A former designation for part of West 120th Street between Broadway and Claremont Avenue. Named in 1921 for the son of William Moylan who had died in World War I. Moylan was a resident of the street.

Mulberry Street Probably named for the presence of mulberry trees nearby. Laid out prior to 1767, the name originally applied only to the portion south of the bend in the street below Bayard. The street was called *Ryndert Street* between the bend and Broome Street. The name was extended to the full street by 1797. By 1825 the street had been extended to Bleecker.

Murray Street. Named for Joseph Murray, a vestryman of Trinity Church and trustee of Columbia College. The street runs through land ceded by the college and the church.

Murray's Wharf. A former wharf that stood along the north side of Wall Street. Operated by the prosperous merchant Robert Murray (1721-1786), whose mansion stood in what is now the Murray Hill neighborhood.

Mustary Street. Probably a misreading of **Mulberry Street**. Said by Post to be a former name of Mulberry Street between Park Row and Park Street (a section now mostly closed).

N.

Nagle Avenue. Named in the late 19th Century for Jan Nagle (or Nagel), a friend of William Dyckman, who had large landholdings in upper Manhattan.

Nassau Street. Named for William of Orange, Prince of Nassau, who became King William III. Laid out around 1689, the portion between Maiden Lane and Ann Streets is mapped as Nassau Street in 1696 and as *Kip Street* below that point. See also **William Street** and *Pie Woman's Lane.*

Nathan D. Perlman Place. Named in 1954 for Nathan David Perlman (1887-1952), a lawyer, judge and philanthropist who also served as president of Beth Israel Hospital. Formerly *Living-ston Place*. See also **Birmingham Street** .

Neilson Place. Formerly located in **Mercer Street** between Waverly Place and 8th Avenue. Of uncertain origin.

New Avenue East. Former name of part of **Madison Avenue** where it borders Marcus Garvey Park between East 120th and 124th Streets. The street was named part of Madison in 1872. It was designated as the "east" New Avenue to distinguish it from the other New Avenue that existed at the time, which was later named Manhattan Avenue.

New Avenue East is also a former name of **Bradhurst Avenue**, which was regulated by that name in 1892. It was so called to distinguish it from *New Avenue West* , which became **Edgecombe Avenue**.

New Avenue West. Former name of **Edgecombe Avenue**. The street was laid out without a name at the same time as the present Bradhurst Avenue, which was called New Avenue East. Both streets were regulated under their current names in 1892.

New Avenue. Original name of **Manhattan Avenue** between 1871 and 1890.

New streets in the grid were not always named at the time they were laid out and were sometimes referred to in generic terms such as "the new avenue." In this case, the street that became Manhattan Avenue was called "New" for nearly twenty years.

New Batavia Street. Alternate name of *Batavia Lane*. The street was renamed from Batavia Lane to Batavia Street in 1817.

New Bowery. Laid out as an extension of the **Bowery** in 1856. Renamed **St. James Place** around 1947. See illustration on page 78.

New Canal Street. When **Walker Street** east of Baxter Street was renamed in 1855 as part of Canal Street, the newly named section was sometimes referred to as New Canal Street.

New Chambers Street. A now obsolete street that extended **Chambers Street** from Park Row to James Slip in 1855. Competing reports were received by the Council from the Street Committee on the proposed extension of the Street. The majority recommended opening the street to James Slip, while a minority report recommended opening it further to Catherine Slip. The majority recommendation was adopted. See illustration on page 78.

New Chapple Street. According to Post, a former name for **Catherine Slip**.

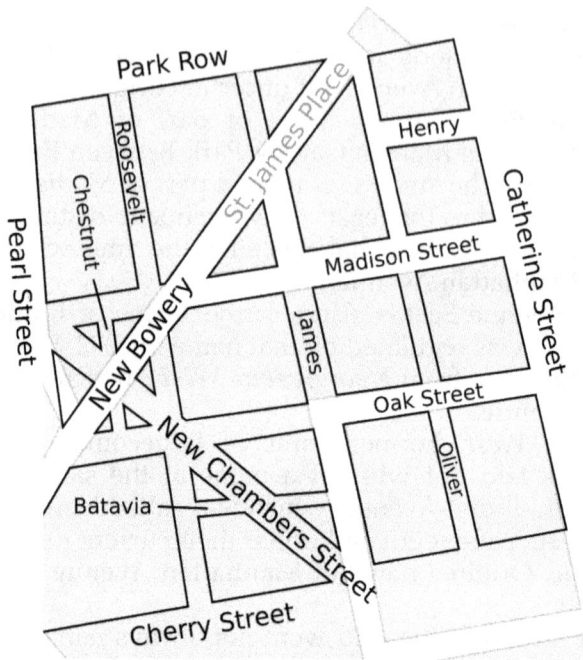

New Bowery / New Chambers

New Market Slip. A former slip located at the foot of Spring Street. The name is a reference to the *Clinton Market,* planned in 1827 and so named in 1829, it was for a time also referred to as the "new market."

New Slip. A name initially used for *James Slip* .

New Street. In Dutch, the *Nieuw Straat.* One of the oldest streets in Manhattan, the street was opened in 1679 and referred to simply as "the new street." This was a common designation for new streets until a name was settled upon. In the case of New Street, a more formal name was never arrived at and the street retains its status as a "new" street over 300 years later.

Newlon's Dock. Former dock on the Hudson River between Beach and Hubert Streets. Of uncertain origin.

Nicholas Street. Former name of **Walker Street** and **Canal Street** between Mulberry Street and the Bowery. Laid out prior to 1755 on what was the Bayard Farm, it was probably named for Nicholas Bayard II. Sometimes mapped as St. Nicholas Street.

Nicholas William Street. A proposed street in the *Stuyvesant Farm Grid* plan laid out in 1788 but never officially adopted. Named for Nicholas William Stuyvesant (1768-1833), the son of

Petrus Stuyvesant (1727-1805). Nicholas William was also the name of Petrus Stuyvesant's grandfather. See illustration on page 103.

Nieuw Straat. See **New Street**.

Norfolk Street. Named for the county of Norfolk in England. Laid out prior to 1767, the street is one of several in on the former *Delancey Farm* that make reference to English places. It is near Essex and Suffolk Streets.

North End Avenue. Named for its location in the northern part of the Battery Park City development. Construction was begun on the street in 1988.

North Moore Street. Named for Bishop Benjamin Moore of Trinity Church, which ceded the land to the city. Moore was also president of Columbia University and the father of Clement C. Moore. Laid out prior to 1797 and named North Moore to distinguish it from Moore Street in lower Manhattan.

North Street. Former name of **Houston Street** east of the Bowery. Extended to meet Houston in 1823 and renamed in 1833. The street was the northernmost proposed street in the east side grid of streets laid out prior to 1797.

North William. Referred to the portion of **William Street** that once extended past Frankfort Street to Park Row. Now closed. See also *King George Street*.

Northern Avenue. Former name of **Cabrini Boulevard**.

Nyack Place. Formerly located at 149 Bank Street and named for the New York village of Nyack.

O.

Oak Street. A closed street that once ran along a line south of **Monroe Street** west of Catherine Street. Originally laid out prior to 1755 as *Rutgers Street* between Pearl and Catherine Streets, the street was known as Oak Street by 1804. The name change was probably to eliminate confusion with the newer **Rutgers Street** that still exists under that name. The street was closed for construction of the Alfred E. Smith Houses, which were completed in 1953. See illustration on page 78.

Obelisk Road. Also the *Road to the Obelisk*. See *Monument Lane*.

Oblique Road. Former name for **Marketfield Street** west of Broadway, now part of **Battery Place**. Presumedly named for its oblique intersection with Broadway.

Observatory Place. A public space created in the 1811 **Commissioners' Plan** bordered by East 89th and 94th Streets between 4th and 5th Avenues. Observatory Place was officially closed in 1865 to open the street grid. Originally chosen as a high place to build a future reservoir, it was so named in the hope that it would serve as a suitable place for an observatory until the reservoir might be completed.

Ogden Street. Modern **Perry Street** is mapped as Ogden Street on the *Mangin-Goerck Plan* in 1799. It is not clear the name was ever in wide use. Of uncertain origin, but Benjamin and Jonathan Ogden were prosperous landowners in the city in the late 18th Century.

Ogilvie's Wharf. A former wharf on the East River at the foot of Grand Street. Peter Ogilvie was granted a water lot at Corlear's Hook in 1808.

Old Boston Road. See *Eastern Post Road* .

Old Broadway. The name Broadway was used for the *Bloomingdale Road* that ran up the western side of the island. When the *Boulevard* was renamed part of Broadway, shifting its route to the west, this section between West 125th and 133rd Streets became known as "Old" Broadway. See **Broadway**.

Old Ditch. Name sometimes used for the **Beaver Street** between Broadway and Broad Street.

Old Dutch Church Street. Referred to **Exchange Place** between Broad and William Streets. The Dutch Reform Church purchased property along what is now the north side of Exchange Place from the City in 1691, where it built its first church building.

Old Greenwich Lane. The same as *Greenwich Lane* .

Old Kiln Road. See *Great Kill Road* .

Old Slip. So called by 1743, Old Slip was one of the first slips established in the city. Part of the slip was formerly part of the *Burgher's Path*.

Old Windmill Lane. See *Pieter Jansen's Lane.*

Oliver Street. A former name for part of **Spring Street** between Broadway and the Bowery. Laid out prior to 1794 on the Bayard East Farm and probably named for a member of the Bayard Family.

Oliver Street. Named for Oliver Desbrosses, one of the children of James Desbrosses, who established a distillery where Catherine, Oliver and James Streets met the East River. The street was laid out between Madison Street and the East River prior to 1755, when it appears mapped as Olav Street (Olav or Olaf being a version of the name). The section below Madison Street was closed for construction of the Alfred E. Smith Houses, completed in 1951. The remaining section of Oliver Street was originally called *Fayette Street*. See illustration on page 78.

Olwers Street. An alternate spelling for **Oliver Street**.

Orange Street. A former name of **Baxter Street**. Named for William, Prince of Orange, who became William III of England in 1689. Laid out prior to 1767 between Chatham Street (now Park Row) and the Fresh Water (at about the bend in the street near present Hogan Place). The name was extended to include *Mary Street* about 1803, extending the street north to just beyond Prince Street. In 1839, the portion below Broome Street was renamed Baxter and the portion to the north of Broome renamed *Marion Street*. The portion between Worth Street and Park Row was closed as part of an effort to clean up the *Five Points* neighborhood.

Orchard Street. Former name of **Broome Street** between Broadway and Thompson Street. So named in 1797, probably in reference to a nearby orchard.

Orchard Street. The street passes through what was once an orchard on the James Delancey farm. Laid out prior to 1767 and opened in 1807.

Oswego Street. A name sometimes used for **Liberty Street**. The first Oswego Market was built in 1738 on the east side of Broadway, opposite the street.

Otters Alley. A former alley that connected Thompson and Sullivan Streets between Broome and Grand Streets.

Overlook Terrace. Laid out prior to 1911 in what was then a largely undeveloped part of Manhattan, the street is named for its location among the highest points on the island.

Oyster Pasty Alley. Former name of **Exchange Alley**. A fortification once stood at the west end of this alley at a time when the waterfront of the Hudson River was near the present Trinity Place. The fortification was called the Oyster Pasty Battery, Pasty Mount, Oyster Pasty Mount, or often just Oyster Pasty. The origin of the name for the fortification is obscure, but may refer to the shape of the mound on which it stood, or the presence of piles of oyster shells. A cannon once mounted at Oyster Pasty now stands in Battery Park. The alley was laid out prior to 1695.

P.

Pacific Place. Formerly located behind 139 West 29th Place.

Paerl Street. See **Pearl Street**.

Pagoda Place. Formerly located at the foot of East 120th Street. So called prior to 1862. Of uncertain origin.

Paisley Place. A former row of houses along the former *Southampton Road* in the block bounded by West 16th and 17th Streets and 6th and 7th Avenues. The group of wooden houses was erected in 1822 by Scottish hand-weavers who had relocated to escape the yellow fever epidemic in lower Manhattan. Named for the town of Paisley in Scotland. Also called Weavers Row.

Paladino Avenue. Named in 1954 for Anthony C. Paladino, a developer and contractor. The name originally applied to **Pleasant Avenue**, including the extension of the street created around the Robert F. Wagner Houses project. The section below East 120th Street returned to its previous name of Pleasant around 1957.

Park Avenue. Originally laid out as 4th Avenue, Park Avenue was so named beginning in the mid 19th Century with the section between East 34th and 36th Streets. The street was primarily used for railroad traffic, which ran through a cut in the native granite through the Murray Hill neighborhood. In the 1850s, the city required the railroads to bridge this cut to allow for cross town traffic, and several park-like areas were created over it which gave the section of street its new name. The cut was eventually completely paved over, with the green areas retained, and survives today as the Park Avenue Tunnel between East 34th and 39th Streets. By 1867 the section between East 34th and 42nd Streets was mapped as Park Avenue and the name was extended for the rest of the length of the street by 1888.

Park Place. Named in 1813 for its location near City Hall Park. Formerly *Robinson Street* and *Lower Robinson Street*.

Park Row. Named for its location along City Hall Park. Laid out as part of *Chatham Street*, the section fronting the park between Broadway and Murray Street was referred to as *Chatham Row* beginning some time prior to 1797. By 1829 it was referred to as Park Row. In 1886, the name was extended to include all of Chatham Street.

Park Street. Former name of **Mosco Street**. Previously *Cross Street*.

Park Terrace East, Park Terrace West. Named in reference to nearby Isham Park.

Partition Street. A name sometimes used for the present day **Fulton Street** west of Broadway. The street marks the southern boundary of the original Company Farm, later the Trinity Church Farm. Also called *Division Street*.

Passage Place. Former name of **Peck Slip**. Perhaps so called for the ferry passage to Brooklyn that operated from this location.

Pasty Alley, Pasty Street. See *Oyster Pasty Alley.*

Patchin Place. Said to be named for Aaron Patchin, the son-in-law of Samuel Milligan, who married Milligan's daughter, Isobel. Mulligan, after whom the nearby Milligan Place is named, gave the property to Patchin and his daughter.

Payson Avenue. Named in 1921 for George S. Payson, pastor of the Fort Washington Presbyterian Church who had retired the previous year. Previously *Prescott Avenue*. The avenue was curtailed and routed to Seaman Avenue near West 204th Street when Inwood Hill Park was created. A path within the park now follows much of this closed part of the route.

Pearl Street. Commonly thought to have been named for its surface of crushed oyster shells from its days as an early waterfront street. The name was first applied to the section between the waterfront (now at State Street) and Whitehall Street when this formed "The Strand" or "The Waterside" at the edge of the East River. The portion east of Broad Street was called *Dock Street*. Between William and Wall Streets the street was called **Hanover Square**, and beyond Wall Street it extended as *Queen Street* to what is now Park Row. In 1794, these four separately-named sections were combined as Pearl Street. In 1811, *Magazine Street* was renamed as an extension of the street at its northern end. Also called Perel Street and Paerl Street. Other early names include "The Waal" and "The Sheet-Pile Street" for the wooden bulkhead that was built along its edge with the river.

Pearsall's Dock. According to Post, a former dock on the East River at Water Street between Catherine and Market Streets. Thomas Pearsall was a successful merchant in the early 19th Century and may have been connected with the dock.

Peck Slip. Named for Benjamin Peck, who operated a wharf next to the slip in the early 18th Century and whose house stood nearby.

Pelham Street. A former one-block street that connected Monroe and Cherry Streets between Pike and Rutgers Streets. Possibly named for the village of Pelham in Westchester County. Closed for the construction of the Rutgers Houses project which was completed in 1965.

Pell Street. Long said to have been named for John Pell, a butcher. The street was laid out some time prior to 1799 and John Pell is shown in an 1808 city directory as living and operating on lower Bowery. The street marks part of the southern line of the Bayard farm.

Penn Street. Probably a misreading of **Pell Street**.

Percel Street, Perel Street. See **Pearl Street**.

Perry Street. Named for Commander Oliver Perry in 1813. Previously *Henry Street.* Called *Ogden Street* on the *Mangin-Goerck Plan.*

Pershing Square. Named in 1918 for General John J. Pershing (1860-1948), leader of the American Expeditionary Forces in World War I.

Peter Cooper Road. A road that serves the Peter Cooper Village housing development completed in the 1940s.

Peter Street. A proposed street in the *Stuyvesant Farm Grid* that was never officially adopted. Named probably for Peter Gerard Stuyvesant, the son of Petrus Stuyvesant (1727-1805), Petrus and Peter being longstanding family names among the Stuyvesants. See illustration on page 103.

Petticoat Lane. Former name of **Marketfield Street** between Broadway and Broad Street. So mapped in 1695, and mapped as Marketfield by 1730. Of uncertain origin. The Huguenot community of New York built the first French church on the lane in 1688, and the name may have been in reference to churchgoers dressed in their Sunday finery.

Phelps Place. Referred to East 30th Street between 1st and 2nd Avenues. Of uncertain origin.

Pie Woman's Lane and *Pie Woman's Street.* Names used to describe the portion of present **Nassau Street** between Wall Street and Maiden Lane. The name is a reference to an unknown merchant of pies who was sufficiently well known so as to be used as a landmark in early official records.

Pieter Jansen's Lane. A former lane that once ran from Broadway west to the Hudson River on a line north of modern Liberty Street, leading to the windmill built by Pieter Jansen Mesier. Appears on maps around 1730, but is gone by the 1750s. Also called Windmill Lane and Old Windmill Lane.

Pike Slip. Named for its location at the foot of **Pike Street**. Formerly *Charlotte Slip*.

Pike Street. Named in 1813 for General Zebulon Pike, who died at the Battle of York in the War of 1812. Previously *Charlotte Street*.

Pine Street. Laid out as *King Street* in 1685 and opened to the waterfront in 1692, this street was given the generic name Pine Street in 1794 when the council removed several references to British royalty from Manhattan street names. Little Queen Street was renamed Cedar Street at the same time. Also sometimes called *French Church Street*.

Pinehurst Avenue. Laid out in the early 20th Century, the avenue is named for the nearby estate of C.P. Bucking, called Pinehurst.

Pitt Street. Named for William Pitt the Younger (1759-1806). Laid out prior to 1797 and extended in 1810, the street was one of two sharing the same name for several years.

Pitt Street. Former name of **Lafayette Street** between Hester and Spring Streets. Laid out on the Bayard Farm prior to 1794 and named for William Pitt the Younger (1759-1806), Prime Minister of Great Britain. Extended to Spring Street prior to 1799. Incorporated into *Elm Street* in 1806.

Platt Street. Named for Jacob S. Platt who purchased property between Pearl and Gold Streets and laid out a street around 1833. Extended from Gold Street to William Street in 1835.

Pleasant Avenue. Formerly part of **Avenue A**, this section north of East 109th Street was renamed Pleasant Avenue in the 1890s for its riverside setting. The portion south of East 114th Street was closed for the creation of Thomas Jefferson Park in 1897. In 1954, the street was renamed **Paladino Avenue** when the portion above East 120th Street was rerouted to accommodate the Robert F. Wagner Houses project. By 1957, the part below 120th was once again known as Pleasant Avenue.

Point Street. A proposed street in the *Mangin-Goerck Plan* that was never adopted. Its proposed path corresponds roughly with modern East 14th Street between 4th and 5th Avenues.

Pollock's Wharf. A former wharf along what is now Washington Street south of Carlisle Street. Named for Carlisle Pollock, who operated the Wharf. See also **Carlisle Street**.

Pomander Walk. Named for the play of the same name, which takes place on an imaginary street in London. Developed by Thomas Healy and opened in 1921.

Poplar Street. A proposed street in the *Mangin-Goerck Plan* that was never adopted. Its proposed path corresponds roughly with the line of modern East 16th Street between Park and 5th Avenues.

Post Avenue. Teunis (or Dennis) and Henry Post owned large farms in northern Manhattan the early 19th Century. The street is named after this family.

Potters Hill. Former name for *Park Street*. Named for the pottery established by John Remmey in 1735 on this hill that once stood northeast of City Hill Park.

Prescott Avenue. Former name of **Payson Avenue**. Possibly named for Colonel William Prescott, who took part in the defense of New York during the Revolutionary War.

Prince Graft. See *Princes Graft*.

Prince Street. Former name of **Rose Street**. First laid out prior to 1730 and named Prince Street by 1755, the name was changed in 1794 when the City was removing references to British royalty from street names. At the same time, the present **Prince Street** was named by Nicholas Bayard.

Prince Street. Laid out prior to 1794 on Nicholas Bayard's farm, the current Prince Street was named about the same time the Common Council removed the name from what is now *Rose Street*. Bayard was on the council at the time. It is not certain to which prince, if any, the name refers.

Princen Straat. See *Princess Street*.

Princes Graft. Also *Princes Gracht*. Referred to **Broad Street** between Beaver and Wall Streets. The canal, or *graft* that ran through Broad Street was called the *Heere Graft* below Beaver Street and *De Princes Graft* above Beaver to where it ended near present Exchange Place. The name Princes Graft was also used for the street that continued past the canal on to Wall Street. The name was in use by 1665 when it appears in a list of property assessments in Dutch court records, suggesting the Prince to which the name referred was William, Prince of Orange. The British continued to use the name for the upper part of present Broad Street for a time after the canal was filled in 1676.

Princess Street. Also *Princes Street*. Former name of **Beaver Street** between Broad and William Streets. First appears as Princes Street in 1695, the spelling was inconsistent on maps and documents until the name was changed in 1794, at which time it was referred to as Princess Street. Probably so named because the street led to the *Princes Graft* in Broad Street at Beaver.

Printing House Square. The offices of four New York newspapers were once located around this triangular intersection.

86

Prospect Street. Former name of **Thompson Street**. The street passes along what was once a piece of high ground north of the Lispenard Meadow, suggesting a possible source for the name.

Provost Street. Former name of **Franklin Street** between West Broadway and West Street. Laid out and named prior to 1797, and ceded by Trinity Church to the City in 1802. Named for Samuel Provoost, Rector of Trinity Church from 1784 to 1800, and first Bishop of the Diocese of New York. Renamed as part of Franklin Street in 1833.

Public Highway. A name sometimes used in reference to lower **Broadway**.

Pump Street. Former name of Walker Street from Centre Street to Canal Street and Canal Street from that point to Division Street. First laid out prior to 1797 between the Bowery and Division Street, Pump Street aligned with *Nicholas Street* on the Bayard farm west of the Bowery. By 1799 the name Pump Street was applied to Nicholas Street as well. Walker Street, established in 1806, aligned with the street west of Centre Street and in 1829 the name Walker was extended for the full street between West Broadway and Division Street. In 1855, Canal Street was extended to meet Walker Street near Mulberry Street and the street was renamed Canal east of that point. Probably named for the presence of a well and pump in the street near Bowery.

Q.

Quay Street. According to Post, referred to **Water Street** between Whitehall Street and Coenties Slip.

Queen Street. Former name of part of **Pearl Street**. See *Great Queen Street.*

Quick Street. A proposed street in the *Stuyvesant Farm Grid* that was never officially adopted. Named for Jacobus Quick (d. 1815), who owned a lot along The Bowery bordering the Stuyvesant estate. When Petrus Stuyvesant (1727-1805) was plotting the grid of streets on his property, one of the proposed streets would have intersected the Bowery on Quick's land. Stuyvesant made a deal with Quick to trade his lot on the Bowery for some lots on the new street, which Stuyvesant named after Quick. See illustration on page 103.

Quick Street is also reportedly a former name for **East Broadway**, possibly after the same Quick family.

R.

Rachel Lane. A short street connecting Mangin and Goerck Streets between Grand and Broome Streets. Now closed. Of uncertain origin.

Raisin Street. See *Reason Street.*

The Ramparts. Referred to **Wall Street** between Broadway and Pearl Street.

Randall Place. Was in East 9th Street between University Place and Broadway. Of uncertain origin.

Randall Street. A proposed street in the *Mangin-Goerck Plan* that was never adopted. Its proposed path corresponds roughly with modern East 11th Street between Broadway and 5th Avenue.

Rapelje Street. A proposed street on the *Glass House Farm* that was never officially adopted. Named for George Rapelje, who owned the farm to the north of the area. See illustration on page 46.

Reade Street. Named for Joseph Reade, warden of Trinity Church when land for the street was ceded to the City by the church in 1761. Also spelled Read, Redd and Redd's Street.

Reason Street. A former name of **Barrow Street** between Bleecker and Bedford Streets. The street was extended past Bedford Street in 1828 to intersect Barrow and the name Barrow was applied to the entire street. Frequently spelled "Raisin" or "Raisen." Thought to have been named to honor Thomas Paine's pamphlet "The Age of Reason."

Rector Place. Named for its location on a line with **Rector Street** to the east. This oval drive was developed as part of the Battery Park City development project undertaken in 1981.

Rector Street Wharf. Former wharf near the foot of **Rector Street** between Washington and West Streets.

Rector Street. The residence of the rector of Trinity Church stood on the street. Originally laid out between Broadway and modern Trinity Place in 1739 as *Robinson Street,* the street was later known as *Auchmuty Street,* some time after 1764 when the Reverend Samuel Auchmuty became rector. Auchmuty died in 1777. By 1797 the street had been extended to the Hudson River and was mapped as Rector Street.

Redd's Street, Redd Street. Alternate spellings of **Reade Street.**

Rensselaer Street. A street in the *Mangin-Goerck Plan* that was never officially adopted. It was laid out as an east-west street in an extension of the *Stuyvesant Farm Grid* and ran parallel to Quick Street one block to the south. The Rensselaer family were prominent in the city from the early days of Dutch settlement.

Renwick Street. Named for the family of William Renwick, who owned the property along Greenwich and Canal Streets through which the street was laid out around 1819. Jane Renwick, the widow of William, is listed as living on Renwick Street in 1820. Her son, James Renwick, a scientist and professor at Columbia University, is often named as the source of the street's name. It is probably more correct to attribute the name to his parents, perhaps specifically to his mother, who owned the land at the time the street was named.

Republican Alley. A former L-shaped alley that ran west from Elk Street between Duane and Reade Streets and turned south to Reade Street. Later called *Manhattan Alley* and *Manhattan Place*. Possibly a reference to the political party or perhaps used in a more general sense.

Rhinelanders Alley. Formerly connected Hubert and Beach Streets in the block west of Greenwich Street. William Rhinelander died in 1777, leaving in his will several lots along Greenwich Street between Chambers and Beach Streets. This alley served some of Rhinelander's property near Beach Street.

Rhinelanders Basin. Also called *Rhinelanders Dock* and Rhinelanders Wharf. Situated along what is now West Street, in the section between Barclay and Murray Streets. In the late 18th Century William Rhinelander acquired extensive waterfront property along the Hudson River between Chambers and Beach Streets. See also *Rhinelanders Alley.*

Rhinelanders Dock. Two Hudson River docks once held the name of William Rhinelander, the property owner. One was at the foot of North Moore Street, the other between Barclay and Murray Streets.

Rhinelanders Lane. A lane that ran from near the present intersection of East 86th Street and 2nd Avenue northeasterly to near the present intersection of East 91st Street and York Avenue. The lane marked the southern border of the country estate of William Rhinelander.

Rider Street, Ridder Street. See **Ryder's Alley**.

Ridge Street. Named in reference to the ridge of land the street followed along its lower path. Laid out prior to 1797 between Broome and Houston Streets and extended south to Division Street in 1825.

Riker's Lane. A former lane that ran from the East Post Road at a point just south of modern East 76th Street and 3rd Avenue easterly along the line of 76th Street to a point east of 2nd Avenue, then southerly along the northern border of Richard Riker's farm to a point east of modern York Avenue just south of East 75th Street.

Ritter's Wharf. A former wharf at the foot of Charlton Street at Washington Street. Owned in 1819 by John P. Ritter.

River Terrace. A street created as part of the Battery Park City project, which was started in the early 1970s. Named for its location winding along a riverside park.

Riverside Avenue. See **Riverside Drive**.

Riverside Boulevard. Named for its location west of Riverside Park South. Laid out as part of the expansion of Riverside Park undertaken in 2000.

Riverside Drive. Named for its location winding along the Hudson River on the east side of Riverside Park. The park and drive were laid out between West 72nd and 125th Streets beginning in 1873, with the street called Riverside Avenue. Over the next several years, the park and the drive were extended to 155th street. In the early 20th Century, Riverside Drive was extended to meet *Lafayette Boulevard* at about 161st Street and the name was extended to Dyckman Street. The portion of the street between 155th and 161st Streets is officially called West Riverside Drive to distinguish it from the renamed remnant of Lafayette Boulevard between Broadway and 161st Street.

Riverview Terrace. Named for its location on a bluff overlooking the East River. The street was developed in 1878 as a row of modest homes.

Rivington Place. Formerly located behind 316 Rivington Street between Lewis and Goerck Streets. Named for its connection to the street. Now closed.

Rivington Street. Named for James Rivington, a loyalist newspaper editor who fled New York and returned after the Revolutionary War. Laid out prior to 1791 and extended from Cannon Street to the East River in 1816. Closed below Cannon for construction of the Baruch Houses which were completed in 1959.

Road to Albany and Boston. See *Eastern Post Road*.

Road to Crown Point. See *Crown Point Road*.

Road to Greenwich. Referred to **Greenwich Street** north of Beach Street.

Road to Stuyvesant's Bowery. An early designation for the old lane that was shortened to **Bowery**. Peter Stuyvesant's farm, or bowery, was located east of the lane north of modern Stuyvesant Street.

Road to the Obelisk. See *Monument Lane.*

Robert Street. A proposed street in the *Mangin-Goerck Plan* that was never adopted. Its proposed path corresponds roughly with modern East 10th Street between Broadway and 5th Avenue.

Robinson Street. The original name of **Rector Street** between present Broadway and Trinity Place. In 1739, the Trinity Church closed a lane along the south side of the church to incorporate its gardens into its churchyard. In exchange for permission to close the lane, the church proposed creating a new lane on the south side of the newly-expanded churchyard to be called Robinsons Street. Probably named for Joseph Robinson, who was warden of the church at the time the street was created.

Robinson Street is also the former name of **Park Place** between Church Street and Broadway, and between Greenwich Street and West Broadway. These two sections of the street were originally separated by the Columbia College campus located between West Broadway and Church Streets, with the western portion called *Lower Robinson.* In 1813, the eastern section was renamed Park Place and Lower Robinson was shortened to Robinson. The street is now closed between West and Greenwich Streets. The remnant between Greenwich Street and West Broadway was changed to Park Place when the street was cut through the former college grounds.

Rockefeller Plaza. Named for John D. Rockefeller, Jr., the developer of the Rockefeller Center complex through which the street runs. The development was started in 1931 and completed in 1939.

Rodman's Slip. A previous name for *Burling Slip.* The adjoining land was granted to John Rodman in 1700.

Romain Street. A proposed street in the *Mangin-Goerck Plan* that was never officially adopted. As laid out, it ran parallel to and one block north of present day East Houston Street between the Bowery and the East River. Dr. Nicholas Romain (also Romaine and Romayne) was a landholder at Corlear's Hook whose land the proposed street would cross.

Romaine's Wharf. A former wharf at the foot of Montgomery Street. See *Romain Street.*

Roosevelt Street. A former street that ran from present Park Row south to the Cherry Street on a line parallel with James Street, meeting the river about where the Brooklyn Bridge now stands. Jacobus Roosevelt and other petitioned the Common Council in 1748 to allow them to construct slips and wharves at their riverside lots between Peck Slip and James Street. Laid out prior to 1754 and regulated in 1764. See illustration on page 78.

Roosevelt's Lane. A former lane that ran southwesterly in a straight line from the village of Harlem at about the present intersection of East 116th Street and Lexington to the edge of the Harlem Marsh, at a point near East 110th Street between 1st and 2nd Avenues. The lane ran along the southwestern border of a large tract of land owned by James Roosevelt, whose country house stood on what is now the eastern side of 1st Avenue within Jefferson Park, about on a line with East 113th Street.

Roosevelt's Slip. Former name of **Peck Slip**. Jacobus Roosevelt operated waterfront facilities along this part of the East River in the 18th Century. See also *Roosevelt Street*.

Rose Hill Lane. See *Abingdon Road.*

Rose Street. Of uncertain origin but possibly in reference to a nearby property holder. Previously called *Prince Street*, the name was changed in 1794.

Roslyn Place. Formerly located in Greene Street between West 3rd and 4th Streets, now closed. Of uncertain origin.

Rotten Row. An alternate name for *Hunter's Key*. Of uncertain origin, however a once-fashionable lane in Hyde Park, London still exists by the same name, perhaps providing a model for the name. The nearby waterfront was a place where refuse accumulated, left by the tide, offering another possible source. The water lots along the row were leased in 1766, at which time the area began to be filled in and improved.

Rotterdam Street. A street in the *Mangin-Goerck Plan* that was never adopted as an official street. Named for the Dutch city.

Rough Street. According to Post, a former name of **Henry Street**. Also spelled Ruff Street. Of uncertain origin, but more likely to be descriptive of the street surface than a figurative reference to the neighborhood.

Roy Road. An abbreviation sometimes used in reference to *Fitzroy Road.*

Rudder Street. An alternate version of **Ryder's Alley**.

Russel Place. Formerly located in **Greenwich Avenue** between Charles and Perry Streets.

Rutgers Hill. Former name for part of **Gold Street** between John Street and Maiden Lane. Named for Anthony Rutgers, Jr., who operated a large brewery on the corner with Maiden Lane.

Rutgers Place. Referred to **Monroe Street** between Jefferson and Clinton Streets. Now closed. Named for the Henry Rutgers family, which once owned the surrounding property.

Rutgers Slip. Named for its location at the foot of **Rutgers Street**.

Rutgers Street. A former street that ran from Pearl Street to Catherine Street on a line just south of modern **Monroe Street** and that was formerly part of Monroe. Laid out prior to 1755, the street was regulated in 1764. The street was the older of two streets by the name Rutgers that existed between about 1797 and 1804. By 1804, the older street was also being called *Oak Street* and was so mapped in 1811. Both Rutgers Streets were named for the family of Henry Rutgers, who owned much of the surrounding area along the East River.

Rutgers Street. The present Rutgers Street was named for the Henry Rutgers family, whose land it was laid out through prior to 1797. At the time there was another Rutgers Street at the western end of the Rutgers property between Pearl and Catherine Streets. While the two streets coexisted, the present Rutgers Street was sometimes referred to as East Rutgers Street. See also *Rutgers Street.*

Rutgers Wharf. Formerly located east of Market Slip. This was part of the Henry Rutgers estate, and other sections of the waterfront between Market and Montgomery Streets were also referred to as Rutgers Wharf or Rutgers Pier at different times.

Rutherford Place. Named for the family of Helen Rutherford, wife of Peter Gerard Stuyvesant (1778-1847). The couple donated the land for Stuyvesant Square Park in 1836. The street forms the west border of the park.

Ryder's Alley. Of uncertain origin. Also called Rider Street or Ridder Street. Laid out prior to 1754, and presumably received its name from an adjacent property owner. See also **Eden's Alley**.

Rynders Street, also *Rhynders* and *Ryndert.* The former name of **Centre Street** between Franklin and Broome Streets. Originally laid out on Nicholas Bayard's East Farm prior to 1794, the name is in reference to the family of Elizabeth Rynders (sometimes spelled Ryndert), the first wife of Nicholas Bayard II. Ryndert Street is shown in 1754 and 1767 as the name of **Mulberry Street** north of the bend in the street near Bayard Street. This street was mapped as *Catherine Street* in a conveyance dated 1794, and it appears the name was transferred from one street to the other by the Bayard family between 1767 and 1794. Although both instances are sometimes said to be a reference to Captain Isaiah Rynders (1804-1885), a notorious New York political boss, the name appeared in 1754 for the name of modern Mulberry Street and in 1794 in the case of present day Centre Street. A simple comparison of dates shows that Isaiah Rynders had not yet been born when the name came into use.

S.

Sackett Street. Former name of **Cherry Street**. Named for Richard Sackett, who owned the property through the which the street was laid.

St. Bridget's Place. Formerly located behind 185 East 7th Street, the present location of the St. Brigid School.

St. Clair Place. Named in 1921 for St. Clair Pollock, a five-year-old boy who drowned in the Hudson River in 1797, and whose grave is located in Riverside Park under a monument to the "amiable child."

St. Clements Place. Formerly located in Macdougal Street between Houston and Bleecker Streets as well as between Waverly Place and East 8th Street. St. Clement Episcopal Church stood on Macdougal near West 3rd Street.

St. David Street. See *David Street.*

St. George's Place. Formerly part of East 13th Street between 1st and 2nd Avenues. Named for the nearby St. George's Episcopal Church on Stuyvesant Square.

St. George's Square. A broad intersection formed by Pearl, Cherry and Dover Streets. Named probably for England's patron saint or possibly for the square of the same name in London. The original site of St. George's Chapel stood about two blocks from the square, at the corner of Beekman and Cliff Streets, suggesting another possible source. The name was changed to *Franklin Square* in 1817.

St. Hevins Street. See *Hevins Street.*

St. James Place. Named in the 1940s for the Church of St. James the Apostle located on James Street north of Madison. Previously called *New Bowery*.

St. James Street. See **James Street**.

St. John's Alley. A name sometimes used for **St. John's Lane**.

St. John's Lane. Named for St. John's Chapel, which formerly stood on Varick Street facing St. John's Square. The street was laid out around 1807, when the chapel was completed. The chapel was demolished in 1918 when Varick Street was widened.

St. John's Street. Same as **John Street**.

St. Luke's Place. So called prior to 1860 and named in reference to the Church of St. Luke in the Fields located at the intersection of Hudson and Grove Streets. Frequently referred to as part of **Leroy Street.**

St. Marks Place. Named for the nearby church of St. Mark's in the Bowery. Laid out as East 8th Street in the Commissioner's Plan.

St. Nicholas Avenue. Named for the "patron saint" of New York City, St. Nicholas, who gained popularity in the city through the works of authors such as Washington Irving and Clement C. Moore. St. Nicholas Avenue was created in 1866 from parts of the *Harlem Lane* and *Kings Bridge Road.*

St. Nicholas Place. Named in association with **St. Nicholas Avenue**, from which it branches at Donnellon Square.

St. Nicholas Street. See *Nicholas Street.*

St. Nicholas Terrace. Runs along the western edge of St. Nicholas Park, west of St. Nicholas Avenue.

St. Peter's Place. Formerly part of **Church Street** between Vesey and Barclay Streets. Named for St. Peter's Church, which stands in the block.

St. Timothy's Place. A past name for part of West 52nd Street between Broadway and 8th Avenue. Named for St. Timothy's Church, established at the location about 1854.

Saltus' Wharf. A former wharf operated by Solomon Saltus located west of the Old Slip. Listed in 1817.

Samuel Street. A street laid out as part of the *Kip's Bay Farm* but never officially adopted. Named for Samuel Kip, eldest son of Samuel Kip, the owner of the farm. See illustration on page 60.

Sand Hill Road. A former name for **Greenwich Avenue.** The road ran from the Bowery along the line of present **Astor Place**, continuing on that line to about the present intersection of Waverly Place and 5th Avenue. The Zantberg was a long "sand hill" that ran between Manhattan and Greenwich Village. The Sand Hill Road crossed the hill.

Scammel Street. A former street laid out prior to 1797 one block east of modern Gouverneur Street. Closed for construction of the Vladeck Houses project, completed in 1940. Probably named after Colonel Alexander Scammel, a Revolutionary War figure.

Schaape Waytie. The "sheep pasture" that stood along the present Broad Street between Exchange Street and Wall Street.

Schermerhorne's Wharf. Formerly located on the waterfront at South Street between John and Fulton Streets. The adjoining water lots were purchased by Arnout Schermerhorne (c.1686-c.1742) in 1730.

Schiff Parkway. This designation for the Delancey Street approach to the Williamsburg Bridge was named for Jacob Schiff (1847-1920) in 1921. Schiff was a banker and philanthropist.

Schreyer's Hook. Referred to the site of present **State Street** between Whitehall and Pearl Streets. This was the location of the first pier built by the Dutch of New Amsterdam in 1648. The name is thought to be a reference to the Schreyers Tower in Amsterdam, sometimes translated as the "tower of tears," a waterside landmark where families made tearful goodbyes to those off to sea.

Schroepel Street, also *Schweppel* and *Schrapple.* A street on the *Glass House Farm* that was never officially adopted. Named for George C. Schroepel, who owned the farm to the south of the area. See illustration on page 46.

Science Street. A proposed street in the *Mangin-Goerck Plan* that was never adopted. Laid out on the approximate line of modern Waverly Place between Sullivan Street and Broadway. The name was probably chosen in association with the existing Art Street (now Astor Place) that was one block to the north.

Scott Street. A proposed street laid out in 1796, part of which later became *Troy Street*, now West 12th Street between Greenwich Avenue and West Street. So named by Abijah Hammond, who owned the surrounding property. Of uncertain origin, but possibly for an associated family.

Scotts Alley. Former name of Franklin Place. The alley served the livery stable of John Scott, which stood on White Street in the 1840s.

Seaman Avenue. Named in reference to the Seaman family, longtime property holders in the area. Henry B. Seaman, an engineer, lived nearby when the avenue was laid out around 1905.

Second Street. Laid out prior to 1767 and until 1817 the name of **Forsyth Street**. See also *First Street*.

Sheep's Pasture. The English translation of the *Schaape Waytie*.

Sheera Street. According to Post, a former name for lower **Broadway** below Wall Street. The word is possibly a misreading of *De Heere Straet*, one of the early designations of the street.

The Sheet Pile Street. See **Pearl Street**.

Sheridan Square. Named in 1918 for Civil War General Philip Henry Sheridan (1831-1888).

Sheriff Street. Named for Sheriff Marinus Willett, who purchased property in the former Delancey farm in 1785. Laid out prior to 1797 between Grand and Houston Streets and extended to East 2nd Street in 1836. Several portions are now closed. See also **Willett Street.**

Sherman Avenue. The Sherman family settled in upper Manhattan in the early 19th Century. A Sherman household is mapped on the *Commissioners' Plan* in 1811 on what is now Broadway near Dongan Place, as well as on the inlet of the Harlem River just below where West 201st Street now stands. The surrounding area is still known as Sherman Creek.

Sherman Square. Named in 1891 for General William Tecumseh Sherman, who lived in the area during his retirement.

Shinbone Alley. A name sometimes used for **Doyers Street**. Probably a reference to the bend at the center of the street, giving it the appearance of a bent leg. The name was also used to refer to *Washington Alley*. See also **Shinbone Alley**.

Shinbone Alley. The L-shaped alley that runs between Lafayette and Bond Streets is still designated Shinbone Alley on official city maps, although the street sign at Lafayette currently marks it as **Jones Alley**. The name appears to be a general term for an alley that contains a bend or turn, like the joint of a leg. See also *Shinbone Alley*.

Shubert Alley. The alley runs to the east of the Shubert Theater, which is named for Sam S. Shubert, one of three brothers who founded the theater and production company now called The Shubert Organization in the late 19th Century.

Sickles Street. Samuel Sickles owned several tracts of land in northern Manhattan in the early 19th Century, including property around Fort George east of 10th Avenue.

Singel. The Singel was the old street inside the wall of New Amsterdam, now corresponding generally to **Wall Street**. Also spelled Cingel and Cingle, the name is a reflection of the Singel Canal in Amsterdam, a canal that encircled the oldest part of that city. The name was also used for the path and buildings along the canal. By extension, the name was applied to the path that encircled New Amsterdam along its northern fortification.

Sixth Street. Laid out prior to 1767 and until 1817 the name of **Ludlow Street**. See also *First Street*.

Skinner Road. A former road that included what is now **Christopher Street** and which continued past Greenwich Avenue to the *Union Road*. One of the roads on the Warren Estate named for Peter Warren's sons-in-law. Colonel William Skinner married Warren's daughter Susan.

Skinner's Lane, Skinner's Street. A former street that once made part of **Cliff Street**. The street intersected Frankfort Street north of Pearl and ran northerly for about a block, with the former *Hague Street* abutting it at a right angle. The street was in the middle of the Swamp, the low-lying area where the tanning industry was centered for many years. Its name comes from its location as a market street for hides and skins. It was renamed part of Cliff Street in 1827.

Slote Lane, also *Sloot Lane.* A former L-shaped street that corresponds approximately to **Beaver Street** between William and Hanover Streets and **Hanover Street** between Beaver and Pearl Streets. Laid out prior to 1730. An English spelling of the Dutch word "sloot" meaning a ditch. Also sometimes called Slaughter House Lane, Slaughter House Street and Sloat's Lane. Later named *Exchange Street,* then *Merchant Street.*

Slyck Steege. Literally *dirty lane.* A name used for part of **South William Street**.

Smee Straat, Smeedes Straat. See *Smith Street.*

Smell Street Lane. A name sometimes used to refer to **Broad Street** between Exchange Place and Wall Street. The smell referred to was probably from the former canal in Broad Street, in which refuse accumulated and which served as an open sewer.

Smith Place. A former court along *Smith Street.* Also called Smith Court. Later *Congress Place.*

Smith Street Lane. A name sometimes used for **Beaver Street** between Broad and William Streets. So named as a lane that led to the former Smith Street, now William Street.

Smiths Vly, also *Smiths Fly, Smees Vly, De Smee's Vly, Smith's Valley, Smith Street Valley.* A former name used for part of **Pearl Street**. A marshy meadow or "vly" stood along the East River between about Pine and Fulton Streets. The name first appears in Dutch, sometimes as *De Smees Vly,* meaning "the smith's valley," perhaps indicating that it was named for a blacksmith who set up operations nearby. Later anglicized to Smiths Fly, then shortened to the Fly. See also *Fly Market Street.*

Smith Street. A former name for **William Street** between Wall and Pearl Streets. Named for the smithy of Burgher Jorissen, originally located near the present intersection of William and Stone Streets. Renamed as part of William Street in 1794.

Sniffen Court. Named for John Sniffen, a builder hired by property developers in the 1860s to convert four regular city lots into ten smaller lots connected by an alley.

South End Avenue. Named for its location at the southern end of the island of Manhattan, South End Avenue was created in the 1980s as part of the Battery Park City project.

South Fifth Avenue. Former name of **La Guardia Place** and **West Broadway** above Canal Street. In 1870, Laurens Street was widened and renamed South Fifth Avenue in an attempt to make it more attractive for commercial development. In an unusual reversal of normal practice, the street was numbered from north to south, beginning at Washington Square. In 1896 the street was incorporated into West Broadway.

South Street. First laid out between Moore and Broad Streets in 1796, and extended from Coenties slip to Catherine Slip in 1798. By 1799 the street had been laid out to the tip of Corlear's Hook. Named for its location as the southernmost street in lower Manhattan.

South William Street. Named when *Mill Street* was extended to William Street in 1836. The lower part of South William Street has had many names, including *Glazier's Street, Slyck Steege, Dirty Lane,* and *Jews Alley.*

Southampton Road. A former road on the Peter Warren estate that ran from the present intersection of Gansevoort Street and 8th Avenue northeasterly to the Abingdon Road at about modern West 21st Avenue east of 6th Avenue. Named for one of Peter Warren's sons-in law, George Fitzroy, Baron Southampton, who married Warren's daughter, Anne, in 1758. See also *Fitzroy Road* and illustration on page 41.

Spencer Place. Referred to West 4th Street between Christopher and West 10th Streets. Of uncertain origin.

Spingler Place. Formerly part of East 15th Street between 5th Avenue and Broadway. Of uncertain origin.

Spring Street. Probably named for a spring on the Bayard farm which is said still to exist in the basement of a Spring Street building. Laid out prior to 1794 as *Oliver Street* between the Bowery and Broadway, the street was laid out to about modern 6th Avenue and mapped as Spring Street by 1799. In 1803 it was joined with *Brannon Street* and in 1807 Brannon was renamed as part of Spring Street.

Spruce Street. A street in the *Mangin-Goerck Plan* that was never officially adopted. It was laid out as an east-west street in an extension of the *Stuyvesant Farm Grid* and ran parallel to Dove Street one block to the north.

Spruce Street. Laid out prior to 1730 as *George Street.* Changed to Spruce in 1817 as part of the renaming of several streets that referred to British royalty. Tree names were used in several instances.

Stadt Huys Lane. See *City Hall Lane.*

Stadt Wall. Former designation for the wall along **Wall Street** and by extension the street itself.

Staff Street. Named in 1921 to honor a local World War I veteran who had died in action. The first name of the veteran is not known for certain. This and two other streets were named at the suggestion of the Inwood Post of the American Legion. Originally called C Street. See also **Henshaw Street** and *Daniels Street*.

Stamer's Slip, also *Stymer's Slip.* According to Post a former slip on the Hudson River between Beach and Hubert Streets.

Stanton Place. Formerly located behind 8 Stanton Street and named for its connection to Stanton Street.

Stanton Street. Probably named for George Stanton, an agent of James Delancey, who had owned the large farms through which the street was laid out before the American Revolution. Regulated in 1805.

Staple Street. Of uncertain origin, but probably named for a local property owner. Usually appears as Staples Street in early city directories. John Staples and later his widow Amelia were a prominent landholders at the time Staple Street appeared, suggesting a possible source. Laid out some time between 1799 and 1803, when it first appears in public records.

State Prison Dock. A former dock near the foot of Christopher Street. The Newgate State Prison was built in the late 18th Century on the river at Washington Street north of Christopher Street.

State Street. Named for its location along the western side of the Government House grounds, which stood on the site of the old fort south of Bowling Green. Laid out in 1792 and called *Copsey Street* the name was changed to State Street in 1793.

Steuben Street. One of the names of what was originally called the *Cross Road* and later *Low's Lane.* Most probably named in honor of Baron Friedrich Wilhelm von Steuben (1730-1794), the Prussian general who trained Washington's revolutionary army at Valley Forge.

Stevens' Wharf. A former wharf at Front Street west of Peck Slip, operated by the trader and merchant Ebenezer Stevens.

Stewart Street. A former lane that was never adopted as a city street. Stewart Street ran from the west side of the Bloomingdale Road (now Broadway) between West 30th and 31st Streets to the west to a point just south of West 30th Street about midway between 6th and 7th Avenues. The lane provided access to the Bloomingdale Road for James Stewart's farm that originally extended from western end of the lane to about 8th Avenue.

Stillwell's Lane or *Road.* A former road that ran southeast from the Bloomingdale Road (now Broadway) at about modern West 87th Street to a point now within Central Park, about where West Drive and the 86th Street Transverse cross. The lane was laid out by Samuel Stillwell, who owned a large piece of property east of the Bloomingdale Road.

Stone Street. Named for its cobblestone surface, this was the first hard surface street in the city. In 1655 the residents of the street petitioned to have it paved. Formerly Brouwer or *Brewer Street*. Also referred to in early records as the *Straet van de Graft*.

Stoney or *Stony Street*. An alternate version of **Stone Street**, between Whitehall and Broad Streets.

Straet van de Graft. Former name for **Stone Street** between Whitehall and Broad Streets. Literally, "the street by the canal," referring to its location leading to the former canal in Broad Street. The name is sometimes translated from Dutch records as *Canal Street*.

The Strand. Refers to the west side of Whitehall, between State and Pearl Streets, and the north side of Pearl Street, between Whitehall and Wall Streets, when these streets were at the water's edge. See also *The Water*.

Striker's Lane, also *Stryker's Lane*. A former lane that ran from the Bloomingdale Road, near the present intersection of Broadway and West 51st Street, in a straight line northwesterly to the Hudson River, to a point now on the western edge of Dewitt Clinton Park on a line with West 53rd Street. Garret Strijker, who anglicized his name to Striker, built his family home along the Hudson River in 1764. Much of the estate now forms Dewitt Clinton Park. The bay that once existed north of Striker's estate was also called after his family. Remnants of Striker's Lane existed into the late 18th Century in the form of a short place behind 743 11th Avenue called Stryker's Lane, and a row of houses on West 52nd Street between 10th and 11th Avenues called Stryker's Row. The slanted alley north of the building at the northeast corner of West 52nd Street and 11th Avenue indicates part of the lane's path.

Striker's Row, also *Stryker's Row*. See *Striker's Lane*.

Stuyvesant Alley. A former alley connecting East 11th and 12th Streets between 2nd and 3rd Avenues. The area was once part of the Stuyvesant farm.

Stuyvesant Place. Formerly located along 2nd Avenue between East 7th and 10th Streets. This area was originally part of the Stuyvesant farm.

Stuyvesant Street. Named for the family of Petrus Stuyvesant (1727-1805), the great-grandson of Governor Petrus Stuyvesant, the last Director-General of New Netherland. The street was laid out around 1788 by the younger Petrus as the central street of the *Stuyvesant Farm Grid*, a proposed street plan that was never completely adopted officially. As proposed, the street extended from The Bowery to the East River. Before the Commissioner's Plan of numbered streets and avenues was adopted, some development had taken place along Stuyvesant Street near the Bowery, including the construction of St. Mark's Church and some fashionable homes. Only this short stretch of the street was officially adopted and remains open today. Other lots had been sold based on the line of the proposed street, however, and some oddly-shaped property lines still exist where the numbered streets ran athwart the older plots.

Suffolk Street. Named for the county in England, as are its neighboring streets Essex and Norfolk. Laid out prior to 1767 in the *Delancey Farm Grid*.

Sugar Loaf Street. Former name of **Franklin Street** between Broadway and Baxter Street. The Sugar Loaf Hill was one of the sandy hills that once stood in lower Manhattan.

Sullivan Street. Named for General John Sullivan (1740-1795), a figure in the Revolutionary War. Originally laid out as *Locust Street* on the Bayard farm, the street was mapped as Sullivan Street in 1799.

Susan Street. A former street in the *Kip's Bay Farm Grid* laid out about 1805. Probably named for Susan Kip, wife of Cornelius Kip, a son of Samuel Kip, after whom *Cornelius Street* was named. See illustration on page 60.

Sutton Place and **Sutton Place South.** This section of **Avenue A** was developed in the 1870s by shipping millionaire Effingham Sutton and James Stokes.

Swartwouts Dock, also *Swartwouts Wharf.* A former dock south of the Albany Basin on the Hudson River, near present Albany Street at Washington Street. Operated by Samuel Swartwout in the late 18th and early 19th Centuries.

Sylvan Place and **Sylvan Court.** Once the center of the village of Harlem, the name is probably a reference to the trees that lined the street when these streets were part of the lane that led to the Dutch Church. The church was constructed in the late 1660s on the town square, which stood about where Sylvan Place intersects with East 120th Street.

Szold Place. Named in 1951 for Henrietta Szold (1860-1845), founder of the Hadassah Women's Organization. Originally laid out in 1847 as *Dry Dock Street*.

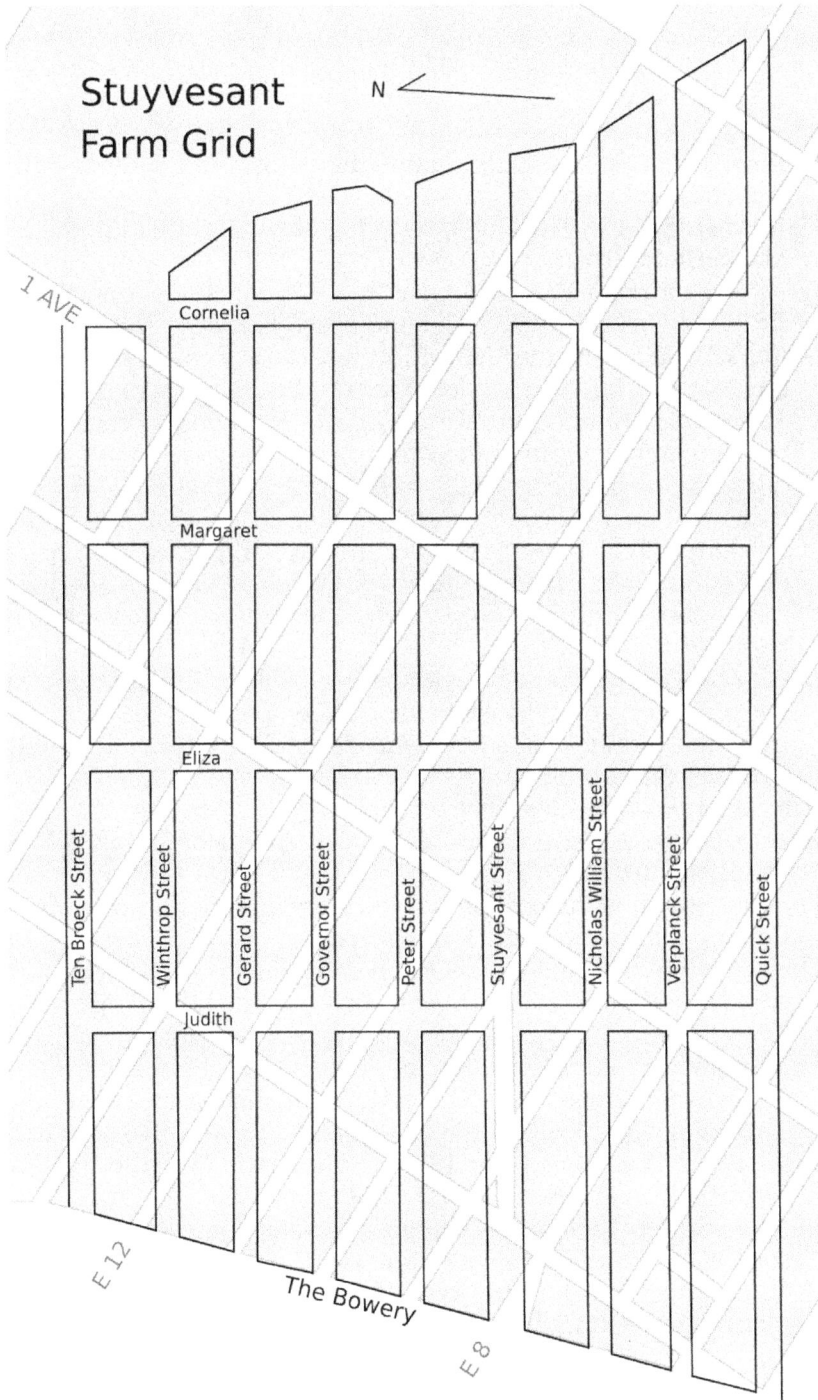

Stuyvesant Farm Grid

N

1 AVE

Cornelia

Margaret

Eliza

Ten Broeck Street

Winthrop Street

Gerard Street

Governor Street

Peter Street

Stuyvesant Street

Nicholas William Street

Verplanck Street

Quick Street

Judith

E 12

The Bowery

E 8

T.

T'Maagde Paatje. The Dutch name meaning "the maidens' path." See **Maiden Lane**.

T'Markvelt Steegie. The Dutch term for "the marketfield path." See **Marketfield Street**.

Taras Shevchenko Place. Named in 1978 for Taras Shevchenko (1814-1861), a Ukrainian poet and artist. Formerly *Hall Street*.

Taylor's Wharf. A former wharf located west of the Fly Market at the foot of Maiden Lane on Front Street. A man named John Taylor is mentioned in city records as applying to construct a building at this location in 1794.

Ten Broeck Street. A proposed street in the *Stuyvesant Farm Grid* that was never officially adopted. Laid out in 1788 and named for Dirck Ten Broeck, the son-in-law of Petrus Stuyvesant (1727-1805). Ten Broeck married Petrus' daughter, Cornelia, after whom *Cornelia Street* was named. See illustration on page 103.

Ten Eyck's Wharf. Named for Mary Ten Eyck, who built a pier on her property along the east side of Coenties Slip. Ten Eyck was from the family of Conraet and Antje Ten Eyck, after which Coenties Slip is named.

Tennecks Wharf. See *Ten Eyck's Wharf*.

Terrace Drive. A Central Park drive that runs along high ground south of a former stream.

Thames Street. Named for the river that runs through the city of London. Formerly *Little Stone Street*.

Theatre Alley. This alley once ran behind the Park Theater, which stood on Park Row near Ann Street. The theater opened in 1798. Prior to that, the street was mapped as *Mews*.

Thelonious Sphere Monk Circle. This short section of West 63rd Street was named in 1983 for the jazz pianist and composer Thelonious Monk (1917-1982).

Third Street. Laid out prior to 1767 and until 1817 the name of **Eldridge Street**. See also *First Street*.

Thomas Street. Named for Thomas Lispenard, great-great-grand-son of Anthony Lispenard, founder of the Lispenard estate. Laid out prior to 1797 between Hudson and Church Streets. Extended from Church to Broadway in 1869.

Thompson Street. Named for General William Thompson (1736-1781), a Revolutionary War figure. Laid out prior to 1797 and so named by 1799.

Thompson's Court. A former alley that ran north from Rivington Street east of Columbia Street, now within the Baruch Houses project.

Tiebout Street. A former street that ran about straight east from The Bowery between 14th and 15th Streets to a point near the present intersection of 16th Street and 3rd Avenue. The street crossed the lower part of a farm owned by Cornelius Tiebout. See illustration on page 107.

Tiemann Place. Named in 1921 for former New York Mayor Daniel Tiemann, whose stately home once stood on the north side of West 127th Street between Broadway and Riverside Drive.

Tienhoven Street. A former street laid out beyond the Wall prior to 1691 along land owned by Lucas Van Tienhoven. The street is associated with both present day **Pine Street** and **Liberty Street**.

Times Square. Named in 1904 after the newspaper offices of the New York Times moved to a new building at 1475 Broadway. Formerly *Long Acre Square*.

Tin Pot Alley. Former name for **Exchange Alley**. An anglicized version of the Dutch "Tuyn Paat" meaning "Garden Path." Named for the formal garden along Broadway to which this old street led. Also called *Oyster Pasty Alley*. See *Garden Street, Garden Street Alley*.

Tompkins Place. Former name for part of East 10th Street between 1st Avenue and Avenue A. Located near Tompkins Square Park.

Tompkins Street. An obsolete street that once ran between Grand Street and East 4th Street one block east of Mangin Street. Probably named for New York Governor Daniel D. Tompkins who was serving as U.S. Vice President under James Monroe when the street was laid out in 1822. Also called *Bushwick Street*, now part of the **FDR Drive**.

Torbert Street, also *Tolbert Street.* A former street that connected Henry and Madison Streets between Catharine and Market Streets. Samuel Torbert owned property nearby in the 1820s. Also called *Moore's Row*.

Townsend's Dock. A former dock on the Hudson River at the foot of West 11th Street.

Townsend's Wharf. A former wharf on the west side of Market Slip.

Trimble Place. Named for George S. Trimble, former president of the board of governors of the Society of New York Hospital, who died in 1872. The street was laid out after 1869 when Thomas Street was opened through what were the grounds of the old New York Hospital on Broadway between Duane and Worth Streets.

Trinity Place. Named in 1843 in reference to the Trinity Church grounds which it borders. Formerly *Lumber Street*. The street has also been considered part of **Church Street** by some mapmakers.

Troy Street. Former name of West 12th Street between Greenwich Avenue and West Street. Opened in 1827. Of uncertain origin but probably named for the city of Troy, New York. Part of the street was originally laid out as *Scott Street*.

Tryon Row. A former street that ran from Centre Street to Park Row just below Chambers Street. "Tryon's Gate," a gate to the British barracks that stood nearby during the revolution, was located near present day Park Row. The short row of buildings was named for its proximity to the gate, which was named for British Governor William Tryon (1729-1788).

Tudor City Place. A private street laid out as part of the Tudor City housing development that was completed in 1932. The area is named for its Tudor Revivial architectural style.

Tulip Street. A proposed street on the *Glass House Farm* that was never officially adopted. See illustration on page 46.

Turin Lane. A former country lane that connected the Bloomingdale and East Post Road around 93rd Street. As described, it appears to be the same road as *Apthorp's Lane*. Of uncertain origin.

Tuyen Street, Tuyn Street. The original Dutch name for *Garden Street*.

U.

Union Place. Former name for the triangle formed by the intersection of **Broadway** and 4th Avenue (formerly **Bowery**), now the wedge-shaped area north of 10th Street and between these two streets. Named for the union of the two thoroughfares. See **Union Square** and illustration on page 107.

Union Road. An obsolete road that ran between the *Skinner Road* and the *Southampton Road*, beginning about halfway between the present 5th and 6th Avenues near 11th Street and running northwest, parallel to the present Greenwich Avenue, to the present intersection of 7th Avenue and 15th Street. Of uncertain origin, but possibly after its location as a connecting road to several smaller lanes, or as a general reference to the United States.

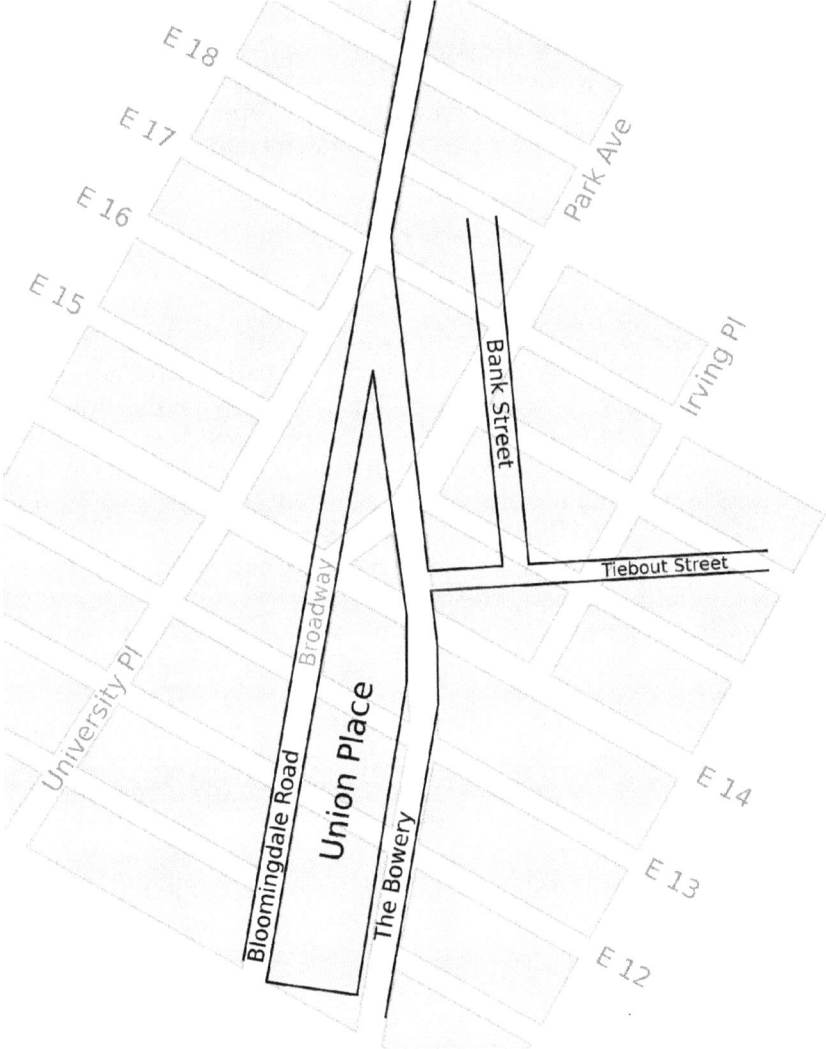

Union Place c.1807

Union Square. Named for the union of the Bloomingdale and Bowery Roads, now **Broadway** and 4th Avenue. Opened as a public space in 1839.

Union Street. Former name of **Greene Street**. So called prior to 1797, the name is perhaps a reference to the newly-formed United States.

United Nations Plaza. Named for its location along the western side of the United Nations complex. Part of 1st Avenue between East 42nd and 48th Streets was so designated in 1952 as construction at the site drew to a close.

University Place. Named in 1836 in reference to the University Building of New York University, which opened on Washington Square in 1837. Formerly *Jackson Avenue* and also part of **Wooster Street**.

V.

Valleau's Wharf. Former wharf located at the foot of *Corlears Street* operated by William Valleau in the early 19th Century.

Van Bruggen Street. According to Post, a former name for both Pine Street and Hanover Square. Carel Van Brugge, an early Dutch settler, owned property in this area in the 1680s. Van Brugge's name was sometimes recorded as Van Bruggen and was later anglicized to Charles Bridges.

Van Nest Place. A former name for part of **Charles Street** between Bleecker and West 4th Streets.

Van Zandt's Wharf. A former wharf on the East River south of Pearl Street between Wall Street and Gouverneur Lane. Johannes Van Zandt established the wharf in the 1770s.

Vandam Street. Named in 1807 for Anthony Van Dam, vestryman of Trinity Church from 1762-1783. Laid out prior to 1799 as *Budd Street*, the street was ceded by Trinity Church to the city in 1808.

Vanderbilt Avenue. Named for the family of Cornelius Vanderbilt, who owned property in the area and built the original Grand Central Depot in 1869. The creation of the street was required by the state legislature in 1869 as part of the act that granted use of part of 4th Avenue to the New York and Harlem Railroad for construction of the new depot.

Vandercliffes Street. Former name of **Gold Street** between John and Beekman Streets. Laid out prior to 1730 and named for Dirck Vandercliff, who had an orchard and tavern in the area. See also **Cliff Street**.

Vandewater Street. A former street that connected Frankfort and Pearl Streets south of present day Rose Street. Laid out prior to 1754 and regulated in 1768. Harman and Hendrick Vandewater were prominent citizens in the first half of the 18th Century. Previously *Duke Street.*

Varick Place. Was located in **Sullivan Street** between West Houston and Bleecker Streets. Probably named in reference to former mayor Richard Varick. See also **Varick Street**.

Varick Street. Named for Richard Varick, Mayor of New York from 1789 to 1801. Laid out prior to 1797, the street was mapped as Varick Street by 1799. In the early 20th Century, the street was widened and extended to meet 7th Avenue.

Verlett's Hill, Varlett's Hill. See *Verlettenberg.*

Verdant Lane. A former country lane that ran from near the present intersection of Broadway and West 45th Street at Times Square, northwesterly to a point near West 49th Street west of 11th Avenue. Certainly named for its idyllic setting.

Verlettenberg. Former name of **Exchange Place** between Broadway and Broad Street. Literally "Verlett's Hill" in Dutch. A reference to Nicolaes Verlett, a prominent early Dutch settler and one of the signers of the Dutch surrender of New Amsterdam in 1698. Also sometimes called Verlettenberg Hill. Anglicized to *Flatten Barrack.*

Vermilyea Avenue. Frederick Vermilye owned a farm west of modern Broadway at about 185th Street in the early 19th Century.

Verplanck Street. A proposed street in the expanded Stuyvesant farm grid of the *Mangin-Goerck Plan* that was never adopted. The Verplanck family were early Dutch settlers, some of whom intermarried with the Stuyvesant family. See illustration on page 103.

Vesey Street. Named for the Reverend William Vesey (1674-1746), first rector of Trinity Church. Ceded by the church to the city and regulated in 1761.

Vestry Street. Named in reference to the elective governing body of Trinity Church, which ceded the land for the street to the city in 1802, and not for the presence of any vestry house as some sources claim. The street was laid out and named prior to 1797, when the area around it was still largely countryside.

Village Street. Original name of **Houston Street** west of Bedford. Named for the village of Greenwich. Changed to *Hamersley Street* in 1807 and then incorporated as part of Houston in 1858.

W-X-Y-Z.

Wadsworth Avenue. Named for Civil War General James Samuel Wadsworth (1807-1864).

Wadsworth Terrace. The street runs parallel to **Wadsworth Avenue.**

The Wagon Road. An early name sometimes used for **Broadway.**

Walker Street. Probably named for John and Ann Walker, whose land the street crossed, and not for Captain Benjamin Walker, the Revolutionary War figure and New York Representative, as is commonly claimed. Ann Walker was a resident of Walker Street when it was first regulated in 1806 between West Broadway and Centre Street. The portion east of Centre was renamed part of **Canal Street** in 1855 after Canal had been extended.

Wall Street. Named for the wooden fortification that ran along the northern edge of New Amsterdam. The wall was ordered built in 1653. The path that ran just inside the wall was first called the *Singel,* and later Wall Street or sometimes simply "the wall."

Walnut Street. Former name of **Jackson Street.**

Walton's Wharf. A wharf located between Peck Slip and Dover Street where William Walton and his family operated a shipyard. William's home, the Walton House, was one of the grandest in the city and stood near Franklin Square.

Wanamaker Place. This block of East 9th Street between Broadway and Lafayette Street marks the location of Joseph Wanamaker's second department store, opened in 1896 at 280 Broadway.

Ward's Wharf or *Pier.* Former wharf on the west side of Peck Slip. Jasper Ward built a house nearby in 1807 which still stands.

Warren Place. Former name for part of **Charles Street** between Waverly Place and Greenwich Avenue. Named perhaps in reference to Sir Peter Warren, who once owned much of the nearby property.

Warren Road. A road on the former Peter Warren estate that ran from the Southampton Road to the Abingdon Road. See illustration on page 41.

Warren Street. Named for Sir Peter Warren whose 300-acre farm stood along the Hudson River north of the Church Farm. Laid out prior to 1754 and ceded to the city by Trinity Church in 1761.

Warren Street. Former name of **Clinton Street** below Division Street. Laid out on the Rutgers farm prior to 1792, when the name was changed to avoid confusion with the older Warren Street that still exists. Possibly also named for Peter Warren.

Washington Alley. See **Washington Mews**.

Washington Mews. Named for its location near Washington Square Park. Originally a row of stables serving houses on East 8th Street, this picturesque alley was renovated in 1915 as a row of small houses intended for use by artists.

Washington Place. Named in 1833 between Broadway and the Washington Parade Ground, now Washington Square Park. Formerly part of East 5th Street. The street on the west side of the park that continues on the same line was originally named as part of **Barrow Street**, but by extension became commonly known as West Washington Place by the 1840s.

Washington Square. Originally laid out as the Washington Parade Ground, the park and surrounding streets are named for George Washington. Washington Square East was originally part of **Wooster Street**.

Washington Street. Former name of **Jefferson Street**. Named for George Washington.

Washington Street. Named for George Washington, Revolutionary War general and first President of the United States. Ceded as part of a grant from the Trinity Church in 1751, Washington was laid out as a waterfront street from Cedar Street to Beach Street by 1797. It was extended several times before reaching Little West 12th Street by 1851. Much of the lower part of the street has been closed for development.

Water Port. The former fortification along Wall Street originally had two gates, one at Broadway and one at the East River, called the Water Port. It was located at the present intersection of Wall and Pearl Streets.

Water Street. Named for its location at the waterside. Water Street started in 1696 when a public street 30 feet wide was established at the low water mark below present Pearl Street at Coenties Lane. By 1730 it had been extended about to present-day John Street with part of it mapped as *Hunter's Key* and *Burnet's Key*. The name Water Street first appears officially in 1736, applied to the portion between Maiden Lane and John Street. By 1754 the street and the name were extended to Catherine Street. In 1767, the oldest part of the street between Coenties Slip and Old Slip was mapped as *Little Dock Street*. Between Wall Street and Beekman's Slip was called *Burnet Street*. In 1784 it was continued across the Herman Rutgers farm to Montgomery Street where it met *Crown Point Street* along the same line.

The Water, also *The Waterside, At the Water,* etc. Referred to the earliest waterfront streets, generally corresponding to **State Street** between Pearl and Whitehall Streets, **Whitehall Street** from State to Pearl Streets, and **Pearl Street** from Whitehall to Hanover Square.

Watkins' Wharf. According to Post a former wharf at the foot of Spring Street. Of uncertain origin.

Watts Street. Named for Robert Watts, vestryman and warden of Trinity Church. Laid out and named in 1794 on Trinity Church property. Ceded to the city between Greenwich Street and the Hudson River in 1802 and between Greenwich and Hudson Streets in 1808.

Waverly Place. Named after Sir Walter Scott's novel. The former 6th Street was renamed Waverly Place in 1833, and the name was extended to include *Factory Street* in 1853.

Weasyes Street. A misspelling of **Vesey Street**.

Weavers Row. See *Paisley Place.*

Weehawken Street. Named for the Weehawken Market, established here in 1829. A wooden house still standing on the west side of the street is a remnant of the former market building constructed in 1834.

Weigh House Street. Former name of **Moore Street**. Named for the weigh house built in 1654 at what is now the southeast corner of Pearl and Moore Streets. Laid out by 1731 and extended to the waterfront (at present South Street) in 1735. By 1786 the street was known as "Moore's Street."

Wendel Street. A former name of *Oak Street.*

Wesley Place. Was located in **Mulberry Street** between Houston and Bleecker Streets. Of uncertain origin.

West Broadway Place. Formerly part of **West Broadway** between Canal and Grand Streets.

West Broadway. In 1837, property owners in *Chapel Street* and *Laurens Street* petitioned the City to combine the streets and change the name to West Broadway, to associate the street with the main thoroughfare of the city. At that time the Street Commission, to which the City had delegated the petition, reported their opinion against changing the name, as the street was neither long enough nor wide enough to warrant being called a broad way. By 1840, the name West Broadway was in use for Chapel Street. It was applied to Laurens Street in 1896, but only after Laurens had been widened and renamed *South Fifth Avenue.*

West Court. According to Post, a former court located behind part of West 22nd Street between 5th and 6th Avenues.

West Drive. A drive situated along the western side of Central Park.

West End Avenue. In 1880, 11th Avenue between 72nd and 108th Streets was renamed West End Avenue at the suggestion of the West Side Association, a neighborhood organization that proposed the renaming of several numbered streets to give them more attractive names. West Side Avenue was also suggested.

West Road. A former road that corresponded generally with 6th Avenue between West 42nd and 92nd Streets.

West Street. Named for its location along the western edge of Lower Manhattan. The street was provided for in 1751 when Trinity Church ceded the surrounding land to the City and laid out as far north as Charles Street in the 1811 Commissioner's Plan.

West Thames Street. Named for the river in London and designated West Thames to distinguish it from the older **Thames Street**. The street was laid out as part of the Battery Park City development which was initiated in the 1970s.

White Place. Formerly located behind 214 West 18th Street. Also called White's Place, suggesting it was named for a local resident. Of uncertain origin.

White Street. A street in the *Mangin-Goerck Plan* that was never officially adopted. It was laid out as an east-west street in an extension of the *Stuyvesant Farm Grid* and ran parallel to Dow Street one block to the north.

White Street. Of uncertain origin. Sometimes said to have been named for Captain Thomas White who owned land in the area of City Hall Park in the 1760s and who died about 1784. White was a loyalist during the American Revolution and seems an unlikely choice to be honored with a street name in 1804, when the name first appears in public records. Ann White, the widow of Thomas, lived into the 1820s and was a prominent member of society, however White was a common surname and the street may have been named for a local property owner or resident. The street was regulated in 1806.

White's Wharf. A former wharf along Washington Street between Battery Place and Morris Street.

Whitehall Slip. Former name of **Whitehall Street** south of Pearl Street. So designated officially in 1793.

Whitehall Street. The large white house built for Peter Stuyvesant, the last governor of New Netherland, stood along the waterfront at what is now the foot of Whitehall Street. When the

British took over New Amsterdam, the house was nicknamed Whitehall after the seat of government in England. The street is one of the oldest in the city and was referred to as *Marckvelt* as early as 1658. See also **State Street**.

Willett's Wharf. A dock and ferry landing owned by Marinus Willett, former Sheriff of New York City, and a Lt. Colonel in the Revolutionary War. The wharf was located on the East River between Broome and Delancey Streets. Sometimes called Colonel Willett's Dock. See also **Willett Street**.

Willett Street. Named for Marinus Willett who purchased several lots along Grand Street in 1785. The street was first laid out prior to 1797 as *Margaret Street* and known by Willett Street by 1807.

William Street. The name William has been applied to several streets. **Broome Street** between the Bowery and Sullivan Street was referred to as William Street on the original map of Nicholas Bayard's East Farm, possibly after a member of the Bayard Family. **Bedlow Street** was called William Street until 1792, probably after William Bedlow, a son-in-law of Henry Rutgers. *Asylum Street*, now part of West 4th Street, was called William until 1813. **Macdougal Street** was reportedly once called William Street.

William Street. Named for William of Orange, who became William III of England (see **Nassau Street**). The street that is now William Street above Wall Street is referred to in a deed dated 1687, however it is not clear whether the street existed at this date or was projected. This street is shown, but not named, in 1695 on the Miller Plan between Wall Street and Maiden Lane, and called William between Maiden Lane and Ann Street on the Shoemakers Plan in 1696. The name William Street was applied prior to 1730 to the street between Wall Street and George Street (now Spruce). Another possible explanation for the name is that it refers to William Beekman, after whom the nearby Beekman Street is named, and whose house and farm were served by the street. As both William and Nassau Streets were laid out about the same time, it seems more likely that William III was the source of the name. In 1794, William, *Smith Street* and *King George Street* were combined under the name William at the same time several other streets that made reference to British royalty were renamed. While this may seem to indicate that the name William held no royal significance to the Council at this time, one must also note that the nearby Nassau Street has retained its name to the present day.

114

Willow Terrace. Formerly located in East 73rd Street near 3rd Avenue.

Winckel Street. A former street that ran along the west side of the Dutch East India Company stores located east of Whitehall between Bridge and Stone Streets. *Winckel* or *winkel* is a Dutch word meaning "shop" or "store." See illustration below.

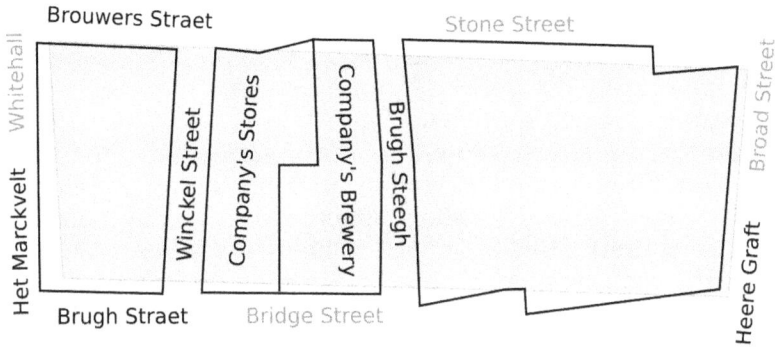

Winckel Street c.1660

Windmill Lane. See *Pieter Jansen's Lane.*

Winne Street, also *Wynne Street.* Former name of **Mott Street** between Bayard and Broome Streets. Laid out on the Bayard Farm by Nicholas Bayard prior to 1794. Possibly named in reference to Peter Winne, to whom Bayard sold property in Albany in 1755 that he had received as dowry from his second wife, Margaritie Beverhout.

Winthrop Place. Formerly located in **Greene Street** between Waverly Place and East 8th Street. Of uncertain origin.

Winthrop Street. A proposed street in the *Stuyvesant Farm Grid* that was never officially adopted. Named for Benjamin Winthrop, who was married to Judith Stuyvesant, daughter of Petrus Stuyvesant (1727-1805), after whom *Judith Street* was named. See illustration on page 103.

Wooster Street. Named prior to 1799, probably for General David Wooster (1711-1777), a revolutionary war figure. Wooster Street was extended from 4th Street to *Art Street* (near the present Waverly Place) in 1825, and extended again between 8th Street and 14th Street in 1833. The portion along Washington Square was renamed **Washington Square East** and the portion north of Waverly Place was renamed *Jackson Avenue* in 1833, then **University Place** in 1836.

Worth Street. Named in 1855 for General William Jenkins Worth (1794-1849), an officer in the Mexican-American War and the War of 1812. Previously *Anthony Street.*

Wynkoop Street. A name sometimes used for **Bridge Street**. The name is in reference to Benjamin Wynkoop, a silversmith who lived near the waterfront in the early 18th Century.

Wynne Street. See *Winne Street.*

Wyoming Place. Referred to **Elizabeth Street** between Houston and Bleecker Streets. The names of the newly-formed western territories became popular in the 1870s and 1880s (when the Dakota Apartments were built, for example).

York Avenue. Named in 1928 for Sgt. Alvin C. York (1887-1964), a World War I veteran. Formerly part of **Avenue A**.

York Street. Of uncertain origin, but probably simply in reference to the city's name. This short street was originally named as part of **Hubert Street** although it has always been separated from the main section of Hubert Street by St. John's Park. In 1823, the residents of this section of the street successfully petitioned the Common Council to change the name to York Street.

NOTES

Some frequently-used sources are abbreviated. Please see the bibliography for full information.

Avenue A. *M.C.C. 1784-1831*, 7:487; *L.S.N.Y 1837*, Chapter 274; "Avenue A Now York Avenue from 59th to 93d." *New York Times* 11 Apr. 1928; (Sutton Place) Federal Writers' Project. *The WPA guide to New York City...* New York: New Press, 1992. 227; Post, 5; "Hearing Advances Big Housing Plan; Further Action Due May 19 on Metropolitan Life Project." *The New York Times* 6 May 1943; (Asser Levy Place) "Honors Jewish Pioneer; City Renames Northern End of Avenue A for Asser Levy." *New York Times* 23 Feb. 1955.

A. Philip Randolph Square. "Council Passes Bill to Honor Rights Leader in Harlem..." *New York Times* 9 Dec. 1964.

Abattoir Place. Edwards, Richard. *New York's Great Industries*. New York: Arno Press, 1973 38; *Report of the New York Produce Exchange*. New York: The Exchange, 1883. 340.

Abeel's Wharf. Longworth, 1816 [58]; "John H. Abeel." (obituary) *New York Times* 20 Apr. 1896.

Abingdon Place. Pasko, W W. *Old New York: A Journal Relating to the History and Antiquities of New York City*. New York: W.W. Pasko, 1889. 109; Post, 3.

Abingdon Road. Post, 3; Commissioners' Plan.

Abingdon Square. Walpole, Horace, and Thomas Park. *A catalogue of the royal and noble authors of England, Scotland and Ireland: with lists of their works*. London: Scott, 1806. 382.

Abraham Kazan Street. "Abraham E. Kazan Dies at 82..." *New York Times* 22 Dec. 1971.

Academy Place. Dripp.

Academy Street. "Tubby Hook's Old School." *The Sun* 26 Mar. 1911.

Achmuty Lane. Post, 3.

Achmuty Street. Post, 3.

Ackerly's Wharf. Hoffman, Murray. *A treatise upon the estate and rights of the corporation of the city of New York, as proprietors*. New York: McSpedon & Baker, 1853. xli.

Ackerman Place. *New York's great industries Exchange and commercial review, embracing also historical and descriptive sketch of the city, its leading merchants and manufacturers*. New York: Historical Pub. Co., 1884. 36; Trow, 1865. 23.

Adam Clayton Powell, Jr. Boulevard. "How Official Is Official?" *New York Times* 10 Oct. 2010.

Adams Place. Post, 3.

Adams Wharf. Post, 3.

Agnew's Alley. Trow, 1877. 25.

Albany Basin. Post, 3 Taylor-Roberts.

Albany Street. Taylor-Roberts.

Albion Place. Post, 3.

Allen Street. *M.C.C. 1784-1831*. 9:71.

Allerton's Wharf. Colonial Dames of America. *Ancestral records and portraits: a compilation from the archives of Chapter I, the Colonial Dames of America*. New York: Grafton Press, 1910. 735.

Amity Alley. Post, 4.

Amity Lane. Post, 4; *M.C.C. 1675-1776*. 4:149; Mangin-Goerck; Hall, Jonathan P, et al. *Reports of Cases Argued and Determined in the Superior Court of the City of New York*. Albany: W.C. Little, 1859. 1:344.

Amity Place. Post, 4.

Amity Street. *M.C.C. 1784-1831*. 4:149.

Amos Street. *M.C.C. 1784-1831*. 5:760; referred to as West 10th: *Proceedings of the Board of Councilmen of the City of New York*. New York: The Board, 1858. 72:740.

Amsterdam Avenue. *M.C.C. 1784-1831*. 8:421; Salwen, Peter. *Upper West Side story: a history and guide*. New York: Abbeville Press, 1989. 67.

Amsterdam Street. Post, 4 Mangin-Goerck.

Ann Street (former). Post, 4 Mangin-Goerck; Taylor-Roberts; *Original grants and Farms*.

Ann Street. (Ann White) Mott, Hopper Striker. *The New York of yesterday...* New York and London: Putnam's, 1908. 107; (Ann Beekman) Moss, Frank, and C. H. Parkhurst. *The American Metropolis from Knickerbocker days to the present time: New York City life in all its various phases*. New York: P.F. Collier, 1897. 298.

Anthony Street. Former Worth Street: John Austin Stevens, Jr. *Colonial Records of the New York Chamber of Commerce 1768-1784, with Historical and Biographical Sketches*. New York: John F. Trow, 1867. 145; *M.C.C. 1784-1831*. 9:191; former Duane Street: Post, 4; *M.C.C. 1675-1776*. 4:496.

Antwerp Street. Mangin-Goerck.

Apthorp's Lane. Stark, James Henry. *The loyalists of Massachusetts and the other side of the American Revolution*. Boston: J.H. Stark, 1910. 352; Commissioners' Plan.

Arch Place. Post, 4.

Arden Street (former). *M.C.C. 1784-1831*. 9:175. 18:129.

Arden Street. *Blue Book*, 23.

Art Street. Commissioners' Plan; *Original Grants and Farms*; *M.C.C. 1784-1831*. 5:35, 14:849.

Arundel Street. Ratzer; *M.C.C. 1784-1831*. 4:12, 19:254; Post, 5.

Ashland Place. Brown, Henry Collins. *Valentine's manual of old New York*. New York, N.Y.: Valentine's Manual Inc, 1922. 69.

Asser Levy Place. "Honors Jewish Pioneer; City Renames Northern End of Avenue A for Asser Levy." *New York Times* 23 Feb. 1955.

Astor Court. Willis, Carol, and Donald Friedman. *Building the Empire State: [a rediscovered 1930s notebook charts the construction of the Empire State Building]*. New York: Norton, 1998. 46.

Astor Place. *L.S.N.Y.*, 1836. Chapter 279.

Asylum Street. Richmond, John Francis. *New York and its institutions, 1609-1871*. New York: E.B. Treat, 1872. 299; *Proceedings of the Board of Assistant Aldermen. 1835*. New York (N.Y.). Board of Assistant Aldermen. 3:232; *M.C.C. 1784-1831*. 7:566; Post, 5; Mangin-Goerck.

Attorney Street. Taylor-Roberts; *M.C.C. 1784-1831*. 14:648.

Auchmuty Street. *M.C.C. 1675-1776*. 4:456; *Trinity Wall Street - History - Guide to Archives - Rector's Office*. Trinity Wall Street. <http://www.trinitywallstreet.org/history/guide/rector>. 11 Jan. 2013

Audubon Avenue. Grinnell, George Bird. *Audubon park; the history of the site of the Hispanic society of America and neighbouring institutions*. New York: Printed by order of the trustees, 1927. 1.

Augusta Street. Post, 5.

Augustus Street. Ratzer; *M.C.C. 1784-1831*. 1:240.

Bache Street. Stevens, John Austin Jr. *Colonial Records of the New York Chamber of Commerce 1768-1784, with Historical and Biographical Sketches.* New York: John F. Trow, 1867. 145; Mangin-Goerck.

Bailey Street. *Blue Book of Farms,* 4.

Bancker Street. Mott, Hopper S. "The Road to the Bouwerij." *Americana.* New York: National Americana Society, 1913. 8:492; Mangin-Goerck; Post, 5.

Bancker's Wharf. Post, 5.

Bank Street (former). Bank of the Manhattan Company, and Walton Advertising and Printing Company (Boston, Mass.). *Historic buildings now standing in New York, which were erected prior to eighteen hundred.* New York City: Printed for Bank of the Manhattan Co., 1914. 44; Commissioners' Plan; *Landmark Map.*

Bank Street. Hardie, James. *An account of the yellow fever, which occurred in the city of New-York, in the year 1822: to which is prefixed a brief sketch of the different pestilential diseases, with which this city was afflicted, in the years 1798, 1799, 1803 & 1805.* New York: Printed by Samuel Marks, 1822. 40; McAtamney, Hugh. *Cradle days of New York: (1609-1825).* New York: Drew & Lewis, 1909. 84.

Barclay Street. Dix, 565; *M.C.C. 1675-1776.* 6:263; Barber, John Warner. *Historical Collections of the state of New York.* New York: S. Tuttle, 1841. 173; Post, 32.

Barley Street. *M.C.C. 1784-1831.* 5:479; Foote, Thelma Wills. *Black and white Manhattan: the history of racial formation in colonial New York City.* Oxford: Oxford University Press, 2004. 119.

Barrack Street. Montresor.

Barrow Street (former). Post, 5.

Barrow Street. *M.C.C. 1784-1831.* 4:423, 17:859; Dix, 579.

Baruch Place. Mangin-Goerck.

Batavia Lane. Ratzer; *M.C.C. 1784-1831.* 9:291; Smith, Alfred E. *Houses.* New York City Housing Authority. <http://www.nyc.gov/html/nycha/html/developments/mansmith.shtml>. 3 Feb. 2013

Battery Place. *L.S.N.Y.,* 1857. Chapter 785.

Battoe Street. Ratzer; Post, 6.

Baxter Street. Pelletreau, William S. *Early New York houses: with historical & genealogical notes.* New York: Francis P. Harper, 1900. 168; "New York Adds a Warrior's Name." *New York Times* 8 Dec. 1918.

Bayard Place. Post, 6.

Bayard Street. Duyckinck; Ratzer; *M.C.C. 1784-1831.* 5:479.

Bayard's Lane. De Voe, 212.

Beach Street. Stevens, John Austin Jr. *Colonial Records of the New York Chamber of Commerce 1768-1784, with Historical and Biographical Sketches.* New York: John F. Trow, 1867. 145; Mangin-Goerck; *M.C.C. 1784-1831.* 3:119, 5:511.

Beach's Wharf. Taylor-Roberts.

Beaver Lane. *M.C.C. 1784-1831.* 17:766; Bradford; Ratzer.

Beaver Street. Post, 6 *M.C.C. 1675-1776.* 1:315.

Bedford Street. Mangin-Goerck.

Bedlow Street. Mott, Hopper S. "The Road to the Bouwerij." *Americana.* New York: National Americana Society, 1913. v8, 492; Whittelsey, Charles B. *The Roosevelt Genealogy, 1649-1902.* Hartford, Conn: Press of J.B. Burr & co, 1902 16; *M.C.C. 1784-1831.* 1:716.

Beekman Place. *Blue Book of Farms,* 7; Hanlon, Pamela. *Manhattan's Turtle Bay: Story of a Midtown Neighborhood.* Charleston SC: Arcadia Pub, 2008. 57.

Beekman Street. Bradford; *M.C.C. 1675-1776.* 5:300, 306; Curry, Daniel. *New York: A Historical Sketch of the Rise and Progress of the Metropolitan City of America.* New

York: Carlton & Phillips, 1853; *Original grants and farms*; *M.C.C. 1784-1831*. 3:531, 8:453.

Belvidere Place. Disturnell, 161.

Bennett Avenue. *Bennett Park Highlights*. City of New York Parks and Recreation. <http://www.nycgovparks.org/parks/bennettpark/history>. 6 Feb. 2013

Benson's Lane. Mangin-Goerck; Goodrich; *M.C.C. 1784-1831*. 1:642,673.

Bethune Street. *M.C.C. 1784-1831*. 16:57.

Beurs Straat. Post, 6.

Billings Row. Disturnell, 161; *Goulding's New York City Directory*. New York: L.G. Goulding, 1878. 109.

Birmingham Street. "Details on Street Naming; Background on Dispute Relative to Changing Name Given." *New York Times* 26 Jun. 1954.

Bishop's Lane. Disturnell, 161.

Bleecker Street. *M.C.C. 1784-1831*. 5:735; Mangin-Goerck.

Bloomfield Street. *Proceedings of the Board of Assistant Aldermen of the City of New York*. New York: The Board, 1873. 130:212.

Bloomingdale Road. *Commissioners' Plan*; Randel;

Bogardus Place. *Blue Book of Farms*, 24.

Bogart Street. *Proceedings of the Board of Assistant Aldermen of the City of New York*. New York: The Board, 1873. 130:212.

Bond Street. *M.C.C. 1784-1831*. 4:116.

Bonsall's Wharf. Stevens, John A, et al. *The Magazine of American History with Notes and Queries*. New York: A.S. Barnes, 1877. 1:261; Taylor-Roberts.

Boorman Place. Scoville, 157; Post, 6.

Boorman Terrace. Post, 7.

Bott Street. Post, 7.

Boulevard Place. Brown, Henry Collins. *Valentine's manual of old New York*. New York, N.Y.: Valentine's Manual Inc, 1922. 70.

Boulevard. *Landmark Map*; "New Names for Up-Town Streets" *New York Times* 1 Feb. 1880; *Insurance maps of the City of New York*. New York City:Sanborn-Perris Map Co., Limited, 1893 *Insurance Maps of New York*. 26 Apr. 2011 *NYPL Digital Gallery*. The New York Public Library. Volume 11 Plates 260, 261 <http://digitalgallery.nypl.org/nypldigital/id?2001785>. 7 Mar. 2013.

Bowery. *M.C.C. 1784-1831*. 7:549.

Bowling Green. *M.C.C. 1675-1776*. 4:179; *M.C.C. 1784-1831*. 9:246.

Bowne's Wharf. Taylor-Roberts.

Bradhurst Avenue. *Blue Book of Farms*, 21; Scoville, 5:118; "No Longer Coogan Avenue." *New York Times* 23 Jan. 1889.

Brannon Street. Mangin-Goerck; *M.C.C. 1784-1831*. 4:677.

Brevoort Place. Post, 8; Brevoort, Henry, and George S. Hellman. *Letters of Henry Brevoort to Washington Irving: Together with Other Unpublished Brevoort Papers*. New York: G. P. Putnam's Sons, 1918. 332.

Brewer Street. City History Club of New York, and Frank Bergen Kelly. *Historical guide to the city of New York*. New York: F. A. Stokes, 1909. 41; New York (N.Y.), Berthold Fernow, and E. B. O'Callaghan. *The records of New Amsterdam from 1653 to 1674 anno Domini*. New York: Pub. under the authority of the city by the Knickerbocker Press, 1897. 1:300; *Map of the Dutch Grants*.

Brewers Hill. Baron, Stanley. *Brewed in America: A History of Beer and Ale in the United States*. Boston: Little, Brown, 1962. 69.

Bride Street. Post, 8.

Bridge Street. *M.C.C. 1675-1776*. 1:314; Bradford.

Broad Street. Costello; Miller; *M.C.C. 1675-1776*. 1:19, 277.

Broadway. *Map of the Dutch Grants; Commissioners' Plan;* Randel; and see further references under entries for former names.

Brook Street. Viele.

Brooks Street. *M.C.C. 1784-1831.* 5:439.

Broome Street. Mangin-Goerck; Scoville, 3:214; *M.C.C. 1784-1831.* 4:181.

Bruce's Wharf. *M.C.C. 1784-1831.* 2:464.

Brugh Steegh. *Map of the Dutch Grants.*

Budd Street. *M.C.C. 1784-1831.* 3:274, 4:423.

Bullock Street. Ratzer; *M.C.C. 1784-1831.* 4:181.

Burgher's Path. *Map of the Dutch Grants.*

Burling Lane. *Commissioners' Plan;* Sandford, Lewis H. *Reports of Cases Argued and Determined in the Superior Court of the City of New York [1847-1852].* New York: Banks, Gould, 1849. 4:234; *Landmark Map.*

Burling Slip. Thompson-Stahr, Jane. *The Burling Books: Ancestors and Descendants of Edward and Grace Burling, Quakers (1600-2000).* Baltimore, MD: Gateway Press, 2001. 82.

Burnet Street. Fernow, Berthold, and Laer A. J. F. Van. *Calendar of Council Minutes 1668-1783.* Albany: University of the State of New York, 1902. 283; Bradford.

Burnet's Key. Fernow, Berthold, and Laer A. J. F. Van. *Calendar of Council Minutes 1668-1783.* Albany: University of the State of New York, 1902 283; Bradford; Ratzer; Wilson, James G. *The Memorial History of the City of New-York: From Its First Settlement to the Year 1892.* New York: New York History Co, 1892. 166.

Burr Street. Taylor-Roberts; Post, 9.

Burr's Corners. American Scenic and Historic Preservation Society. *Annual report of the American Scenic and Historic Preservation Society to the legislature of the State of New York.* Albany, N.Y., 1901. 156.

Burrows Street. *M.C.C. 1784-1831.* 7:566, 18:45.

Burton Street. Post, 9; Doggett, John. *Doggett's New-York City Directory, for.* New-York: J. Doggett, Jr, 1848. 488; *Journal and Documents of the Board of Assistants, of the City of New York.* New York: The Board, 1845. 25:559; Craig, John S. *Craig's Daguerreian Registry.* Torrington, Conn: J.S. Craig, 1994. 2:22.

Bushwick Street. Post, 9; Wilson, James G. *The Memorial History of the City of New-York: From Its First Settlement to the Year 1892.* New York: New York History Co, 1892. 21.

Bussing's Wharf. *M.C.C. 1784-1831.* 7:566, 3:560.

Byvanck Street. *Columbia Studies in the Social Sciences.* New York: Columbia University Press, etc., 1902. 14:233; *Commissioners' Plan.*

Cabrini Boulevard. *L.S.N.Y.* 1939. Chapter 232.

Camden Place. Post, 9.

Canal Street (former). New York (N.Y.), Berthold Fernow, and E. B. O'Callaghan. *The records of New Amsterdam from 1653 to 1674 anno Domini.* New York: Pub. under the authority of the city by the Knickerbocker Press, 1897. 1:300.

Canal Street. *M.C.C. 1784-1831.* 2:217, 3:708, 6:109, 10:612.

Cannon Street. Taylor-Roberts; Mangin-Goerck; Scoville, 3:34.

Cannon's Dock. Taylor-Roberts.

Cannon's Wharf. Pelletreau, William S, and John Keller. *Abstracts of Wills on File in the Surrogate's Office: City of New York.* New York: Printed for the Society, 1893. 30:185 [note]

Carlisle Street. Longworth, 1816. 259; *M.C.C. 1784-1831.* 2:341.

Carmine Street. Mangin-Goerck; *Commissioners' Plan; M.C.C. 1784-1831.* 9:332.

Caroline Street. Post, 54; *Landmark Map; M.C.C. 1784-1831.* 16:151.

Carroll Place. Post, 9.

Cathedral Parkway. *L.S.N.Y.* 1891. Chapter 275.

Catherine Lane. Taylor-Roberts; Post, 9.

Catherine Market. Disturnell, 161.

Catherine Street (former). Taylor-Roberts; *M.C.C. 1784-1831.* 7:566.

Catherine Street. Scoville, 5:278.

Cato's Lane. Mott, Hopper Striker. "Cato's Tavern." *Americana.* New York: National Americana Society. April, 1916. 123.

Cedar Street. *M.C.C. 1784-1831.* 2:73.

Central Park West. *M.C.C. 1784-1831.* 8:421; Salwen, Peter. *Upper West Side story: a history and guide.* New York: Abbeville Press, 1989. 67.

Centre Market Place. *Journal and Documents of the Board of Assistants, of the City of New York.* New York: The Board, 1839. 13:311

Centre Street. Post, 11; Bridges; *M.C.C. 1784-1831.* 13:106.

Chambers Street. *M.C.C. 1675-1776.* 6:263.

Chapel Street. Willis, Samuel J, D T. Valentine, Joseph Shannon, John Hardy, and Otto Hufeland. *Manual of the Corporation of the City of New York.* New York, 1869 783; *M.C.C. 1784-1831.* 8:421.

Charlotte Street. Taylor-Roberts; *M.C.C. 1784-1831.* 7:567.

Charlton Street. *M.C.C. 1784-1831.* 4:423; Mangin-Goerck; Dix, 577.

Chatham Square. *M.C.C. 1784-1831.* 1:484, 7:6, 8:449.

Cheapside Street. Taylor-Roberts.

Cheeseman Street. *Proceedings of the Commissioners of the Sinking Fund of the City of New York 1866-1867.* New York, 1903. 936; McKay, Richard C. *South Street: A Maritime History of New York.* New York: G.P. Putnam's sons, 1934. 36.

Chelsea Lots. Disturnell, 161.

Cherry Street. Cutter, William Richard. *New England families, genealogical and memorial; a record of the achievements of her people in the making of commonwealths and the founding of a nation.* New York: Lewis Historical Pub. Co., 1913. 304; Barr, Amelia Edith Huddleston. *The house on Cherry street.* New York: Dodd, Mead, 1909. 1.

Chestnut Street. Taylor-Roberts.

Chrystie Street. *M.C.C. 1784-1831.* 9:71; Taylor-Roberts.

Church Street. Ratzer; *Commissioners' Plan*; "The Church Street Extension." *New York Times* 6 May 1869.

City Hall Lane. Kelly, Frank B. *Historical Guide to the City of New York.* New York: F. A. Stokes company, 1909. 30; Barber, John W. *The History and Antiquities of New England, New York and New Jersey…* Worcester: Published by Dorr, Howland & Co, 1841. 129; Post, 10.

Claremont Avenue. *Documents of the Assembly of the State of New York, 1912.* 130; *Riverside Park Monuments.* City of New York Parks and Recreation. <http://www.nycgovparks.org/parks/riversidepark/monuments/1206>. 13 Feb. 2013; "New Names for Up-Town Streets." *New York Times* 1 Feb. 1880.

Clark Street. *M.C.C. 1784-1831.* 5:376; Dix, 573.

Clarkson Street. *M.C.C. 1784-1831.* 4:223; Dix, 579.

Clendening's Lane. *Commissioners' Plan*; Randel.

Clermont Street. Post, 11.

Cleveland Place. "In the Real Estate Field." *New York Times* 20 Jun. 1908.

Cliff Street. Duycknick; Pelletreau, William S. *Early New York houses: with historical & genealogical notes.* New York: Francis P. Harper, 1900. 163; *M.C.C. 1784-1831* 16:442.

Clinton Alley. Disturnell, 162.

Clinton Market. Disturnell, 162; *M.C.C. 1784-1831.* 17:504.

Clinton Place. Disturnell, 162.

Coenties Slip. Moss, Frank, and C H. Parkhurst. *The American Metropolis: From Knickerbocker Days to the Present Time : New York City Life in All Its Various Phases : an Historiograph of New York.* New York: P.F. Collier, 1897. 44.

Coffee House Slip. Stevens, John A. *Colonial Records of the New York Chamber of Commerce, 1768-1784: With Historical and Biographical Sketches.* New York: B. Franklin, 1971. 340; Ukers, William H. *All About Coffee.* New York: The Tea and Coffee Trade Journal Company, 1922. 122.

Colden Street. *M.C.C. 1784-1831.* 5:479.

Collays Place. Disturnell, 163.

Collect Street. *M.C.C. 1784-1831.* 5:114.

College Place. *M.C.C. 1784-1831.* 19:706.

Collister Street. Dix, 170; *M.C.C. 1784-1831.* 10:30.

Columbia Street (former). Mangin-Goerck; *M.C.C. 1784-1831.* 6:543, 7:566.

Columbia Street. Ratzer.

Columbian Alley. Post, 11; Goodrich.

Columbus Avenue. Salwen, Peter. *Upper West Side story: a history and guide.* New York: Abbeville Press, 1989. 67.

Columbus Circle. *Central Park Highlights.* City of New York Parks and Recreation. <http://www.nycgovparks.org/parks/centralpark/highlights/7738>. 16 Feb. 2013.

Commerce Street. Mangin-Goerck; *M.C.C. 1784-1831.* 16:538.

Commons Street. Post, 11.

Concord Street. Post, 11.

Congress Place. Disturnell, 162.

Congress Street. *Commissioners' Plan; Atlas of the borough of Manhattan.* New York City: Bromley, G. W., & Company, 1916. Plate 33.

Convent Avenue. *Atlas of the borough of Manhattan.* New York City: Bromley, G. W., & Company, 1916. Plate 150.

Coogan Avenue. "No Longer Coogan Avenue." *New York Times* 23 Jan. 1889.

Cooper Square. *Cooper Triangle Highlights.* City of New York Parks and Recreation. <http://www.nycgovparks.org/parks/M016/history>. 16 Feb. 2013.

Cooper Street (former). Post, 11; Stokes, 5:1304.

Cooper Street. *Annual Report of the Department of Public Works of the City of New York for the Year Ending December 31, 1896.* New York: Martin B. Brown, 1896. 100; *Atlas of the borough of Manhattan.* New York City: Bromley, G. W., & Company, 1916. Plate 183.

Copsey Street. Dunlap, William, and Walt Whitman. *History of the New Netherlands, Province of New York, and State of New York, to the Adoption of the Federal Constitution: By William Dunlap.* New York: Printed for the author by Carter & Thorp, 1839 CLXIV; *M.C.C. 1784-1831.* 2:5.

Corlears Street. *Commissioners' Plan;* Post, 13; *M.C.C. 1784-1831.* 4:420.

Cornelia Street (former). Post, 11; Mangin-Goerck; Reynolds, Cuyler. *Genealogical and family history of southern New York and the Hudson River Valley: a record of the achievements of her people in the making of a commonwealth and the building of a nation.* New York: Lewis Historical Pub. Co., 1914. 3:1013.

Cornelia Street. Pelletreau, William S. *Early New York houses: with historical & genealogical notes.* New York: Francis P. Harper, 1900. 71.

Cornelius Street. Post, John J. *Abstract of title of Kip's Bay Farm of New York.* New York: S.V. Constant, 1894; Mangin-Goerck; Post, 12.

Cortlandt Street. "Missing for 50 Years, a Bit of Cortlandt Street Will Return." *The New York Times Online.* 25 Oct. 2012 <http://cityroom.blogs.nytimes.com/2012/10/25/missing-for-60-years-a-bit-of-cortlandt-street-will-return/>. 3 Feb. 2013; *M.C.C. 1675-1776.* 4:180.

Cottage Place. Mangin-Goerck; Post, 12; Trow, 1872.

Countess' Slip. Post, 12.

Cozine Street. *New York Marriages Previous to 1784*. Baltimore: Genealogical Pub. Co, 1968. 153; *M.C.C. 1784-1831*. 5:765.

Crabapple Street. Post, 12.

Crane Wharf. Ratzer; Taylor-Roberts.

Crosby Street. *Genealogical Record of the Saint Nicholas Society: Advanced Sheets, First Series*. New York: Printed for the Society, 1902. 80; Taylor-Roberts; *26th Annual Report of the American Scenic and Historic Preservation Society to the Legislature of the State of New York*. Albany, N.Y, 1922 256; *M.C.C. 1784-1831*. 5:183.

Cross Road. Post, 43.

Cross Street. Pelletreau, William S. *Early New York houses: with historical & genealogical notes*. New York: Francis P. Harper, 1900 167; *Commissioners' Plan*.

Croton Street. *Atlas of the borough of Manhattan*. New York City: Bromley, G. W., & Company, 1916. Plate 183.

Crown Point Road. Montresor; Post, 12.

Crown Point Street. Post, 13.

Crown Street. *M.C.C. 1784-1831*. 2:74.

Cruger Street. Mangin-Goerck; Post, 13; *Blue Book of Farms*, 4.

Cruger's Wharf. Taylor-Roberts; "Old New York Coffee Houses." *Harper's New Monthly Magazine, March to May 1882*. 421.

Custom House Street. *M.C.C. 1784-1831*. 4:403.

Cuyler's Alley. *Collections of the New York Historical Society for the Year 1902*. New York: Printed for the Society, 1902. 197.

Daniels Street. "War Hero Street Names" *New York Times* 5 Jun. 1921; *Insurance maps of the City of New York*. Surveyed and published by Sanborn-Perris Map Co., Limited, 11 Broadway, 1900. Volume 12 Plate 16.

David Street. Post, 13; Mangin-Goerck; *M.C.C. 1784-1831*. 9:575; Johnson, William, Samuel M. Hopkins, Alonzo C. Paige, Oliver L. Barbour, Charles Edwards, Murray Hoffman, Charles L. Clarke, Lewis H. Sandford, and Stewart Rapalje. *Reports of Cases Adjudged in the Court of Chancery of New York*. New York: Banks & Bros, 1887. 2:53.

Davies Place. Disturnell, 163; Trow, 1877. 310.

Decatur Place. Post, 13; Longworth, 1838. 468. *Proceedings of the Board of Aldermen*. New York, N.Y: The Board, 1837. 459.

Delafield's Wharf. Taylor-Roberts; *M.C.C. 1784-1831*. 4:218.

Delameter Square. "Seek Mementos of Monitor' Builders." *Greater New York: Bulletin of the Merchants' Association of New York*. 8 May 1922.

Delancey Street. *M.C.C. 1784-1831*. 1:373.

Depau Place. Scoville, 1:211; McKay, Richard C. *South Street: A Maritime History of New York*. New York: G.P. Putnam's sons, 1934. 165.

Depew Place. "Plans Submitted for Great Grand Central" *New York Times* 24 Dec. 1904; "Central Must Pay Damages." *New York Times* 17 Jul. 1907; "Plan Big Building to Span Park Avenue," *New York Times* 11 Oct. 1922.

Depeyster Street. Duyckinck; Taylor-Roberts; *M.C.C. 1784-1831*. 1:80.

Depeyster's Lane. *Blue Book of Farms*, 15.

Desbrosses Street. *Commissioners' Plan*; Dix, 577; *M.C.C. 1784-1831*. 12:808.

Dey Street. *Original Grants and Farms*; Ratzer; Post, 6.

Division Street (former). Ratzer; *Landmark Map*.

Division Street. *Landmark Map*; *Seward Park Highlights*. City of New York Parks and Recreation. <http://www.nycgovparks.org/parks/sewardpark/history>. 9 Feb. 2013.

Dixon's Row. Trow, 1872. 48.

Dock Street. Miller; Bradford; Post, 14.
Dominic Street. Post, 11.
Dominick Street. Dix, 579.
Donovan's Lane. Trow, 1877. 67.
Dove Street. Mangin-Goerck; Post, 14.
Dover Street. Ratzer.
Dow Street. Mangin-Goerck; Post, 14.
Downing Street. Mangin-Goerck.
Doyers Street. Longworth, 1808. 31.
Dry Dock Street. *L.S.N.Y.* 1847. v.2, Chapter 356.
Duane Street. Mangin-Goerck; *M.C.C. 1784-1831.* 5:479; McAtamney, Hugh.
  Cradle days of New York: (1609-1825). New York: Drew & Lewis, 1909. 104.
Duffy Square. "Duffy Sq. Signs to be Put Up Today." *New York Times* 13 Jun. 1939.
Duggan Street. Post, 14; *M.C.C. 1784-1831.* 7:247.
Duke Ellington Circle. "Returning Duke's Love for a City." *New York Times* 2 Jul.
  1997.
Duke Street. Bradford; Duyckinck; *M.C.C. 1784-1831.* 2:73; Post, 14.
Duncomb Place. Trow, 1872; Disturnell, 164.
Dunham Place. Trow, 1877. 72.
Dustan's Wharf. *M.C.C. 1784-1831.* 4:180; Hardie, James. *An Account of the Malig-
  nant Fever, Lalely [sic] Prevalent in the City of New-York€¦* New-York: Printed by
  Hurtin and M'Farlane,€¦, 1799. 21.
Dutch Street. Evetts.
Dwars Street. *Map of the Dutch Grants.*
Dyckman Street. *Blue Book of Farms,* 24; "City and Suburban News." *New York
  Times* 28 Mar. 1888.
Dyer Avenue. "39th St. Tube Gets Name of Lincoln" *New York Times* 17 Apr. 1937.
Eagle Street. Ratzer; Taylor-Roberts.
East Bank Street. *Blue Book of Farms.*
East Broadway. *M.C.C. 1784-1831.* 19:435.
East Clinton Place. Disturnell, 163; Trow, 1872.
East End Avenue. *Commissioners' Plan.*
East George Street. Post, 15.
East Place. Trow, 1872. 59; Disturnell, 163.
East Street. Mangin-Goerck; *Commissioners' Plan*; Post, 15.
East Tompkins Place. Disturnell, 163; Trow, 1872; *Tompkins Square Park Highlights.*
  City of New York Parks and Recreation.
  <http://www.nycgovparks.org/parks/tomponssquarepark/history>. 17 Feb.
  2013.
Eastern Post Road. *Landmark Map; Blue Book of Farms.*
Eden Street. Post, 16.
Eden's Alley. Duyckinck; Ratzer; *M.C.C. 1784-1831.* 2:143; Pelletreau, William S,
  and John Keller. *Abstracts of Wills on File in the Surrogate's Office: City of New
  York.* New York: Printed for the Society, 1893; Hardie, James. *An Account of the
  Yellow Fever ...* New-York: Printed by Samuel Marks, 1822. 2.
Edgar Street (former). Post, 16.
Edgar Street. *M.C.C. 1784-1831.* 2:134, 153; Taylor-Roberts.
Edgar's Alley. *Longworth's American Almanac: New-york Register and City Directory.*
  New York: T. Longworth, 1808. 137.
Edgecombe Avenue. "The Application of the Board Of Street Opening And Im-
  provement Of The City Of New York relative to acquiring title, wherever the
  same has not been heretofore acquired, to Edgecombe Road (although not yet

named by proper authority)..." [*Records and Briefs - New York Court of Appeals*]. Albany, 1899.

Edward M. Morgan Place. *Board of Aldermen Ordinance and Resolutions, etc.* New York, 1926. 53.

Elbert Street. Post, John J. *Abstract of title of Kip's Bay Farm of New York.* New York: S.V. Constant, 1894.

Elbow Street. Duyckinck; Post, 16.

Eldridge Street. *M.C.C. 1784-1831.* 9:71.

Elephant Wharf. *M.C.C. 1784-1831.* 17:237; Goodrich.

Eliza Street. Post, John J. *Abstract of title of Kip's Bay Farm of New York.* New York: S.V. Constant, 1894; Reynolds, Cuyler. *Genealogical and family history of southern New York and the Hudson River Valley: a record of the achievements of her people in the making of a commonwealth and the building of a nation.* New York: Lewis Historical Pub. Co., 1914. 3:1013; Mangin-Goerck; *Original Grants and Farms.*

Elizabeth Street. Pelletreau, William S. *Historic Homes and Institutions and Genealogical and Family History of New York.* New York: The Lewis Pub. Co, 1907. 1:101; *M.C.C. 1784-1831.* 8:421.

Elk Street. "It's Elk Street Now, Not Elm." *New York Times* 17 Feb. 1939.

Ellet's Alley. Innes, J. H. *New Amsterdam and its people; studies, social and topographical, of the town under Dutch and early English rule.* New York: C. Scribner's sons, 1902 160 (note).

Elm Street. Taylor-Roberts; Mangin-Goerck; *M.C.C. 1784-1831.* 4:311, 6:777; Kelly, Frank B. *Historical Guide to the City of New York.* New York: F. A. Stokes company, 1909. 92.

Emerson Street. *Annual Report of the Department of Public Works of the City of New York for the Year Ending December 31, 1896.* New York: Martin B. Brown, 1896 100; *Atlas of the borough of Manhattan.* New York City: Bromley, G. W., & Company, 1916 Plate 183.

Ericsson Place. "Seek Mementos of Monitor' Builders." *Greater New York: Bulletin of the Merchants' Association of New York.* 8 May 1922; "The Former Beach Street, Now Ericsson Place, in TriBeCa..." *New York Times* 28 May 2000.

Erie Place. *Annual Report on the Railroads of New York.* Albany, 1858. 173; Post, 17.

Essex Market Place. Disturnell, 164.

Essex Market. Disturnell, 164.

Essex Street. Ratzer.

Everett Row. Disturnell, 164.

Exchange Place, Exchange Street, *Hazard's United States Commercial and Statistical Register.* S.l: s.n., 1839. 5:336

Exterior Street. Proceedings of the Board of Councilmen of the City of New York. New York: The Board, 1858. 72:518.

Extra Place. *Collections of the New York Historical Society for the Year 1902.* New York: Printed for the Society, 1903. 34.

Factory Street. *M.C.C. 1784-1831.* 7:566.

Fair Street. *M.C.C. 1784-1831.* 7:730, 8:630.

Father Demo Square. *Father Demo Square Highlights.* City of New York Parks and Recreation. <http://www.nycgovparks.org/parks/M191/history>. 11 Feb. 2013.

Fayette Street. *M.C.C. 1784-1831.* 1:73, 741; Taylor-Roberts.

Feitner's Lane. Mott, Hopper S. *The New York of Yesterday...* New York and London: Putnam's, 1908. 375.

Ferry Place. Post, 17.

Ferry Street. Taylor-Roberts; *M.C.C. 1784-1831.* 5:253; Post, 17.

Finn Square. "Name Square for Philip S. Finn" *New York Times* 7 Feb. 1919.

Fir Street. *Commissioners' Plan*; Post, 18.

First Street. Ratzer; *M.C.C. 1784-1831*. 9:71;

Fisher Street. *M.C.C. 1784-1831*. 5:479.

Fitzroy Road. Janvier, Thomas A. *In Old New York*. New York: Harper & Bros, 1894. 112; Randel; *Commissioners' Plan*; *M.C.C. 1784-1831*. 18:684.

Flatten Barrack Street. Bradford; Post, 19; *M.C.C. 1675-1776*. 2:321.

Fletcher Street. Bradford; *M.C.C. 1675-1776*. 4:327.

Fly Market Street. *M.C.C. 1784-1831*. 13:694.

Foley Square. *Thomas Paine Park Highlights*. City of New York Parks and Recreation. <http://www.nycgovparks.org/parks/thomaspainepark/history>. 18 Feb. 2013.

Forsyth Street. Taylor-Roberts; *M.C.C. 1784-1831*. 9:71.

Fort George Avenue. Mays, Terry M. *Historical Dictionary of the American Revolution*. Lanham, Md: Scarecrow Press, 2010. 116.

Fort Washington Place. "War Hero Street Names" *New York Times* 5 Jun. 1921.

Fourth Street. *M.C.C. 1784-1831*. 9:71.

Frankfort Street. Hoffman, Murray. *Treatise Upon the Estate and Rights of the Corporation of the City of New York, As Proprietors*. New York: E. Jones & Co., printers, 1862. 223.

Franklin Alley. Disturnell, 164.

Franklin Market. Disturnell, 164; *M.C.C. 1784-1831*. 12:405.

Franklin Square. *M.C.C. 1784-1831*. 9:64.

Franklin Street. *Commissioners' Plan*; *M.C.C. 1784-1831*. 8:393; .

Franklin Terrace. Disturnell, 164.

Frawley Circle. "Frawley's Name Given to Plaza." *The New York Times* 8 Dec. 1926.

Frederick Douglass Circle. "City Circle Named in Negro's Honor." *New York Times* 18 Sep. 1950.

Freedom Place. "New Street to Honor Slain Rights Workers." *New York Times 18* Nov. 1967.

Freeman Alley. *Maps of the city of New York*. New York: Perris & Browne, 1857-1862. Plate 33; "Sales for the Present Week." *New York Times* 15 Oct. 1893.

French Church Street. Dunlap, David W. *From Abyssinian to Zion: A Guide to Manhattan's Houses of Worship*. New York: Columbia University Press, 2004. 202.

Front Street. *M.C.C. 1784-1831*. 1:309, 3:598; *Commissioners' Plan*; Dripp.

Fulton Market. *M.C.C. 1784-1831*. 1:508; Disturnell, 164; Devoe, 1:508.

Fulton Street. *M.C.C. 1784-1831*. 8:630.

Gansevoort Street. *Proceedings of the Board of Aldermen*. New York, N.Y: The Board, 1837. 12:199.

Garden Row. *Landmark Map*; Brown, Henry C. *Valentine's Manual of Old New York*. New York, N.Y: Valentine's Manual Inc, 1922. 82.

Garden Street. Costello; *Map of the Dutch Grants*; Taylor-Roberts.

Gardiner Street. Post, 19.

Gates Street. Mangin-Goerck; Post, 19.

Gay Street. *M.C.C. 1784-1831*. 16:680.

General Green Street. Post, 20.

George Slip. *M.C.C. 1784-1831*. 7:567; Taylor-Roberts.

George Street. *M.C.C. 1784-1831*. 7:567, 9:229; Mangin-Goerck; Post, 20.

Gerard Street. Mangin-Goerck; Reynolds, Cuyler. *Genealogical and family history of southern New York and the Hudson River Valley: a record of the achievements of her people in the making of a commonwealth and the building of a nation*. New York: Lewis Historical Pub. Co., 1914. 3:1015.

Germain Street. *Commissioners' Plan*.

Gibbs' Alley. Post, 20; Hardie, James. *An Account of the Malignant Fever, Lately Prevalent in the City of New-York*. New-York: Printed by Hurtin and M'Farlane at the Literary Printing Office ... and sold by the author ... by John Low ... the other booksellers and the printers, 1799. 105.

Gilbert Street. *M.C.C. 1784-1831*. 5:765, 16:441.

Gilford Place. *Proceedings of the Board of Aldermen*. New York, N.Y: The Board, 1899. 2:193.

Glass House Farm. *Blue Book of Farms*, 5; Weeks, Joseph D. *Report on the Manufacture of Glass*. Washington: Govt. Print. Off, 1884 93; Hunter, Frederick W. *Stiegel Glass*. Boston: Houghton Mifflin Co, 1914. 148.

Glaziers Street. Duyckinck, Whitehead C, and John Cornell. *The Duyckinck and Allied Families: Being a Record of the Descendants of Evert Duyckinck : Who Settled in New Amsterdam, Now New York, in 1638*. New York: T.A. Wright, 1908. [ix].

Glover Place. Doggett 1848. 169.

Goelets Street. *M.C.C. 1675-1776*. 3:482; Pelletreau, William S. *Historic Homes and Institutions and Genealogical and Family History of New York*. New York: The Lewis Pub. Co, 1907. 1:187; *M.C.C. 1784-1831*. 17:766; Taylor-Roberts.

Goerck Street. Mangin-Goerck.

Gold Street. Bradford.

Golden Hill Street. Bradford.

Golden Hill. Tiedemann, Joseph S. *Reluctant Revolutionaries: New York City and the Road to Independence, 1763-1776*. Ithaca: Cornell University Press, 2008. 148.

Gouverneur Alley. Post, 20 *M.C.C. 1784-1831*. 2:241.

Gouverneur Lane. Scoville, 2:253; *M.C.C. 1784-1831*. 2:241, 271.

Gouverneur Slip. Disturnell, 164.

Gouverneur Street. *M.C.C. 1784-1831*. 2:434.

Governor Street. Mangin-Goerck; Reynolds, Cuyler. *Genealogical and family history of southern New York and the Hudson River Valley: a record of the achievements of her people in the making of a commonwealth and the building of a nation*. New York: Lewis Historical Pub. Co., 1914. 3:1013.

Grand Army Plaza. *Grand Army Plaza Landmark Designation Report* City of New York Landmarks Preservation Commission. 23 Jul. 1974.

Grand Street. Montresor; Ratzer; *M.C.C. 1784-1831*. 12:808.

Great George Street. *M.C.C. 1784-1831*. 2:65.

Great Jones Street. *M.C.C. 1784-1831*. 4:116.

Great Kill Road. Post, 21; *Proceedings of the Board of Aldermen*. New York, N.Y: The Board, 1837. 12:199.

Great Queen Street. Miller; Bradford; *M.C.C. 1784-1831*. 2:65.

Greeley Square. Stevens, G A. *New York Typographical Union No. 6: Study of a Modern Trade Union and Its Predecessors*. Albany: J.B. Lyon Co., State Printers, 1913. 633.

Green Lane. *M.C.C. 1675-1776*. 1:273.

Greene Street. Taylor-Roberts; Mangin-Goerck.

Greenwich Avenue. *M.C.C. 1784-1831*. 14:306; *Proceedings of the Board of Aldermen*. New York, N.Y: The Board, 1843. 24:428.

Greenwich Street. *M.C.C. 1675-1776*. 4:463.

Grove Street. *M.C.C. 1784-1831*. 7:566, 18:45; *Documents of the Senate of the State of New York*. Albany: J.B.Lyon, 1909. 13: Doc. 35, 24.

Hague Street. Duyckinck; "School is Named for Bergtraum." *New York Times* 7 Jul. 1974.

Hall Street. *M.C.C. 1784-1831*. 17:533.

Hamersley Place. Post, 21.

Hamersley Street. Mangin-Goerck; *M.C.C. 1784-1831.* 4:423; *Proceedings of the Board of Councilmen of the City of New York.* New York: The Board, 1858. 72:916.

Hamilton Place. *Blue Book of Farms*, 21; *Commissioners' Plan.*

Hamilton Street. *M.C.C. 1784-1831.* 16:298; Post, 10.

Hammond Street. Mangin-Goerck; *Report of Cases Argued and Determined in the Superior Court of the City of New York.* New York: Banks and Bros., 1859. 3:328.

Hancock Street. Bridges; *Commissioners' Plan*; Post, 8.

Hanover Square. Bradford; *M.C.C. 1784-1831.* 2:65, 19:19.

Hanover Street. *M.C.C. 1784-1831.* 19:19.

Hariot Street. Mangin-Goerck; Post, 22.

Harlem Bridge Road. *Commissioners' Plan*; Post, 22.

Harlem Lane. Post, 22.

Harlem Road. Post, 24; *Commissioners' Plan.*

Harman Street. *M.C.C. 1784-1831.* 19:435; Samuel J. Willis, D. T. Valentine, Joseph Shannon, John Hardy, and Otto Hufeland. *Manual of the corporation of the city of New York.* New York, 1842. 782.

Harrison Street. Montresor.

Harsen's Road. *Blue Book of Farms*, 9.

Harwood Place. Disturnell, 165; *Goulding's New York City Directory.* New York: L.G. Goulding, 1877. 598.

Haven Avenue. *Minutes and Documents of the Board of Commissioners of the Department of Parks for the Year Ending April 30, 1898*, New York City: Martin B. Brown Co., 1898. 50.

Hawthorne Street. *Annual Report of the Department of Public Works of the City of New York for the Year Ending December 31, 1896.* New York: Martin B. Brown, 1896. 100; *Atlas of the borough of Manhattan.* New York City: Bromley, G. W., & Company, 1916. Plate 183.

Hazard Street. *M.C.C. 1784-1831.* 4:423; Mangin-Goerck.

Heere Graft. *M.C.C. 1675-1776.* 1:19, 277.

Henderson Place. "Henderson Place Historic District Designation Report," Landmarks Preservation Commission, 11 Feb. 1966.

Henry Street (former). Mangin-Goerck; Bridges; *M.C.C. 1784-1831.* 7:578.

Henry Street. Taylor-Roberts.

Henshaw Street. "War Hero Street Names." *New York Times* 5 Jun. 1921; *Insurance maps of the City of New York.* Surveyed and published by Sanborn-Perris Map Co., Limited, 11 Broadway, 1900. Volume 12 Plate 16.

Herman Place. Disturnell, 165; Trow, 1872. 49.

Herring Street. Mangin-Goerck; *M.C.C. 1784-1831.* 7:567.

Hester Street. Duyckinck; *26th Annual Report of the American Scenic and Historic Preservation Society to the Legislature of the State of New York.* Albany, N.Y: s.n., 1922. 256; Pelletreau, William S. *Historic Homes and Institutions and Genealogical and Family History of New York.* New York: The Lewis Pub. Co, 1907. 1:101.

Hetty Street. *M.C.C. 1784-1831.* 4:423; Mangin-Goerck.

Hevins Street. Duyckinck; Post, 23.

High Street. Taylor-Roberts.

Hoboken Street. *Documents of the Board of Assistants of the City of New York.* New York, 1835. 1:583.

Hoffman Street. *Blue Book of Farms*, 11.

Hogan Place. "City Changes a Street Name." *New York Times* 2 Dec. 1980.

Hopper's Lane. Randel.

Horatio Street. Post, 71.

Horse and Cart Lane Moss, Frank, and C. H. Parkhurst. *The American Metropolis from Knickerbocker days to the present time: New York City life in all its various phases*. New York: P.F. Collier, 1897. 298.

Houston Street. Pelletreau, William S. *Historic Homes and Institutions and Genealogical and Family History of New York*. New York: The Lewis Pub. Co, 1907 102; *M.C.C. 1784-1831*. 13:127; *Proceedings of the Board of Assistant Aldermen of New York*. New York: The Board, 1833. 3:216, 1858. 72:1041.

Howard Street. *Commissioners' Plan*; *M.C.C. 1784-1831*. 11:165.

Hubert Street. Taylor-Roberts; Dix, 582.

Hudson Place. Disturnell, 165; Post, 24.

Hudson Street. *M.C.C. 1784-1831*. 8:421, 9:88.

Hull Street. Miller; *M.C.C. 1675-1776*. 1:315.

Hunter's Key. Duyckinck; Bradford.

India Wharf. Scoville, 1:33.

Indian Road. *Insurance maps of the City of New York, Borough of Manhattan. Volume Twelve*. Published by the Sanborn Map Company, 11 Broadway, New York, 1913. Plates 72, 74.

Irving Place. *Proceedings of the Board of Assistant Aldermen of New York*. New York: The Board, 1833. 2:299.

Isham Street. *Isham Park Highlights*. City of New York Parks and Recreation. <http://www.nycgovparks.org/parks/ishampark/history>. 10 Feb. 2013.

Jackson Avenue. *Proceedings of the Board of Assistant Aldermen of New York*. New York: The Board, 1833. 2:400.

Jackson Place. Disturnell, 165.

Jackson Street. Taylor-Roberts; Mangin-Goerck.

Jacob Street. Ratzer; Taylor-Roberts; Scoville, 1:265.

James Slip. Disturnell, 165.

James Street. Scoville, 5:278; Duyckinck; *Smith, Alfred E. Houses*. New York City Housing Authority. <http://www.nyc.gov/html/nycha/html/developments/mansmith.shtml>. 3 Feb. 2013.

Jane Street. *Commissioners' Plan*; *M.C.C. 1784-1831*. 16:205.

Jauncey Court. Post, 24.

Jay Street. Taylor-Roberts; Dix, 578.

Jefferson Market. *Proceedings of the Board of Assistant Aldermen of New York*. New York: The Board, 1833 2:257.

Jefferson Street. Taylor-Roberts.

Jersey Street. *M.C.C. 1784-1831*. 17:760.

Jersey Street (former). Post, 24; *Blue Book of Farms*, 6.

Jew Street. Innes, J H. *The Old Bark Mill: Or First House of Religious Worship in New York, and Its Surroundings. the Ministry of Dominie Jonas Michaelis - Some Notes Respecting the Site of the First Jewish Synagogue in New York*. New York, 1905. 14.

Jews Alley. Montresor.

Joe DiMaggio Highway. "Pataki Agrees to DiMaggio Highway as Aides Talk of Rift." *New York Times* 17 Mar. 1999.

John Street. Evetts; "History of John Street, New York," 20th *Annual Report of the American Scenic and Historic Preservation Society, 1915*. Albany, N.Y: J.B. Lyon company, 1915. 100.

Jones Lane. *Landmark Map*; Disturnell, 165.

Jones Street. *M.C.C. 1784-1831*. 4:206.

Judith Street. Post, 25 Duyckinck; Mangin-Goerk; Reynolds, Cuyler. *Genealogical and family history of southern New York and the Hudson River Valley: a record of the*

130

achievements of her people in the making of a commonwealth and the building of a nation. New York: Lewis Historical Pub. Co., 1914. 3:1013.

Jumel Terrace. Shelton, W H. *The Jumel Mansion: Being a Full History of the House on Harlem Heights Built by Roger Morris Before the Revolution. Together with Some Account of Its More Notable Occupants.* Boston & New York: Houghton Mifflin Co, 1916. 152.

Kenmare Street. "Need of Amendment No. 1." *New York Times* 2 Nov. 1913; *Petrosino Square Highlights*, City of New York Parks and Recreation. <http://www.nycgovparks.org/parks/petrosinosquare/history>. 16 Feb. 2013.

King George Street. Bradford.

King Street (former). *M.C.C. 1784-1831*. 2:74.

King Street. *M.C.C. 1784-1831*. 4:423; Dix, 579.

Kings Bridge Road. *Landmark Map.*

Kings Road. Post, 25.

Kip Street. Miller.

Kip's Bay Street. Post, John J. *Abstract of title of Kip's Bay Farm of New York*. New York: S.V. Constant, 1894.

Kirkpatrick Place. Disturnell, 165.

Knapp's Place. Trow, 1872. 54; Disturnell, 165.

La Grange Terrace. Kelly, Frank B. *Historical Guide to the City of New York*. New York: F. A. Stokes company, 1909 93; Homberger, Eric. *Mrs. Astor's New York: Money and Social Power in a Gilded Age*. New Haven: Yale University Press, 2004. 105.

Lafayette Boulevard. *Insurance maps of the City of New York*. Surveyed and published by Sanborn-Perris Map Co., Limited, 115 Broadway, 1893 Volume 11 Plates 260, 261; *Insurance maps of the City of New York*. Surveyed and published by Sanborn-Perris Map Co., Limited, 11 Broadway, 1900. Volume 12 Plates 1, 2, 9, 10, 15, 16; "Riverside Drive Extension." *New York Times* 6 Nov. 1897.

Lafayette Place. Homberger, Eric. *Mrs. Astor's New York: Money and Social Power in a Gilded Age*. New Haven: Yale University Press, 2004. 105; *M.C.C. 1784-1831*. 15:470.

Lafayette Street. Kelly, Frank B. *Historical Guide to the City of New York*. New York: F. A. Stokes company, 1909. 92.

LaGuardia Place. "Part of West Broadway to be La Guardia Place." *New York Times* 25 Sep. 1967.

Laight Street. Dix, 577.

Lamartine Place. Powell, John, Derek W. Blakeley, and Tessa Powell. 2001 *Biographical dictionary of literary influences: the nineteenth century, 1800-1914*. Westport, Conn: Greenwood Press. 240; "Lamartine Place Historic District Designation Report," NYC Landmarks Preservation Commission, 2009.

Lasalle Street. *Manhattan College History*. Manhattan College. <http://www.manhattan.edu/about/who-we-are/manhattan-college-history>. 12 Feb. 2013; "War Hero Street Names." *New York Times* 5 Jun.1921.

Laurens Street. Taylor-Roberts; Mangin-Goerck; "More Belgian Pavement to be Laid." *New York Times* 25 Dec. 1870.

Leanderts Place. Disturnell, 165.

Leary Street. Michael J. O'Brien. "The Story of Old Leary Street." *The journal of the American Irish Historical Society*. New York, N. Y. [etc.]: The Society, 1917.15:112.

Leather Street. Post, 26.

Legget's Lane. Mott, Hopper S. *The New York of Yesterday:...* New York and London: Putnam's, 1908. 375.

Lennox Place. Trow, 1872. 61.

Lenox Avenue. "Honoring the Lenox Family." *New York Times* 5 Oct. 1887.

Leonard Street. John Austin Stevens, Jr. *Colonial Records of the New York Chamber of Commerce 1768-1784, with Historical and Biographical Sketches.* New York: John F. Trow, 1867. 145; *M.C.C. 1784-1831.* 7:605.

Leroy Place. Post, 26.

Leroy Street. *M.C.C. 1784-1831.* 4:423; Doggett, 1848. 488; Craig, John S. *Craig's Daguerreian Registry.* Torrington, Conn: J.S. Craig, 1994. 2:22; Dix, 579.

Lewis Street. Taylor-Roberts; Mangin-Goerck; *Commissioners' Plan*; *M.C.C. 1784-1831.* 4:629.

Lexington Avenue. *Journal and Documents of the Board of Assistants of the City of New York.* 1836, 8:[85] Document 30; *L.S.N.Y.,* 1832. Chapter 101; *L.S.N.Y.,* 1833. Chapter 309; *L.S.N.Y.,* 1838. Chapter 148; *L.S.N.Y.,* 1870. Chapter 753; Goodrich.

Liberty Court. Disturnell, 165.

Liberty Street. *M.C.C. 1784-1831.* 2:74.

Lillian Wald Drive. *Wald, Lillian Houses.* New York City Housing Authority. <http://www.nyc.gov/html/nycha/html/developments/manwald.shtml>. 12 Feb. 2013.

Lispenard Street. *Commissioners' Plan*; *M.C.C. 1784-1831.* 5:712; Goodrich.

Little Division Street. Ratzer; Taylor-Roberts; *M.C.C. 1784-1831.* 1:569.

Little Dock Street. Bradford; *M.C.C. 1784-1831.* 1:705; Post, 27.

Little George Street. *M.C.C. 1784-1831.* 9:229.

Little Queen Street. Miller; *M.C.C. 1655-1776.* 6:15; *M.C.C. 1784-1831.* 2:73.

Little Stone Street. Bradford; Ratzer; Post, 27.

Little Water Street. Pelletreau, William S. *Early New York houses: with historical & genealogical notes.* New York: Francis P. Harper, 1900 168; *M.C.C. 1784-1831.* 5:494; *Insurance maps of the City of New York.* Sanborn-Perris Map Co: New York, 1894 Volume 1 Plate 14.

Livingston Street. Mangin-Goerck; Post, 27.

Locust Street. Mangin-Goerck; Post, 27; *Documents of the Assembly of the State of New York.* Albany, N.Y: Weed, Parsons and Co. 1880. 9:897.

Lombard Street. *M.C.C. 1784-1831.* 5:466.

Lombardy Street. *M.C.C. 1784-1831.* 5:494.

London Terrace. London Terrace. Alpern, Andrew. *Luxury apartment houses of Manhattan: an illustrated history.* New York: Dover Publ.,1992. 145.

Long Acre Square. "The Naming of Long Acre Square." *New York Times* 8 Mar. 1903; "To be Called Times Square." *New York Times* 6 Apr. 1904.

Lord's Court. Disturnell, 166; Trow, 1872.56.

Lorillard Place. Blackmar, Elizabeth. *Manhattan for rent, 1785-1850.* Ithaca: Cornell University Press, 1989. 167.

Louisa Street. Post, John J. *Abstract of title of Kip's Bay Farm of New York.* New York: S.V. Constant, 1894.

Love Lane. *M.C.C. 1784-1831.* 15:371.

Low's Lane. *Documents of the Assembly of the State of New York.* Albany: Printed by E. Croswell, 1831 18:153; Willis, Samuel J., D. T. Valentine, Joseph Shannon, John Hardy, and Otto Hufeland. *Manual of the corporation of the city of New York.* New York, 1857. 530.

Lower Robinson Street. *M.C.C. 1784-1831.* 7:549.

Ludlow Place. Disturnell, 166.

Ludlow Street. *M.C.C. 1784-1831.* 9:71.

Lumber Street. *M.C.C. 1784-1831.* 1:717; *Commissioners' Plan*; *Proceedings of the Board of Aldermen.* New York, N.Y: The Board, 1843. 25:138.

Macdougal Alley. *Map of the City of New York.* Map. New York: Perris & Hutchinson, 1849-1850. *Maps of New York City and State.* 16 May 2012 *NYPL Digital Gal-*

lery. The New York Public Library. 11 Mar. 2013.
<http://digitalgallery.nypl.org/nypldigital/id?1253201>.

Macdougal Street. Mangin-Goerck.

Macomb's Place. *23rd Annual Report of the American Scenic and Historic Preservation Society*. Albany, N.Y: J.B. Lyon company, 1918. 134.

Madison Avenue. *L.S.N.Y.,* 1833. Chapter 309.

Madison Court. Disturnell, 166.

Madison Square. *Madison Square Park Highlights*. City of New York Parks and Recreation. <http://www.nycgovparks.org/parks/madisonsquarepark/history>. 1 Mar. 2013

Madison Street. *M.C.C. 1784-1831.* 15:642.

Magaw Place. Himes, Charles F. *Col. Robert Magaw, the defender of Fort Washington, major in Colonel William Thompson's "Battalion of Pennsylvania riflemen" ... colonel of the Fifth Pennsylvania regiment*. [Carlisle]: Hamilton library association, 1915 40; "War Hero Street Names." *New York Times* 5 Jun. 1921.

Magazine Street. Taylor-Roberts; *M.C.C. 1784-1831.* 6:574.

Maiden Lane. Wilson, Rufus Rockwell. *New York, old and new: its story, streets, landmarks*. Philadelphia: J.B. Lippincott, 1909. 69.

Maiden Slip. *M.C.C. 1675-1776.* 5:93.

Mail Street. Livingstone, Colin H. *The Sun's Guide to New York: Replies to Questions Asked Every Day by the Guests and Citizens of the American Metropolis*. Jersey City: Jersey City Print. Co., 1892. 202.

Mangin Street. Mangin-Goerck.

Manhattan Avenue (former). *M.C.C. 1784-1831.* 2:216.

Manhattan Avenue. "The West Side Association." *New York Times* 25 Jan. 1890; "Manhattan Avenue Historic District Designation Report." New York City Landmarks Preservation Commission, 2007.

Manhattan Lane. Randel.

Manhattan Road. Randel.

Manhattan Street. Goodrich; "War Hero Street Names." *New York Times* 5 Jun. 1921.

Mansfield Place. Disturnell, 166.

Maple Street. Post, 29 *Blue Book of Farms*, 6.

Maretta Street. Mangin-Goerck.

Margaret Corbin Drive. James, Edward T., Janet Wilson James, and Paul S. Boyer. *Notable American women, 1607-1950; a biographical dictionary*. Cambridge, Mass: Belknap Press of Harvard University Press, 1971. 385; "Revolutionary War Heroine Finally Given Recognition." *New York Times* 8 Jul. 1977.

Margaret Street. Mangin-Goerck; Reynolds, Cuyler. *Genealogical and family history of southern New York and the Hudson River Valley: a record of the achievements of her people in the making of a commonwealth and the building of a nation*. New York: Lewis Historical Pub. Co., 1914. 3:1013; Columbia University. Faculty of Political Science. *Columbia studies in the social sciences*. New York: Columbia University Press, 1891. 228.

Marie Curie Avenue. "Mayor Dedicates Marie Curie Av." *New York Times* 10 Jun. 1935.

Marion Street. *Journal and Documents of the Board of Assistants, of the City of New York*. New York: The Board, 1839. Document 38, [297].

Market Slip. Taylor-Roberts.

Market Street. *M.C.C. 1784-1831.* 7:567.

Marketfield Street. *Map of the Dutch Grants*.

Martha Street. Mangin-Goerck; Post, 30.

Martin Terrace. Disturnell, 166.

Mary Street. *26th Annual Report of the American Scenic and Historic Preservation Society to the Legislature of the State of New York.* Albany, N.Y, 1921. 257.

McCreas Dock. Post, 28.

McKees Dock. Post, 28.

Meadow Street. Taylor-Roberts; Mangin-Goerck; Post, 30.

Mechanics Alley, Mechanics Place. "F.Y.I." *New York Times* 26 Mar. 2000; *Landmark Map.*

Meek's Court. Trow, 1877. 931.

Mercer Street. Taylor-Roberts; Mangin-Goerck; Goolrick, John T. *The Life of General Hugh Mercer: With Brief Sketches of General George Washington...* New York: Neale Pub. Co, 1906.

Merchant's Court. Post, 34.

Merchant's Place. Post, 34.

Messier's Alley. *Collections of the New York Historical Society for the Year 1902.* New York: Printed for the Society, 1902. 197.

Mews. Taylor-Roberts; Mangin-Goerck; Homberger, Eric. *The Historical Atlas of New York City: A Visual Celebration of Nearly 400 Years of New York City's History.* New York, NY: Holt, 2005. 156.

Middle Road. *M.C.C. 1784-1831.* 1:145.

Middle Street. Taylor-Roberts; Post, 31.

Mill Lane. *Map of the Dutch Grants.*

Mill Street. Innes, J H. *The Old Bark Mill: Or First House of Religious Worship in New York, and Its Surroundings. the Ministry of Dominie Jonas Michaelis - Some Notes Respecting the Site of the First Jewish Synagogue in New York.* New York, 1905. 5.

Miller Place. Disturnell, 166.

Milligan Lane. Post, 31.

Milligan Place. *Commissioners' Plan;* Disturnell, 166.

Millward Place. Post, 31 Disturnell, 166.

Minetta Lane. Goodrich; Stiles.

Minetta Place. Disturnell, 166.

Minetta Street. Taylor-Roberts; Post, 8.

Minthorne Street. Mangin-Goerck; *Original Grants and Farms.*

Mission Place. *Insurance maps of the City of New York.* Sanborn-Perris Map Co: New York, 1894. Volume 1 Plate 14.

Mitchell and Agnew's Basin Post, 31.

Mitchell Place. Disturnell, 166; *Proceedings of the Board of Alderman* New York, 1899. 2:328.

Moll Street. Post, 31.

Monroe Street. *M.C.C. 1784-1831.* 19:434.

Monroe Street. Disturnell, 166.

Montgomery Street. Ratzer; Taylor-Roberts; Shelton, Hal T. *General Richard Montgomery and the American Revolution: From Redcoat to Rebel.* New York: New York University Press, 1994; *M.C.C. 1784-1831.* 1:704.

Monument Lane. 19th Annual report of the American Scenic and Historic Preservation Society to the legislature of the State of New York. Albany, N.Y., 1914. 19:121.

Moore Street. *The Saint Nicholas Society of the City of New York: History, Customs, Record of Events, Constitution, Certain Genealogies, and Other Matters of Interest.* V. 2. New York, 1905. 108; *M.C.C. 1784-1831.* 1:241.

Morningside Avenue. *Morningside Park Highlights.* City of New York Parks and Recreation. <http://www.nycgovparks.org/parks/morningsidepark/history>. 11 Mar. 2013

Morris Place. Trow, 1877. 66; Disturnell, 166.

Morris Street. *M.C.C. 1784-1831.* 17:766.

Mortkile Street. Post, 32; Barber, John Warner. *Historical Collections of the State of New York.* New York: S. Tuttle, 1841. 173.

Morton Street (former). Clark, Emmons. *History of the Seventh Regiment of New York, 1806-1889.* New York: Seventh Regiment, 1890; *M.C.C. 1784-1831.* 4:423; Post, 4.

Morton Street. *M.C.C. 1784-1831.* 4:423, 9:287; Clark, Emmons. *History of the Seventh Regiment of New York, 1806-1889.* New York: Seventh Regiment, 1890.

Mosco Street. "F.Y.I." *New York Times* 1 Feb. 2004.

Moses Street. *Blue Book of Farms,* 5; Post, 32.

Mott Street. Duyckinck; *M.C.C. 1784-1831.* 5:570, 6:321; Pelletreau, William S. *Early New York Houses: With Historical & Genealogical Notes.* New York: Francis P. Harper, 1900. 167; "Road to the Bouwerij" *Americana.* New York: National Americana Society, 1913. 8:496.

Mott's Lane. Mott, Hopper S. *The New York of Yesterdayâ€¦* New York and London: Putnam's, 1908. 350.

Mount Carmel Place. Almeida, Linda D. *Irish Immigrants in New York City, 1945 - 1995.* Bloomington, Ind. : Indiana Univ. Press, 2001. 97.

Mount Morris Place. Disturnell, 166; *Marcus Garvey Park Highlights.* City of New York Parks and Recreation. <http://www.nycgovparks.org/parks/marcusgarveypark/history>. 22 Feb. 2013.

Mount Morris Park West *Marcus Garvey Park Highlights.* City of New York Parks and Recreation. <http://www.nycgovparks.org/parks/marcusgarveypark/history>. 22 Feb. 2013.

Moylan Place. "War Hero Street Names." *New York Times* 5 Jun. 1921.

Mulberry Street. Ratzer; Taylor-Roberts; *M.C.C. 1784-1831.* 14:436.

Murray Street. *M.C.C. 1784-1831.* 6:263, 305; Dix, 575.

Murray's Wharf. Scoville, 4:137, 145.

Mustary Street. Post, 32.

Nagle Avenue. *Documents of the Assembly of the State of New York,* 1914. 35:148.

Nassau Street. *21st Annual Report of the American Scenic and Historic Preservation Society to the Legislature of New York.* Albany, N.Y:1916. 130; Evetts; Miller.

Nathan D. Perlman Place Stone, Kurt F. *The Jews of Capitol Hill: a compendium of Jewish congressional members.* Lanham, Md: Scarecrow Press, 2011. 110; "Area Named for Juristâ€¦" *New York Times* 28 Mar. 1954.

Neilson Place. Trow, 1877. 65; Disturnell, 166.

New Avenue West. City of New York. *Law Department Report, 1901.* 538.

New Avenue East. Dripp; *L.S.N.Y.,* 1872.Chapter 222; City of New York. *Law Department Report, 1901.* 538.

New Bowery. Disturnell, 166; *Proceedings of the Board of Councilmen of the City of New York.* New York: The Board, 1856. 63:183.

New Canal Street. Post, 32.

New Chambers Street. *Proceedings of the Board of Councilmen of the City of New York.* New York: The Board, 1855. 60:1015.

New Chapple Street. Post, 32.

New Market Slip. *M.C.C. 1784-1831.* 16:52; Post, 32.

New Slip. *Collections of the New York Historical Society for the Year 1905.* New York: Printed for the Society, 1906. 274.

New Street. Miller.

Newlon's Dock. Post, 32.

Nicholas Street. Duycknick; Taylor-Roberts; *26th Annual Report of the American Scenic and Historic Preservation Society to the Legislature of the State of New York*. Albany, N.Y: s.n., 1921. 256.

Nicholas William Street. Reynolds, Cuyler. *Genealogical and family history of southern New York and the Hudson River Valley: a record of the achievements of her people in the making of a commonwealth and the building of a nation*. New York: Lewis Historical Pub. Co, 1914. 3:1013; Mangin-Goerck.

Norfolk Street. Ratzer.

North End Avenue. "Battery Park City: A New Phase Begins." *New York Times* 19 Jun. 1988.

North Moore Street. Taylor-Roberts; Dix, 565.

North Street. Taylor-Roberts; *M.C.C. 1784-1831*. 16:52; *Proceedings of the Board of Assistant Aldermen of the City of New York*. New York: The Board, 1833. 3:216.

North William Street. Disturnell, 166.

Nyack Place. Disturnell, 167; Trow, 1877. 56.

Oak Street. Disturnell, 167; Duyckinck; Taylor-Roberts; *Commissioners' Plan*; *Smith, Alfred E. Houses*. New York City Housing Authority. <http://www.nyc.gov/html/nycha/html/developments/mansmith.shtml>. 24 Feb. 2013.

Oblique Road. Mangin-Goerck; Post, 33.

Observatory Place. *Commissioners' Plan*; *L.S.N.Y.*, 1865 Chapter 135.

Ogden Street. Vermilye, Anna S. *Ogden Family History in the Line of Lieutenant Benjamin Ogden of New York: (born June 22, 1735 - Died August 16, 1780) of the Prince of Wales' American Regiment, and His Wife Rachel Westervelt, with Some Account of His Ancestry and Descendants*. Orange, N.J: The Orange Chronicle Co., printers, 1906. 45.

Ogilvie's Wharf. Post, 42; *M.C.C. 1784-1831*. 4:726.

Old Broadway. *Commissioners' Plan*;

Old Ditch. Post, 34.

Old Dutch Church Street *M.C.C. 1675-1776*. 1:260, 7:443.

Old Slip. Bradford; *M.C.C. 1675-1776*. 5:113.

Oliver Street (former). *26th Annual Report of the American Scenic and Historic Preservation Society to the Legislature of the State of New York*. Albany, N.Y: s.n., 1922. 256; Post, 34.

Oliver Street. *M.C.C. 1675-1776*. 5:113; Scoville, 5:278; *Smith, Alfred E. Houses*. New York City Housing Authority. <http://www.nyc.gov/html/nycha/html/developments/mansmith.shtml>. 24 Feb. 2013.

Olwers Street. Bradford; Post, 34.

Orange Street. Ratzer.

Orchard Street (former). Taylor-Roberts; Post, 35.

Orchard Street. Jones, Thomas, and De Lancey E. F. *History of New York During the Revolutionary War: And of the Leading Events in the Other Colonies at That Period*. New York: Printed for the New York Historical Society, 1879. 2:544; Ratzer; *M.C.C. 1784-1831*. 4:361.

Oswego Street. Duyckinck; *M.C.C. 1675-1776*. 4:423.

Otters Alley. Post, 35; Longworth, 1834. 725.

Overlook Terrace. [191st Subway Station Opened] *New York Times* 22 Jan. 1911; *Insurance maps of the City of New York, Borough of Manhattan. Volume Twelve*. Published by the Sanborn Map Company, 1913. Plate 17.

Oyster Pasty Alley. Miller; Pelletreau, William S. *Historic Homes and Institutions and Genealogical and Family History of New York*. New York: The Lewis Pub. Co, 1907. 67.

Pacific Place. Disturnell, 167.

Pagoda Place. Disturnell, 167 Trow, 1877. 66; *Communication from the Superintendent of Buildings*. New York: New York City Department of Buildings, 1862. 65.

Paisley Place. Wilson, Rufus Rockwell. *New York: old & new; its story, streets, and landmarks*. Philadelphia: J.B. Lippincott,1909. 233.

Park Avenue. *Commissioners' Plan*; Dripp.

Park Place. *M.C.C. 1784-1831*. 7:549.

Park Row. Taylor-Roberts; *M.C.C. 1784-1831*. 18:396. "Divver's New Street" *New York Times* 11 Apr. 1886.

Partition Street. *Landmark Map*; Ratzer.

Passage Place. Post, 35.

Patchin Place. Kayton, Bruce. *Radical Walking Tours of New York City*. New York: Seven Stories Press, 2003. 41.

Payson Avenue. "War Hero Street Names." *New York Times* 5 Jun. 1921; *Insurance maps of the City of New York*. Surveyed and published by Sanborn-Perris Map Co., Limited, 11 Broadway, 1900. Volume 12 Plate 18.

Pearl Street. Miller; Bradford; *The Wpa Guide to New York City: The Federal Writers' Project Guide to 1930s New York*. New York: Pantheon Books, 1982. 67; *M.C.C. 1784-1831*. 2:65.

Pearsall's Dock. Post, 35.

Peck Slip. Scoville, 1:103.

Pelham Street. Disturnell, 167; *Rutgers Houses*. New York City Housing Authority. <http://www.nyc.gov/html/nycha/html/developments/manrutgers.shtml>. 12 Feb. 2013.

Pell Street. Duyckinck; Longworth, 1808. 254.

Penn Street. Post, 35.

Perry Street. *M.C.C. 1784-1831*. 7:578.

Pershing Square. "New York Adds a Warrior's Name" *New York Times* 8 Dec. 1918.

Peter Street. Mangin-Goerck; Reynolds, Cuyler. *Genealogical and family history of southern New York and the Hudson River Valley: a record of the achievements of her people in the making of a commonwealth and the building of a nation*. New York: Lewis Historical Pub. Co., 1914. 3:1013.

Petticoat Lane. Miller; Bradford; Burrows, Edwin G, and Mike Wallace. *Gotham: A History of New York City to 1898*. New York: Oxford University Press, 1999. 95.

Phelps Place. Disturnell, 167.

Pie Woman's Lane. Post, 35.

Pieter Jansen's Lane. Miller; Bradford; Saint Nicholas Society of the City of New York. *History, Customs, Record of Events, Constitution, Certain Genealogies, and Other Matters of Interest. V. 1*. New York, 1905. 237.

Pike Street. *M.C.C. 1784-1831*. 7:567.

Pine Street. *M.C.C. 1655-1776*. 1:273; Fernow, Berthold, and Laer A. J. F. Van. *Calendar of Council Minutes 1668-1783*. Albany: University of the State of New York, 1902. 47.

Pitt Street (former). Taylor-Roberts; Mangin-Goerck; *26th Annual Report of the American Scenic and Historic Preservation Society to the Legislature of the State of New York*. Albany, N.Y: s.n., 1922. 256; *M.C.C. 1784-1831*. 4:311.

Pitt Street. Taylor-Roberts; Mangin-Goerck.

Platt Street. Post, 74 Haswell, Chas H. *Reminiscences of New York by an Octogenarian (1816 to 1860)*. New York: Harper, 1896. 273.

Pleasant Avenue. Post, 5; *Thomas Jefferson Park Highlights*. City of New York Parks and Recreation. <http://www.nycgovparks.org/parks/thomasjeffersonpark/history>. 28 Feb. 2013; *Wagner, Robert F. Senator Houses*. New York City Housing Authority.

<http://www.nyc.gov/html/nycha/html/developments/manwagner.shtml>. 28 Feb. 2013.

Point Street. Mangin-Goerck; Post, 36.

Pollock's Wharf. Taylor-Roberts.

Pomander Walk. "New York to have a Pomander Walk.'" *New York Times* 19 Apr. 1921.

Poplar Street. Mangin-Goerck; Post, 36.

Post Avenue. Randel; *Blue Book of Farms*, 26.

Potters Hill. Post, 36; Ries, Heinrich, and Henry Leighton. *History of the Clay-Working Industry in the United States*. New York: J. Wiley & Sons, 1909. 154.

Prince Street (former). *26th Annual Report of the American Scenic and Historic Preservation Society to the Legislature of the State of New York*. Albany, N.Y., 1921. 256; Bradford; Duyckinck; *M.C.C. 1784-1831*. 2:74.

Prince Street. *26th Annual Report of the American Scenic and Historic Preservation Society to the Legislature of the State of New York*. Albany, N.Y: s.n., 1921. 256.

Princes Graft. *Map of the Dutch Grants*; Fernow, Berthold. *The Records of New Amsterdam: From 1653 to 1674 Anno Domini*. New York: Knickerbocker Pr, 1897. 5:224; *M.C.C. 1675-1776*. 1:184.

Princess Street. Miller; *M.C.C. 1784-1831*. 2:74.

Printing House Square. *21st Annual Report of the American Scenic and Historic Preservation Society to the Legislature of the State of New York*. Albany, N.Y. 1916. 151.

Prospect Street. Post, 36; *M.C.C. 1784-1831*. 3:171.

Provost Street. Taylor-Bradford; *M.C.C. 1784-1831*. 3:119; Dix, 565; *Proceedings of the Board of Assistant Aldermen of the City of New York*. New York: The Board, 1833. 3:400.

Public Highway. *Map of the Dutch Grants*;

Pump Street. Duyckinck; Taylor-Roberts; *M.C.C. 1784-1831*. 17:598; Post, 43.

Quay Street. Post, 36.

Quick Street. Post, 37 Johnson, William, et al. *Reports of cases adjudged in the Court of Chancery of New York*. New York: Banks & Bros, 1887. 5:791.

Rachel Lane. Disturnell, 167; Trow, 1877. 63.

Ramparts. Post, 37.

Randall Place. Dripps; Post, 37.

Randall Street. Mangin-Goerck.

Rapelje Street. *Blue Book of Farms*, 5; Post, 37.

Reade Street. Dix, 575.

Reason Street. *M.C.C. 1784-1831*. 17:358, 859.

Rector Place. "6 Builders Chosen for Housing at Battery Park City." *New York Times* 19 Aug. 1981.

Rector Street Wharf. Post, 37.

Rector Street. Wilson, Rufus Rockwell. *New York: old & new; its story, streets, and landmarks*. Philadelphia & London: J.B. Lippincott Co, 1902. 2:61; Dix, 565; Taylor-Roberts.

Redd's Street. Ratzer.

Rensselaer Street. Mangin-Goerck; Post, 37.

Renwick Street. *M.C.C. 1784-1831*. 9:537, 11:327; Fitch, Charles E. *Encyclopedia of Biography of New York: A Life Record of Men and Women Whose Sterling Character and Energy and Industry Have Made Them Preeĩminent in Their Own and Many Other States*. Boston: The American historical society, inc, 1916. 305.

Republican Alley. Post, 37.

Rhinelanders Alley. Post, 37; *Landmark Map*; Stover, Rowland M, William H. Silvernail, Charles H. Mills, and Willard S. Gibbons. *The New York State Reporter: Containing All the Current Decisions of the Courts of Record of New York State,*

Namely: Court of Appeals, Supreme Court, New York Superior Court, New York Common Pleas, Superior Court of Buffalo, City Court of New York, City Court of Brooklyn, and the Surrogates' Courts. Albany: W.C. Little & Co, 1892. 41:476.

Rhinelanders Basin. Post, 38.

Rhinelanders Dock. Post, 38.

Rhinelanders Lane. *Commissioners' Plan*; Post, 38; *Blue Book of Farms*, 12.

Ridge Street. Taylor-Roberts; Viele; *M.C.C. 1784-1831*. 14:437.

Riker's Lane. Randel; Brown, Henry C. *Valentine's Manual of Old New York*. New York, N.Y: Valentine's Manual Inc, 1922. 102.

Ritter's Wharf. *M.C.C. 1784-1831*. 10:328; Post, 38.

Riverside Avenue. *Insurance maps of the City of New York. Borough of Manhattan.* Surveyed and published by Sanborn Map Co., 11 Broadway, 1902 Volume 7 Plate 1.

Riverside Boulevard. *Riverside Park Highlights*. City of New York Parks and Recreation. <http://www.nycgovparks.org/parks/riversidepark/history>. 6 Mar. 2013.

Riverside Drive. *Riverside Park Highlights*. City of New York Parks and Recreation. <http://www.nycgovparks.org/parks/riversidepark/history>. 6 Mar. 2013.

Riverview Terrace. "Streetscapes/Riverview Terrace..." *New York Times* 18 Feb. 1996.

Rivington Place. Disturnell, 167; Trow, 1877. 67.

Rivington Street. Taylor-Roberts; *M.C.C. 1784-1831*. 1:652, 8:209; Homberger, Eric. *The Historical Atlas of New York City: A Visual Celebration of Nearly 400 Years of New York City's History*. New York, NY: Holt, 2005. 61; *Baruch Houses*. New York City Housing Authority. <http://www.nyc.gov/html/nycha/html/developments/manbaruch.shtml>. 24 Feb. 2013.

Road to Albany and Boston. Post, 38.

Road to Crown Point. Post, 38.

Road to Greenwich. Ratzer; Post, 38.

Road to Stuyvesants Boury. Post, 38.

Road to the Obelisk. Post, 38.

Robert Street. Mangin-Goerck; Post, 38.

Robinson Street. Bradford; *M.C.C. 1675-1776*. 4:456; *M.C.C. 1784-1831*. 7:549; Dix, 575.

Rockefeller Plaza. "Rockefeller Center Designation Report." City of New York Landmarks Preservation Commission, 1985.

Rodman's Slip. *M.C.C. 1675-1776*. 2:134; Valentine, D T. *Manual of the Corporation of the City of New York*. New York, 1855. 501.

Romain Street. Mangin-Goerck; *M.C.C. 1784-1831*. 2:559; Longworth, 1808 274.

Roosevelt Street. Duyckinck; *M.C.C. 1675-1776*. 6:400.

Roosevelt's Lane. *Blue Book of Farms*, 17; *Commissioners' Plan*.

Roosevelt's Slip. Post, 39.

Rose Street. King Street. *M.C.C. 1784-1831*. 2:74.

Roslyn Place. Trow, 1877. 67; Disturnell, 167.

Rotten Row. Taylor-Roberts; *M.C.C. 1675-1776*. 7:37.

Rotterdam Street. Mangin-Goerck.

Rough Street. Post, 39.

Russel Place. Trow, 1877. 67; Disturnell, 167.

Rutgers Hill. Taylor-Roberts; Baron, Stanley. *Brewed in America: A History of Beer and Ale in the United States*. Boston: Little, Brown, 1962. 69.

Rutgers Place. Trow, 1877. 67; Disturnell, 167.

Rutgers Slip. Taylor-Roberts.

Rutgers Street (former). Duyckinck; *M.C.C. 1675-1776.* 6:400; *M.C.C. 1784-1831.* 3:548; *Commissioners' Plan.*

Rutgers Street. Taylor-Roberts.

Rutgers Wharf. Taylor-Roberts; Post, 37-8.

Rutherford Place. *Stuyvesant Square Highlights.* City of New York Parks and Recreation. <http://www.nycgovparks.org/parks/stuyvesantsquare/history>. 8 Nov. 2012.

Ryder's Alley. Duyckinck.

Rynders Street. (Centre Street) Taylor-Roberts; Mangin-Goerck; *Collections of the New York Historical Society for the Year 1897.* New York: Printed for the Society, 1897. 228; *26th Annual Report of the American Scenic and Historic Preservation Society to the Legislature of the State of New York.* Albany, N.Y: s.n., 1922. 256; (Mulberry Street) Duyckinck; Ratzer; Asbury, Herbert; *The Gangs of New York: An Informal History of the Underworld.* New York: Vintage Books, 2008.

Sackett Street. "Abstract of Wills - Liber 23," *Collections of the New York Historical Society for the Year 1897.* New York: New York Historical Society, 1897. 210 (note).

St. Bridget's Place. Disturnell, 167.

St. Clair Place. Rider, Fremont, Frederic T. Cooper, and Mary A. Hopkins. *Rider's New York City and Vicinity, Including Newark, Yonkers and Jersey City: A Guide-Book for Travelers, with 16 Maps and 18 Plans, Comp. and.* New York: H. Holt and Co, 1916. 255; "War Hero Street Names" *New York Times* 5 Jun. 1921; *Riverside Park Fund: Amiable Child Monument.* Riverside Park Conservancy. <http://www.riversideparkfund.org/visit/amiable-child-monument/>. 22 Feb. 2013.

St. Clements Place. Longworth, 1838. 696; Trow, 1877. 167

St. George's Place. Disturnell, 167.

St. George's Square. *M.C.C. 1784-1831.* 9:64; Anstice, Henry. *History of St. George's Church in the city of New York, 1752-1811-1911.* New York: Harper, 1911.

St. James Place. "Plans Drawn for East Side Housing..." *New York Times* 11 May 1947.

St. John's Alley. Post, 43.

St. John's Lane. *Commissioners' Plan; 24th Annual Report of the American Scenic and Historic Preservation Society* Albany, N.Y: J.B. Lyon company, 1919. 149.

St. John's Street. Post, 43.

St. Luke's Place. "Cleaning the City Streets" *New York Times* 6 Mar. 1860.

St. Mark's Place. *Commissioners' Plan.*

St. Nicholas Avenue. *L.S.N.Y.,* 1866. Chapter 367.

St. Peter's Place. Post, 43.

St. Timothy's Place. Clarkson, David. *History of the Church of Zion and St. Timothy of New York 1797-1894.* New York: G.P. Putnam's Sons, 1894. 221.

Saltus' Wharf. McKay, Richard C. *South Street: A Maritime History of New York.* New York: G.P. Putnam's sons, 1934. 451.

Samuel Street. Post, John J. *Abstract of title of Kip's Bay Farm of New York.* New York: S.V. Constant, 1894.

Sand Hill Road. Montresor; *Landmark Map.*

Scammel Street. Taylor-Roberts; Disturnell, 167; *Vladeck.* New York City Housing Authority. <http://www.nyc.gov/html/nycha/html/developments/manvladeck.shtml> 19 Feb. 2013.

Schaape Waytie. Valentine, David T, and William I. Paulding. *History of the City of New York.* New York: G.P. Putnam, 1853. 311.

Schermerhorne's Wharf. Post, 40; Taylor-Roberts; Bergen, Tunis G. *Genealogies of the State of New York: A Record of the Achievements of Her People in the Making of a Commonwealth and the Founding of a Nation*. New York: Lewis Historical Pub. Co, 1915 1:459.

Schiff Parkway. "Lehman Will Manage Schiff Parkway Day." *New York Times* 6 May 1921; Schiff, Jacob H, and Cyrus Adler. *Jacob H. Schiff; His Life and Letters*. Garden City, N.Y: Doubleday, Doran, 1928.

Schreyer's Hook. *A Maritime History of New York*. Garden City, NY: Doubleday, 1941. 33; *8th Annual Report of the American Scenic and Historic Preservation Society to the Legislature of the State of New York*. Albany, N.Y, 1913. 141.

Schroepel Street. *Blue Book of Farms*, 6; Post, 40.

Science Street. Mangin-Goerck; Post, 40.

Scott Street. *Reports of Cases Argued in the Superior Court of the City of New York*. New York: Banks Brothers, 1859. 1:325.

Scotts Alley. Post, 40; Doggett, 1840. 322.

Seaman Avenue. City of New York. *The City Record*, V.4, pt.8:7539.

Second Street. *M.C.C. 1784-1831*. 9:71.

Sheera Street. Post, 41.

Sheridan Square. "New York Adds a Warrior's Name." *New York Times* 8 Dec. 1918.

Sheriff Street. Taylor-Roberts; *L.S.N.Y.*, 1836. Chapter 282.

Sherman Avenue. Randel; *Commissioners' Plan*.

Sherman Square. *Sherman Square Highlights*. City of New York Parks and Recreation. <http://www.nycgovparks.org/parks/shermansquare/history>. 25 Feb. 2013.

Shinbone Alley. Post, 41.

Shubert Alley. Lane, Stewart F. *Jews on Broadway: An Historical Survey of Performers, Playwrights, Composers, Lyricists and Producers*. Jefferson: McFarland & Co., Publishers, 2011. 24.

Sickles Street. Randel.

Singel. *Map of the Dutch Grants*.

Sixth Street. *M.C.C. 1784-1831*. 9:71.

Skinner Road. Harrison, Burton, and Martha J. Lamb. *History of the City of New York: Externals of Modern New York*. New York: A.S. Barnes and Co, 1896. 2:606; *Commissioners' Plan*; Randel; Post, 41.

Skinner's Lane. Norcross, Frank W. *A History of the New York Swamp*. New York: Chiswick Press, 1901. 35.

Slote Lane. Bradford; *Commissioners' Plan*.

Smell Street Lane. Brown, Henry C. *Valentine's Manual of Old New York*. New York, N.Y: Valentine's Manual Inc, 1922. 106; Post, 42.

Smith Place. Post, 42.

Smith Street Lane. Brown, Henry C. *Valentine's Manual of Old New York*. New York, N.Y: Valentine's Manual Inc, 1922. 106; Post, 42.

Smith Street. Innes, J H. *New Amsterdam and Its People: Studies, Social and Topographical, of the Town Under Dutch and Early English Rule*. New York: C. Scribner's sons, 1902. 225; Post, 42.

Smiths Vly. Benson, Egbert. *Memoir Read Before the Historical Society of the State of New-York, December 31, 1816*. Jamaica N.Y.: Henry C. Sleight, 1825. 81.

Sniffen Court. "Sniffen Court Historic District Designation Report," City of New York Landmarks Preservation Commission. 1966.

South End Avenue. "Plenty of Plans for Battery Place..." *New York Times*. 26 Sep. 1985.

South Fifth Avenue. "More Belgian Pavement to be Laid." *New York Times* 25 Dec. 1870.

South Street. *M.C.C. 1784-1831*. 2:260, 428; Mangin-Goerck.

South William Street. *Proceedings of the Board of Aldermen*. New York, N.Y: The Board, 1837. 12:575.

Southampton Road. Burke, Bernard, and Ashworth P. Burke. *A Genealogical and Heraldic History of the Colonial Gentry*. London: Harrison, 1891. 112; Post, 42; *Commissioners' Plan*.

Spencer Place. Trow, 1877. 68.

Spingler Place. Disturnell, 168; Post, 42.

Spring Street. Post, 34; Taylor-Roberts; Mangin-Goerck; *M.C.C. 1784-1831*. 3:241, 4:677.

Spruce Street (former). Mangin-Goerck; Post, 42.

Spruce Street. *M.C.C. 1784-1831*. 9:228; Bradford.

Staff Street. "War Hero Street Names" *New York Times* 5 Jun. 1921; *Insurance maps of the City of New York*. Surveyed and published by Sanborn-Perris Map Co., Limited, 11 Broadway, 1900. Volume 12 Plate 16.

Stamer's Slip. Post, 42.

Stanton Place. Disturnell, 168.

Stanton Street. Taylor-Roberts; *M.C.C. 1784-1831*. 4:12; Burrows, Edwin G, and Mike Wallace. *Gotham: A History of New York City to 1898*. New York: Oxford University Press, 1999. 281.

Staple Street. *M.C.C. 1784-1831*. 3:207; Randel; Longworth, 1827. 458.

State Prison Dock. Post, 42; Kornwolf, James D, and Georgiana W. Kornwolf. *Architecture and Town Planning in Colonial North America*. Baltimore: Johns Hopkins University Press, 2002. 1415.

State Street. *M.C.C. 1784-1831*. 1:747, 2:5; Taylor-Roberts.

Steuben Street. Post, 43; *6th Annual report of the American Scenic and Historic Preservation Society to the legislature of the State of New York*. Albany, N.Y., 1901. 156.

Stevens' Wharf. Taylor-Roberts; McKay, Richard C. *South Street: A Maritime History of New York*. New York: G.P. Putnam's sons, 1934. 29.

Stewart Street. Randel; Post, 42.

Stillwell's Lane. Randel; *Commissioners' Plan*; *The New York State Reporter*. Albany, N.Y: W.C. Little & Co, 1891. 40:105.

Stone Street. Berthold Fernow, and E. B. O'Callaghan. *The records of New Amsterdam from 1653 to 1674 anno Domini*. New York: Pub. under the authority of the city by the Knickerbocker Press, 1897. 1:300.

The Strand. *Map of the Dutch Grants*.

Striker's Lane. Disturnell, 168; *Commissioners' Plan*; Mott, Hopper S. "Major General Garrit Hopper Striker." *The New York Genealogical and Biographical Record*. New York: New York Genealogical and Biographical Society, 1908. v. 39, no. 3, 153.

Striker's Row. Disturnell, 168.

Stuyvesant Alley. *NYCityMap*.

Stuyvesant Place. Post, 43; *Commissioners' Plan*.

Stuyvesant Street. Mangin-Goerck; Reynolds, Cuyler. *Genealogical and family history of southern New York and the Hudson River Valley: a record of the achievements of her people in the making of a commonwealth and the building of a nation*. New York: Lewis Historical Pub. Co, 1914. 3:1013.

Suffolk Street. Ratzer.

Sugar Loaf Street. Montresor; Post, 43.

Sullivan Street. Mangin-Goerck; Post, 27; *Documents of the Assembly of the State of New York*. Albany, N.Y: Weed, Parsons and Co. 1880. 9:897.

Susan Street. Post, John J. *Abstract of title of Kip's Bay Farm of New York*. New York: S.V. Constant, 1894.

Sutton Place. Federal Writers' Project. *The WPA guide to New York Cityâ€¦* New York: New Press, 1992. 226.

Swartwout's Dock. Taylor-Roberts; *M.C.C. 1784-1831*. 15:482.

Sylvan Place. Gill, Jonathan. *Harlem: The Four Hundred Year History from Dutch Village to Capital of Black America*. New York: Grove Press, 2011. 42.; *Commissioners' Plan*.

Szold Place. "Street is Renamed for Woman Zionist" *New York Times* 23 Mar. 1951.

Taras Shevchenko Place. "Metropolitan Briefs." *New York Times* 5 May 1978.

Taylor's Wharf. Taylor-Roberts; Post, 44; *M.C.C. 1784-1831*. 2:74.

Ten Broeck Street. Mangin-Goerck; Reynolds, Cuyler. *Genealogical and family history of southern New York and the Hudson River Valley: a record of the achievements of her people in the making of a commonwealth and the building of a nation*. New York: Lewis Historical Pub. Co, 1914. 3:1013.

Ten Eyck's Wharf. Hoffman, Murray. *Treatise Upon the Estate and Rights of the Corporation of the City of New York, As Proprietors*. New York: E. Jones & Co., printers, 1862. 2:91.

Terrace Drive. Viele. *NYCityMap*.

Thames Street. Post, 27; Bradford; Ratzer.

Theatre Alley. Taylor-Roberts; Mangin-Goerck; Homberger, Eric. *The Historical Atlas of New York City: A Visual Celebration of Nearly 400 Years of New York City's History*. New York, NY: Holt, 2005. 156.

Thelonious Sphere Monk Circle. "New York Day by Day" *The New York Times* 27 Jun. 1983.

Third Street. *M.C.C. 1784-1831*. 9:71.

Thomas Street. Stevens, John Austin, Jr. *Colonial Records of the New York Chamber of Commerce 1768-1784, with Historical and Biographical Sketches*. New York: John F. Trow, 1867. 145; "An Old Landmark Disappearing." *New York Times* 14 May 1869.

Thompson Street. Taylor-Roberts; Mangin-Goerck.

Thompson's Court. Brown, Henry C. *Valentine's Manual of Old New York*. New York, N.Y: Valentine's Manual Inc, 1922. 109.

Tiebout Street. *Landmark Map; Map of Original Grants and Farms*; Randel.

Tiemann Place. "War Hero Street Names" *New York Times* 5 Jun. 1921.

Tienhoven Street. Hoffman, Murray. *A Treatise Upon the Estate and Rights of the Corporation of the City of New York, As Proprietors*. New York: McSpedon & Baker, printers to the Common council, 1853. ciii; Post, 46.

Times Square. "To Be Called Times Square: Aldermen Vote to Rename Long Acre Square, Site of New Times Building." *New York Times* 6 Apr. 1904.

Tin Pot Alley. Costello; *Map of the Dutch Grants*.

Tompkins Place. *M.C.C. 1784-1831*. 12:801.

Torbert Street. Post, 46; *M.C.C. 1784-1831*. 17:205.

Townsend's Dock. Post, 46.

Townsend's Wharf. Post, 46.

Trimble Place. *Commissioners' Plan*; Stiles; Dripps; *NYCityMap*; "An Old Landmark Disappearing" *New York Time* 14 May. 1869; "George S. Trimble [obituary]." *New York Times* 20 May 1872.

Trinity Place. Post, 46; *Proceedings of the Board of Aldermen*. New York, N.Y: The Board, 1843. 25:138.

Troy Street. *M.C.C. 1784-1831*. 16:57.

Tryon Row. Disturnell, 168; Watson, John. *Annals and Occurrences of New York City and State in the Olden Time*. Applewood Books, 2009. 183.

Tudor City Place. "Tudor City Historic District Designation Report." City of New York Landmarks Preservation Commission, 1988.

Tulip Street. *Blue Book of Farms*, 6; Post, 46.

Turin Lane. Brown, Henry Collins. *Valentine's manual of old New York*. New York, N.Y.: Valentine's Manual Inc, 1922. 110.

Union Place. *M.C.C. 1784-1831.* 7:41.

Union Road. Randel; *Cmmissioners' Plan*.

Union Square. *Union Square Park Highlights*. City of New York Parks and Recreation. <http://www.nycgovparks.org/parks/unionsquarepark/history>. 3 Mar. 2013.

Union Street. Taylor-Roberts.

United Nations Plaza. "New Top Hat Area May Be U.N. Plaza" *New York Times* 7 May 1952.

University Place. Frusciano, Thomas J, and Marilyn H. Pettit. *New York University and the City: An Illustrated History*. New Brunswick, NJ: Rutgers Univ. Press, 1997 29.

Valleau's Wharf. Post, 17; *M.C.C. 1784-1831.* 6:268.

Van Bruggen Street. Post, 17; *Collections of the New York Historical Society for the Year 1902*. New York: Printed for the Society, 1903. 140; Greene, Richard H, et al. *The New York Genealogical and Biographical Record*. New York: New York Genealogical and Biographical Society, 1880. 8:97.

Van Nest Place. trow, 1877. 57; Dusturnell, 168.

Van Zandt's Wharf. Post, 17; Hamilton, Alexander, Julius Goebel, and Joseph H. Smith. *The Law Practice of Alexander Hamilton: Documents and Commentary*. New York: Published under the auspices of the William Nelson Cromwell Foundation by Columbia University Press, 1964. 4:440.

Vandam Street. Mangin-Goerck; *M.C.C. 1784-1831.* 4:423; Dix, 577.

Vanderbilt Avenue. *L.S.N.Y.*, 1869. Chapter 919.

Vandercliffes Street. Bradford; *The Chronotype*. New York, N.Y: The College, 1873. 257.

Vandewater Street. Duyckinck; Ratzer; *M.C.C. 1675-1776.* 7:124.

Varick Place. Disturnell, 168; Trow, 1877. 70.

Varick Street. Taylor-Roberts; Mangin-Goerck.

Verdant Lane. Post, 47; *Commissioners' Plan*.

Verlettenberg. *M.C.C. 1675-1776.* 2:282.

Vermilyea Avenue. *Blue Book of Farms*, 24.

Verplanck Street. Post, 47; Mangin-Goerck.

Vesey Street. *M.C.C. 1675-1776.* 6:263, 249.

Vestry Street. Taylor-Roberts; *M.C.C. 1784-1831.* 3:119.

Village Street. *M.C.C. 1784-1831.* 4:423; *Proceedings of the Board of Councilmen of the City of New York*. New York: The Board, 1858. 72:1041.

Wadsworth Avenue. "New York Adds a Warrior's Name." *New York Times* 8 Dec. 1918.

Wagon Road. *Map of the Dutch Grants*; Post, 48.

Walker Street. *M.C.C. 1784-1831.* 4:149; *26th Annual Report of the American Scenic and Historic Preservation Society to the Legislature of the State of New York*. Albany, N.Y, 1921 256; *Proceedings of the Board of Councilmen of the City of New York*. New York: The Board, 1855. 59:827.

Wall Street. *The records of New Amsterdam from 1653 to 1674 anno Domini*. New York: Pub. under the authority of the city by the Knickerbocker Press, 1897. 1:65.

Walnut Street. Taylor-Roberts.

Walton's Wharf. Scoville, 1:103; Allgeyer, David. *The Tip of the Island: The Saga of Lower Manhattan.* Conway, AR: Oldbuck Press, 1994. 141.

Wanamaker Place. "Bought by Mr. Wanamaker." *New York Times* 29 Sep. 1896.

Ward's Wharf. Post, 48; Taylor-Roberts; White, Norval, Elliot Willensky, and Fran Leadon. *AIA Guide to New York City.* Oxford: Oxford University Press, 2010. 34.

Warren Place. Disturnell, 168; Trow, 1877. 57.

Warren Road. Post, 48; *Commissioners' Plan*; Randel.

Warren Street (former). *M.C.C. 1784-1831.* 1:716.

Warren Street. Duyckinck; *M.C.C. 1675-1776.* 6:263.

Washington Mews. "Washington Mews to Become a Latin Quarter." *New York Times* 19 Dec. 1915.

Washington Place. *Proceedings of the Board of Assistant Aldermen. 1833.* New York (N.Y.). Board of Assistant Aldermen, 1833. 2:318; Doggett, 1842. 50.

Washington Square. *Washington Square Park Highlights.* City of New York Parks and Recreation. <http://www.nycgovparks.org/parks/washingtonsquarepark/history>. 25 Feb 2013.

Washington Street (former). Post, 48; Taylor-Roberts.

Washington Street. *M.C.C. 1675-1776.* 5:330; Taylor-Roberts; *L.S.N.Y.*, 1851. Chapter 443.

Water Port. Post, 48.

Water Street. *M.C.C. 1675-1776.* 1:406, 4:331; Bradford; *M.C.C. 1784-1831.* 1:704.

The Water. Post, 45.

Watkins' Wharf. Post, 48.

Watts Street. *M.C.C. 1784-1831.* 3:119; Dix, 577.

Waverly Place. *Proceedings of the Board of Assistant Aldermen. 1833.* New York (N.Y.). Board of Assistant Aldermen, 1833. 2:362.

Weasyes Street. Post, 48.

Weavers Row. Wilson, Rufus Rockwell. *New York: old & new; its story, streets, and landmarks.* Philadelphia: J.B. Lippincott, 1909. 233.

Weehawken Street. "Weehawken Street Historic District Designation Report." New York City Landmarks Preservation Commission. 2006.

Weigh House Street. Bradford; Taylor-Roberts; *M.C.C. 1675-1776.* 4:66, 267.

Wendel Street. Post, 48.

Wesley Place. Disturnell, 169; Trow, 1877. 66.

West Broadway Place. Disturnell, 169; Trow, 1877. 71.

West Broadway. *Proceedings of the Board of Aldermen.* New York, N.Y: The Board, 1837 12:260; *Journal and Documents of the Board of Assistants, of the City of New York.* New York: The Board, 1840. v.16, Doc. 70; Taylor-Roberts; Mangin-Goerck.

West Court. Post, 49.

West End Avenue. "New Names for Up-Town Streets" *New York Times* 1 Feb. 1880.

West Street. *M.C.C. 1675-1776.* 5:330; *Commissioners' Plan.*

White Place. Disturnell, 169; Trow, 1877.

White Street (former). Post, 49; Mangin-Goerck.

White Street. *M.C.C. 1784-1831.* 3:802, 4:149.

White's Wharf. *M.C.C. 1784-1831.* 3:608.

Whitehall Slip. *M.C.C. 1784-1831.* 2:57.

Whitehall Street. Booth, Mary L. *History of the City of New York, from Its Earliest Settlement to the Present Time.* New York: W.R.C. Clark & Meeker, 1859. 321.

Willett Street. Taylor-Roberts; *Commissioners' Plan.*

Willett's Wharf. *Commissioners' Plan.*

William Street (former). (Broome) *L.S.N.Y.*, 1796. Chapter 27; Post, 49; (Bedlow) *M.C.C. 1784-1831.* 1:716, 7:566. (Macdougal) Post, 49.

William Street. Bradford; Evetts; *21st Annual Report of the American Scenic and Historic Preservation Society to the Legislature of the State of New York, 1916*. Albany, N.Y, 1916. 130; *M.C.C. 1784-1831*. 2:73.

Willow Terrace. Disturnell, 169; Trow, 1877. 73.

Winckel Street. *Map of the Dutch Grants.*

Winne Street. *Collections of the New York Historical Society for the Year 1898*. New York: Printed for the Society, 1898. 345; *6th Annual Report of the American Scenic and Historic Preservation Society to the Legislature of the State of New York*. Albany, N.Y, 1922. 256.

Winthrop Place. Disturnell, 169.

Winthrop Street. Mangin-Goerck; Reynolds, Cuyler. *Genealogical and family history of southern New York and the Hudson River Valley: a record of the achievements of her people in the making of a commonwealth and the building of a nation*. New York: Lewis Historical Pub. Co, 1914 3:1013.

Wooster Street. Mangin-Goerck.

Worth Street. "New York Adds a Warrior's Name" *New York Times* 8 Dec. 1918.

Wynkoop Street. *M.C.C. 1784-1831*. 3:348.

Wyoming Place. Disturnell, 169; Trow, 1877. 62.

York Avenue. "Avenue A Now York Avenue From 59th to 93d Street." *New York Times* 11 Apr. 1928.

York Street. Goodrich; *M.C.C. 1784-1831*. 12:682.

Illustrations

Amity Lane. *Commissioners' Plan; NYCityMap*

Cheapside Street. *NYCityMap.*

Depeyster's Lane. Randel; *NYCityMap.*

Glass House Farm. *Blue Book of Farms*; Randel.

Kip's Bay Farm Grid. *Commissioners' Plan; NYCityMap.*

Minetta Brook. Viele; *NYCityMap.*

New Bowery. *Landmark Map; NYCityMap.*

North-South Roads. Viele; *NYCityMap.*

Roads on the Warren Estate. *Commissioners' Plan; NYCityMap.*

Stuyvesant Farm Grid. Mangin-Goerck; *NYCityMap.*

Union Place. *Commissioners' Plan; NYCityMap.*

Verdant Lane. Randel; *NYCityMap.*

Winckel Street. *Map of the Dutch Grants; NYCityMap.*

BIBLIOGRAPHY

Asbury, Herbert. *The Gangs of New York: An Informal History of the Underworld*. New York: Vintage Books, 2008.

Barnard, Charles. *The City of New York: A Complete Guide ... and a Complete New Street Directory*. New York: Taintor Bros., Merrill, 1876.

Benson, Egbert. *Memoir Read Before the Historical Society of the State of New-York, December 31, 1816*. Jamaica [N.Y.:] Henry C. Sleight, 1825.

Biographical Directory of the State of New York, 1900. New York City: Biographical Directory Co, 1900.

[*Blue Book of Farms*] *Maps of farms commonly called the Blue book, 1815: drawn from the original on file in the street commissioner's office in the City of New York, together with lines of streets and avenues / laid out by John Randel, jr., 1819-20*. Map. New York City: Sackersdorff, 1868. *Atlases of New York city*. 25 Mar. 2011. *NYPL Digital Gallery*. The New York Public Library <http://digitalgallery.nypl.org/nypldigital/id?1531804> 7 Mar. 2013.

Bolton, Reginald P. *Indian Paths in the Great Metropolis*. New York: Museum of the American Indian, Heye Foundation, 1922.

Booth, Mary L. *History of the City of New York, from Its Earliest Settlement to the Present Time*. New York: W.R.C. Clark & Meeker, 1859.

Bradford, William. *A Plan of the City of New York from an actual Survey*. Map. New York, 1730. Reprinted in Andrews, William L, and James Lyne. *The Bradford Map: The City of New York at the Time of the Granting of the Montgomery Charter*. New York: Printed at the DeVinne Press, 1893.

Burrows, Edwin G, and Mike Wallace. *Gotham: A History of New York City to 1898*. New York: Oxford University Press, 1999.

Chapin, Anna A. *Greenwich Village*. New York: Dodd, Mead and Co, 1920.

Clinton, George, Hugh Hastings, and James A. Holden. *Public Papers of George Clinton, First Governor of New York, 1777-1795, 1801-1804*. New York: State of New York, 1899.

Dawson, Henry B, and William J. Davis. *Reminiscences of the City of New York and Its Vicinity*. New York, 1855.

De Voe, T. F. *The Market Book: Containing a Historical Account of the Public Markets in the Cities of New York, Boston, Philadelphia and Brooklyn, with a Brief Description of Every Article of Human Food Sold Therein, the Introduction of Cattle in America, and Notices of Many Remarkable Specimens*. New York: 1862.

Disturnell, John. *New York As It Was and As It Is: Giving an Account of the City from Its Settlement to the Present Time : Forming a Complete Guide to the Great Metropolis of the Nation, Including the City of Brooklyn and the Surrounding Cities and Villages : Together with a Classified Business Directory*. New York: D. Van Nostrand, 1876.

Dix, Morgan, John Adams Dix, Leicester Crosby Lewis, Charles Thorley Bridgeman, and Clifford P. Morehouse. *A history of the parish of Trinity Church in the city of New York*. New York: Putnam, 1898.

[*Commissioners' Plan*] Randel, John. *A Map of the City of New York*. New York, 1811.

Doggett, John. *Doggett's New-York City Directory*. J. Doggett, Jr., 1840, 1842, 1848.

Dripps, Matthew. *Map of New York and Vicinity*. Map. New York, 1865. Issued in Valentine, D. *Manual of the Corporation of the City of New York*. New York, 1865.

Dunshee, Kenneth H. *As You Pass by*. New York: Hastings House, 1952.

[Duyckinck] Maerschalck, F. *A Plan of the City of New York from an Actual Survey Anno Domini M, DCC, LV.* Map. New York: Duyckinck, 1755. Reprinted in Stokes, v1, plate 34.

Evetts, James. *A Map or Chart of a Certain Tract of Land Commonly Call'd the Shoemakers Land.* Map. New York, 1696. Reprinted in Stokes, v1, plate 24-a.

Feirstein, Sanna. *Naming New York: Manhattan Places & How They Got Their Names.* New York: New York University Press, 2001.

Goodrich, A.T. *A Map of the City of New York.* Map. New York, Goodrich, [1836]. Reprinted in Stokes, v3, plate 99.

Grim, Charles F. *An Essay Towards an Improved Register of Deeds: City and County of New-York, to Dec. 31, 1799, Inclusive.* New-York: Gould, Banks & Co, 1832.

Hardie, James. *The Description of the City of New York: To Which Is Prefixed, a Brief Account of Its Settlement by the Dutch, in the Year 1629 : and of Most Remarkable Events Which Have Occurred in Its History, from That to the Present Period.* New York: S. Marks, 1827.

Innes, J H. *New Amsterdam and Its People: Studies, Social and Topographical, of the Town Under Dutch and Early English Rule.* New York: C. Scribner's sons, 1902.

Kelly, Frank B. *Historical Guide to the City of New York.* New York: F. A. Stokes company, 1909.

King, Moses. *King's How to See New York: A Complete Trustworthy Guide Book ; 100 Illustrations, the Latest Map, Complete Index.* New York: King, 1914.

Koeppel, Gerard T. *Water for Gotham: A History.* Princeton, N.J: Princeton University Press, 2000.

Lathrop, Elise. *Early American Inns and Taverns.* New York: Tudor Pub. Co, 1936.

[*Landmark Map*] Stokes, I.N. Phelps, Macarthy, Jennie F., Macarthy, Clinton H. *The Landmark Map.* 1918. Reprinted in Stokes, v3, plates 174-180.

Longworth's American Almanac: New-york Register and City Directory. New York: T. Longworth, 1808, 1816, 1834, 1838.

Lossing, Benson J. *History of New York City: Embracing an Outline Sketch of Events from 1609 to 1830, and a Full Account of Its Development from 1830 to 1884.* New York: Perine Engraving and Pub. Co, 1884.

[*L.S.N.Y*] *Laws of the State of New York,* Albany.

[Mangin-Goerck] Mangin, Joseph and Goerck, Casimir. *A Plan and Regulation of the City of New-York.* Map. New York, 1803. Reprinted in Stokes, v1, plate 70.

[*Map of the Dutch Grants*] Macarthy, J.F. and C.H. *Map of the Dutch Grants*, published in Stokes' Iconography v2. plate 87.

[*M.C.C. 1675-1776*] Osgood, Herbert L, Austin B. Keep, and Charles A. Nelson. *Minutes of the Common Council of the City of New York, 1675-1776.* New York: Dodd, Mead, 1905.

[*M.C.C. 1784-1831*] Peterson, Arthur Everett. *Minutes of the Common Council of the City of New York, 1784-1831.* New York: City of New York. 1917.

Miller, John. *New Yorke.* Map. [1696] Reprinted in Stokes, v1 plate 23-a.

Montresor, John. *A Plan of the City of New-York and its Environs...* Map. [London], 1775. Reprinted in Stokes, v1, plate 40.

Morrison, John H. *History of New York Ship Yards.* New York: Sametz & Co, 1970.

Moscow, Henry. *The Book of New York Firsts.* Syracuse: Syracuse U. Press, 1995.

Moscow, Henry. *The Street Book: An Encyclopedia of Manhattan's Street Names and Their Origins.* New York: Fordham University Press, 1990.

Moss, Frank, and C H. Parkhurst. *The American Metropolis: From Knickerbocker Days to the Present Time : New York City Life in All Its Var-ious Phases : an Historiograph of New York.* New York: P.F. Collier, 1897.

Moulton, Joseph W. *New York 170 Years Ago: With a View, and Explanatory Notes.* New York: W.G. Boggs, printer, 1843.

148

[*NYCityMap*] New York, City of. *NYCityMap*.
  <http://maps.nyc.gov/doitt/nycitymap/>. 23 Mar. 2013.
O'Callaghan, E B. *Calendar of Historical Manuscripts in the Office of the Secretary of State, Albany, N.Y.* Albany: Weed, Parsons and company, printers, 1865.
[*Original Grants and Farms*] Macarthy, J.F. and C.H. *Original grants and farms*, published in Stokes' *Iconography* v6. following p. 64i.
Pasko, W. W. *Old New York: A Journal Relating to the History and Antiquities of New York City.* New York: W.W. Pasko, 1889.
Pelletreau, William S. Early New York Houses: With Historical & Genealogical Notes. New York: Francis P. Harper, 1900.
Peterson, Arthur E, and George W. Edwards. *New York As an Eighteenth Century Municipality.* New York: Longmans, Green, 1917.
Post, John J. *Old streets, roads, lanes, piers and wharves of New York. Showing the former and present names, together with a list of alterations of streets, either by extending, widening, narrowing or closing. In three parts. 1st. Former name and present name of location. 2d. Present name and former name. 3d. Street alterations.* New York: R. D. Cooke, 1882.
Pritchard, Evan T. *Native New Yorkers: The Legacy of the Algonquin People of New York.* San Francisco: Council Oak Books, 2007.
[Randel] *Randel Farm Maps.* Museum of the City of New York.
  <http://www.mcny.org/sidebars/randel-farm-maps-online.html>.
  17 Feb. 2013.
Ratzer, B. *Plan of the City of New-York in North-America.* Map. London: Jefferys and Faden, 1776. Reprinted in Stokes, v1, plate 41.
Rider, Fremont, and Frederic T. Cooper. *Rider's New York City: A Guide-Book for Travelers, with 13 Maps and 20 Plans.* New York: H. Holt, 1923.
Scoville, Joseph Alfred, George Washington Carleton, David McDowell, and Albert Ulmann. *The old merchants of New York city.* New York: Carleton, 1863.
Selyns, Henricus, Garret Abeel, Winkle E. Van, and William L. Brower. *Records of Domine Henricus Selyns of New York, 1686-7.* New York: Holland Society of New York, 1916.
Smith, Joseph M, Alden March, and James H. Armsby. *Report on the Medical Topography and Epidemics of the State of New York: Submitted to the American Medical Association at Its Annual Meeting at New Haven in June, 1860.* Philadelphia: Collins, printer, 1860.
Stiles, S. *Topographical Map of the City and County of New York.* New York: J.H. Colton and Co., 1836.
Stokes, I N. P, Victor H. Paltsits, and F C. Wieder. *The Iconography of Manhattan Island, 1498-1909: Compiled from Original Sources and Illustrated by Photo-Intaglio Reproductions of Important Maps, Plans, Views, and Documents in Public and Private Collections.* New York: Robert H. Dodd, 1915.
Tauber, Gilbert. *A Guide to Former Street Names in Manhahttan.*
  <http://www.oldstreets.com>. 17 Mar. 2013.
[Taylor-Roberts] Taylor, B. and Roberts, J. *A New and Accurate Plan of the City of New York in the State of New York, in North America.* Map. New York, 1797. Reprinted in Stokes, v1, plate 64.
Trow, John F. *Trow's New York City Directory.* New York: J.F. Trow, 1865.
Trow, John F. *Trow's New York City Directory.* New York: J.F. Trow, 1872.
Trow, John F. *Trow's New York City Directory.* New York: J.F. Trow, 1877.
Van, Winkle E, Joan Vinckeboons, and Kiliaen Rensselaer. *Manhattan, 1624-1639.* New York, 1916.
Watson, John. *Annals and Occurrences of New York City and State in the Olden Time.* Applewood Books, 2009.

www.ingramcontent.com/pod-product-compliance
Lightning Source LLC
Chambersburg PA
CBHW072010040426
42447CB00009B/1565